Banking Supervision at the Crossroads

Banking Supervision at the Crossroads

Edited by

Thea Kuppens, Henriëtte Prast and Sandra Wesseling

Supervision Department, De Nederlandsche Bank, the Netherlands

Edward Elgar
Cheltenham, UK • Northampton, MA, USA

Published by
Edward Elgar Publishing Limited
Glensanda House
Montpellier Parade
Cheltenham
Glos GL50 1UA
UK

Edward Elgar Publishing, Inc.
136 West Street
Suite 202
Northampton
Massachusetts 01060
USA

A catalogue record for this book
is available from the British Library

Library of Congress Cataloguing in Publication Data

Banking supervision at the crossroads/edited by Thea Kuppens,
     Henriëtte Prast and Sandra Wesseling.
          p.   cm.
     Includes bibliographical references and index.
     1. Banks and banking—Europe—State supervision. 2. Financial
institutions—Europe—State supervision. 3. Banking law—Europe.
4. Financial institutions—Law and legislation—Europe. 5. Banks and
banking—Netherlands—State supervision. 6. Financial institutions—
Netherlands—State supervision. 7. Banking law—Netherlands.
8. Financial institutions—Law and legislation—Netherlands. 9. Banks
and banking, International—State supervision. 10. Financial institutions,
International—State supervision. 11. Banks and banking, International—
Law and legislation. 12. Financial institutions, International—Law and
legislation. I. Kuppens, Thea, 1971– . II. Prast, Henriëtte, 1955– .
III. Wesseling, Sandra, 1965– .
     HG1778.E85B357   2004
     354.8'28'094—dc21

                                                                    2003049215
     ISBN 1 84376 308 7

Typeset by Manton Typesetters, Louth, Lincolnshire, UK

Printed and bound in Great Britain by MPG Books Ltd, Bodmin, Cornwall

Contents

List of figures   vii
List of tables   viii
List of contributors   ix

PART I   INTRODUCTION

1. Banking supervision at the crossroads: background and overview   3
   Klaas Knot

2. A brief history of the institutional design of banking supervision in the Netherlands   10
   Joke Mooij and Henriëtte Prast

PART II   CONVERGENCE OF SUPERVISORY PRACTICES

3. Opening remarks   41
   Nout Wellink

4. A functional approach to fifty years of banking supervision   44
   Kees van Dijkhuizen

5. The new single regulator in Germany   55
   Jochen Sanio

6. The role of the Eurosystem in prudential supervision   59
   Wim Duisenberg

7. Convergence in supervision: a commercial banker's perspective   64
   Tom de Swaan

PART III   ISSUES IN THE THEORY OF BANKING SUPERVISION

8. The optimal regulatory environment   69
   David Llewellyn
   Comment   105
   Annemarie van der Zwet

9. The effectiveness of deposit insurance   110
    Gillian G.H. Garcia
    Comment   131
    Wilko Bolt

10. Credit risk measurement and procyclicality   136
    Philip Lowe
    Comment   164
    Henriëtte Prast

11. Economic versus regulatory capital for financial conglomerates   169
    Jaap Bikker and Iman van Lelyveld
    Comment   217
    Gaston Siegelaer

Index   225

Figures

9.1	Convergence to good practice	123
9.2	Decade of system initiation	124
9.3	Moving toward agreement	126
9.4	Convergence on exclusions	127
9.5	Exclusions in 2001	127
9.6	Divergences in 2001	128
10.1	Expected probability of default of US companies currently rated BBB	143
10.2	Proposed risk weights for corporate loans	148
10.3	Capital ratio using EDF and S&P rating PDs for the probability of default	153
10.4	Mexican output gap and hypothetical IRB capital requirements	155

Tables

2.1	Landmarks in the history of supervision	17
4.1	Banking problems in the OECD, 1980–2002	47
4.2	The structure of supervision in the Netherlands	49
9.1	Convergence to good practices	118
9.2	Areas of agreement and disagreement	121
9.3	Countries with explicit, limited deposit insurance systems	125
11.1	Arguments for supervision of financial conglomerates	173
11.2	Overview of risk types in economic capital models	182
11.3	The effects of two percentage point interest rate shocks on net interest income of domestic activities of banks and insurers (in billions of guilders)	191
11.4	The effects of two percentage point interest rate shocks on profits of banks, insurers and (imaginary) financial conglomerates	193
11.5	The revaluation effects of a two percentage point interest rate rise on the fair value balance sheets of banks, insurers and (pro forma) financial conglomerates	196
11.6	Overview of interest rate and share price change effects	198
11.7	Median correlation of stock prices between the sectors, by country, 1990–2000	200
11.8	Median correlation of stock prices of small firms between the sectors, by country, 1990–2000	201
11.9	Risk and return characteristics by country and industry	203
11.10	The effects of pro forma mergers, weighted by market capitalization	204
11.11	The effects of pro forma mergers of small firms, weighted by market capitalization	205
11.12	Aggregated balance sheets of Dutch banks and insurance firms (domestic, 2000)	209

Contributors

Jaap Bikker, Directorate of Supervision, De Nederlandsche Bank

Wilko Bolt, Research Department, De Nederlandsche Bank

Kees van Dijkhuizen, Treasurer-General, Ministry of Finance, the Netherlands

Wim Duisenberg, Governor, European Central Bank

Gillian G.H. Garcia, Consultant

Klaas Knot, Directorate of Supervision, De Nederlandsche Bank

Iman van Lelyveld, Directorate of Supervision, De Nederlandsche Bank

David Llewellyn, Loughborough University, United Kingdom

Philip Lowe, Bank for International Settlements

Joke Mooij, Research Department, De Nederlandsche Bank

Henriëtte Prast, Directorate of Supervision, De Nederlandsche Bank

Jochen Sanio, President, Bundesanstalt für Finanzdienstleitungsaufsicht, Germany

Gaston Siegelaer, Pension and Insurance Board, the Netherlands

Tom de Swaan, Member of the Managing Board, ABN AMRO Holding

Nout Wellink, Governor, De Nederlandsche Bank

Annemarie van der Zwet, Monetary Policy Department, De Nederlandsche Bank

PART I

Introduction

PART I

1. Banking supervision at the crossroads: background and overview

Klaas Knot

This volume contains the proceedings of a conference hosted by De Nederlandsche Bank (DNB) on 24 and 25 April 2002. The conference has been organized to celebrate the adoption of the Act on the Supervision of the Credit System in the Netherlands 50 years ago, when banking supervision was first formalized.

BANKING SUPERVISION ...

The first Act on the Supervision of the Credit System in the Netherlands replaced a system of voluntary arrangements between DNB and the private banks. It was a response to the major changes in the financial and economic environment that had taken place in the inter-war years. The increasing role of the banking sector in the economy and the unfortunate experience of the great depression made it clear that a sound functioning of the banking system was too important to be arranged informally. In Chapter 2 of this volume, Joke Mooij and Henriëtte Prast – both from De Nederlandsche Bank – sketch the historical evolution of banking supervision in the Netherlands, including the run-up to and the consequences of the coming into force of the Act in 1952.

Over time, DNB's tasks and responsibilities in the area of banking supervision have increasingly been viewed as an integral part of its broader mandate for maintaining financial stability in the Netherlands. This concern with the stability of the financial system has also broadened the focus of banking regulation from comparatively narrow creditor protection issues towards problems of systemic risk. While these problems are connected to the financial system more broadly (encompassing markets, several types of financial institutions, and payment systems) the banking system is of particular relevance as it can be prone to contagion through credit and/or liquidity channels, with widespread financial fragility as a result.

The established economic theory of regulation is built on the notion of market failure. Regulation is justified in order to prevent or mitigate the potentially adverse effects of market power, externalities, and asymmetric information between market participants. For bank depositors in particular, the value of longer-term investments that are not publicly traded is difficult to establish. The first-come-first-served constraint applicable for demand deposits implies a strong incentive for depositors to be in the front of the queue, should their confidence in the safety and soundness of the institution fade.[1]

In order to be able to safeguard financial stability under such circumstances, it is vital to establish a financial safety net. Such a safety net typically includes prudential supervision, deposit insurance, emergency liquidity assistance and orderly winding-down procedures.[2] It is worth noting that a well-devised safety net combines elements aimed at preventing as well as resolving financial crises. In the absence of either of these elements, (perceived) risks of destabilization of the banking system will grow. This, in turn, may lead to international repercussions such as the reluctance on the part of foreign institutions to hold claims on domestic banks and the emergence of a country premium for international inter-bank deposits.

The main risk of any financial safety net, however, is that it encourages moral hazard. Financial discipline may be reduced by providing incentives for excessive risk-taking by banks and insufficient monitoring by depositors whose claims are protected by the safety net. To the extent that the specific features of a deposit insurance scheme cannot sufficiently mitigate the occurrence of moral hazard (that is, where risk-based funding is deemed infeasible or inappropriate), the case for public oversight of banks' major activities is reinforced. Otherwise banks would be incented to accumulate overly risky assets, since the downside of their investments is covered by the deposit insurance guarantee. In Chapter 9 of this volume, Gillian Garcia – an international financial consultant – discusses the effectiveness of deposit insurance schemes as well as its interplay with banking supervision.

While this 'classical' line of thought tends to focus on creditor protection in order to prevent bank failures and consequent runs, recent thinking on banking supervision is much more couched in terms of reducing systemic risk and maintaining financial stability. Financial instability is usually thought to be of a systemic nature when significant portions of financial markets break down, causing widespread and substantial losses both in financial markets and, critically, in the real economy. Systemic risk typically refers to the *ex ante* probability and expected severity of such systemic financial instability.

Systemic financial instability may have its origins in the banking sector when credit or liquidity problems of one or more institutions create widespread and substantial credit or liquidity problems for participants elsewhere in the financial system. On top of contagion through direct and 'real' link-ages, financial stress emerging in one bank may also insinuate and thereby prompt similar difficulties in others, as it is often impossible for individual creditors to distinguish bank-specific from industry-wide shocks (a confidence channel). Markets may then break down because institutions being run upon hold assets that cannot easily be liquidated to meet the demands of those participating in the run.

Failure or financial distress of a number of key large banks could result in a credit or liquidity crunch in which market participants are temporarily unable to obtain sufficient working capital or back-up lines of credit to trade in public equity, debt, commodities, currency or derivatives markets. The likeli-hood of these systemic effects occurring as the result of a single bank failure logically increases with the degree of concentration in the banking industry.

In view of the ongoing consolidation within the financial services industry, nowadays three core objectives of financial regulation can be distinguished:[3]

- to sustain systemic stability (that is, limiting the risk of correlated failures as laid out above);
- to maintain the safety and soundness of financial institutions (that is, limiting idiosyncratic rather than systemic risk); and
- to protect the consumer. Consumer protection issues arise for two main reasons: because an institution where clients hold funds might fail, or because of unsatisfactory conduct of business of a firm with its cus-tomers (depositors and investors alike).

By and large, these objectives translate into three generic types of financial regulation and supervision/oversight:

- systemic regulation and oversight, which focuses on the safety and soundness of the financial system as a whole;
- microprudential regulation and supervision, which focuses on the safety and soundness of individual financial institutions; and
- conduct-of-business regulation and supervision, which focuses on how financial firms conduct business with their customers.

While it is difficult to provide a clearly delineated definition of what constitutes systemic oversight, it is clear that it entails typical central banking functions such as ongoing assessment of financial vulnerabilities, the lender-of-last-resort facility and oversight of the payments system. To bring out the contrast with microprudential supervision, Crockett suggests thinking of the financial system as a (mixed) portfolio of institutions. The macroprudential or systemic perspective would focus on the overall performance of the port-

folio; the microprudential vision would give separate weight to the performance of each of its constituencies.[4]

... AT THE CROSSROADS

The theme of the conference has given rise to multiple interpretations, as is
reflected in several of the papers. The leitmotiv has been to chart the consequences for banking supervision of two stylized developments that, over the
last decade or so, have characterized the financial landscape within the Netherlands and elsewhere: the joint occurrence of cross-sector and cross-border
integration of financial services. In Chapter 3 of this volume, Nout Wellink,
Governor of De Nederlandsche Bank, observes that both developments inevitably call for a supervisory response. The somewhat orthogonal relation
between the two, however, implies that banking supervision currently indeed
stands 'at the crossroads'. This is not to say that policy-makers must choose
one of either directions and turn their backs on the other. The theme developed *inter alia* by David Llewellyn in Chapter 8 of this volume is precisely
the opposite: regulators need to proceed in several directions simultaneously
by optimizing the combination of the several components of what he terms
the 'regulatory regime'.

Recent discussions on the optimal institutional structure of financial service regulation and supervision in the Netherlands and elsewhere have been
dominated by the desire to formulate a response to the blurring of distinctions
between banking, insurance and securities activities. After all, consistency in
regulation and supervisory practice is an important prerequisite for achieving
a level playing field between various financial service providers. In Chapter 4
of this volume, Kees van Dijkhuizen – Treasurer-General of the Dutch Ministry of Finance – highlights the main features of the new institutional set-up of
financial supervision in the Netherlands. In a nutshell, the new model ac-
knowledges the predominance of financial conglomerates in the Dutch financial
landscape, the fundamental difference between prudential supervision and
conduct-of-business supervision, and the close linkages between systemic
stability and microprudential supervision in a highly concentrated financial
sector.

In Chapter 5 of this volume, Jochen Sanio – President of the newly established Bundesanstalt für Finanzdienstleistungsaufsicht (BAFin) – compares
the new Dutch model with the recently approved German model of a cross-
sector structure for financial supervision. For roughly the same reasons that
led to the institutional reform in the Netherlands, the German legislator drew
a rather different conclusion. Whereas the Dutch model combines systemic
and microprudential supervision and separates conduct-of-business supervi-

sion, the German model combines microprudential and conduct-of-business supervision within a newly established supervisory authority (BaFin) separate from the Bundesbank's systemic responsibilities. A Financial Markets Regulation Forum representing both institutions will be responsible for the co-ordination of microprudential and macroprudential issues. The comparison between the two countries illustrates that, in the end, each new regime will have its peculiarities often tailored to meet specific national characteristics. It will be interesting to monitor how, over the coming years, the different supervisory strategies will succeed in meeting the fundamental objectives of financial regulation as defined above.

The current supervisory landscape in other European Union countries, as well as at the Community level, is also far from being static. In Chapter 6 of this volume, Wim Duisenberg – President of the European Central Bank – reviews these developments, concentrating on the role of national central banks and the European System of Central Banks (ESCB) in prudential supervision. The role of the ESCB is rooted in the Maastricht Treaty, which assigns it the task of contributing to microprudential supervision and financial stability, while keeping the primary responsibilities in these areas at the national level. Having reviewed the pros and cons of the various institutional structures, the ESCB strongly supports a continued involvement of national central banks in prudential supervision. Any solution other than direct responsibility would have to be coupled with close co-operation and operational involvement of central banks in order to allow the potential synergies between central banking and microprudential supervision to be exploited.

While the blurring of sectoral distinctions has had far-reaching consequences for the institutional set-up of financial supervision, the blurring of geographical distinctions has thus far mainly evoked calls for increasing international co-operation. Prime examples of the fruits of such co-operation are the supervisory standards developed by the Basle Committee on Banking Supervision (BCBS). Under the leadership of its chairman Bill McDonough, the BCBS is currently finalizing the new capital adequacy framework for large internationally active banks ('Basle 2'). In Chapter 7 of this volume, Tom de Swaan – Chief Financial Officer at ABN Amro and former Chairman of the BCBS – stresses the importance of the convergence of supervisory practices around the globe. As Basle 2 would entail an increase in supervisory discretion relative to the old accord, the international level playing field can only be maintained by further convergence of supervisory practices.

In Chapter 8 of this volume, David Llewellyn – professor of Money and Banking at Loughborough University – argues that the real significance of the Basle 2 proposals is the setting of regulation within the wider context of the 'regulatory regime' with a clear recognition that mechanisms other than rules are important in sustaining the safety and soundness of banks and systemic stability. In terms of the 'regulatory regime' paradigm, Basle 2 offers more precision in the regulation component while at the same time also gives emphasis to other mechanisms such as market discipline. His theme is that, while much attention has been given to refining the many and very detailed capital adequacy rules in pillar one (refinement of risk weights and so on), the real challenge lies in how the three proposed pillars (1. minimum capital requirements; 2. supervisory review; and 3. market discipline) are related and are to be co-ordinated. In particular, it is deemed likely that pillars two and three will prove to be more important and significant than the details of capital adequacy rules in pillar one.

Philip Lowe – from the Bank for International Settlements – evaluates a different aspect of Basle 2's capital adequacy rules: its inherent degree of procyclicality. As such, Chapter 10 of this volume provides a telling example of the natural interplay between microprudential regulation and macroeconomic ramifications. It examines the two-way linkages between the credit risk measurement approach underlying Basle 2 and macroeconomic fluctuations. Lowe concludes that much remains to be done in integrating macroeconomic considerations into risk measurement, particularly during the upswing of business cycles that are characterized by rapid increases in credit lending and asset prices.

Finally, in Chapter 11 of this volume Jaap Bikker and Iman van Lelyveld – both from De Nederlandsche Bank – investigate the extent to which Basle 2's increasing reliance on internal risk measurement approaches can be extrapolated to the group-wide supervision of financial conglomerates. Internal risk models are relatively well developed for market and credit risks but for other risks many issues remain to be resolved. An even greater challenge is the development of models that aggregate risks across risk areas and business units, in particular across bank and insurance activities. An important building block of such models is the diversification effect that the combination of different activities might offer. The results suggest substantial potential for diversification that may, however, be offset by increased contagion risks.

In closing, I would like to thank everyone who helped make this conference so successful. We appreciate both the speakers giving their valuable time to share their expertise and the discussants as well as the audience participants who actively contributed to the policy debates. In this context, I should specifically mention Arnoud Boot, Wilko Bolt, Henriëtte Prast, Gaston Siegelaer and Annemarie van der Zwet. I also want to thank the members of DNB's staff who devoted so many hours to developing the program, organizing and directing the conference. In this context, a special articulation of gratitude is owed to Thea Kuppens, Henriëtte Prast and Sandra Wesseling. Once again, the conference provided an excellent forum to address the regulatory and supervisory consequences of cross-sector and cross-border integration of financial services.

NOTES

1. D.W. Diamond and P.H. Dybvig (1983), 'Bank runs, deposit insurance, and liquidity', *Journal of Political Economy*, **91**, 401–19.
2. FSF Working Group on Deposit Insurance (2001), *Guidance for Effective Deposit Insurance Systems*, Basle: BIS.
3. D.T. Llewellyn (1999), *The Economic Rationale for Financial Regulation*, FSA Occasional Paper 1, London.
4. A. Crockett (2001), *Marrying the Micro- and Macroprudential Dimensions of Financial Stability*, Basle: BIS.

2. A brief history of the institutional design of banking supervision in the Netherlands

Joke Mooij and Henriëtte Prast

INTRODUCTION

This chapter describes how banking supervision in the Netherlands has evolved over time. It concentrates on how legal and institutional arrangements and the practice of banking regulation and supervision have responded to developments in the financial environment. In 1952 a law was passed that provided the legal basis for the regulation and supervision of the banking sector by the Nederlandsche Bank (hereafter, the Bank). But prior to that, the Bank already carried out supervisory activities in an informal way. To put the developments of the past 50 years in a broader perspective, the chapter therefore also contains a brief history of the Bank and the commercial banking industry in the Netherlands up to 1952.

The chapter is structured as follows. The next section gives a brief overview of the early history of the banking sector in the Netherlands, from the establishment of the Bank in 1814 to the Bank Act of 1948, which formally entrusted banking supervision to the Bank. The third section describes the main features of the first Act on the Supervision of the Credit System of 1952. The fourth section discusses the Amendment of 1956 and the practice of supervision carried out until 1978. The fifth section examines the extension and revision of the Bank Act in 1978 and the practice of financial supervision until 1990. The penultimate section studies the interaction between changes in the financial environment and in banking supervision and regulation in the Netherlands between 1990 and 2002. It includes the lifting of the prohibition of mergers between banks and insurance companies, the 1990 Protocol on the supervision of financial conglomerates, the new Act on Supervision of the Credit System introduced in 1993 and the developments resulting in the major change in the institutional design in the Netherlands in 2002, when the traditional model of sectoral supervision was replaced by a model of functional supervision, with a separation between prudential supervision on the one hand and conduct-of-business supervision on the other. The final section summarizes the main conclusions.

1814–1948: PATERNAL SUPERVISING

The Bank was founded in 1814 on the initiative of King William I. Initially its purpose was to help revive the Dutch economy. Its first Charter makes no mention of its responsibility for monetary or financial stability. The Bank in those days can be characterized as a commercial bank, which was permitted to issue banknotes. During the first decades its activities – among which were discounting trade bills, lending against securities and trading precious metals – were limited in size. Furthermore, the public and the corporate sector did not have much confidence in the new banknotes. As long as there was no economic upswing, corporate sector demand for loans was small. The banks traded securities, and there were international lending activities as a remnant of the colonial past. What are nowadays called the traditional activities of banks – taking deposits and granting credit to private sector enterprises – were virtually absent in the Netherlands at that time. In fact, until 1860 the Bank was the largest commercial bank in the country (De Vries, 1989). During the second half of the nineteenth century the Netherlands saw a distinct economic recovery. From then onwards, the Dutch banking sector started growing and, by 1900, had taken over the Bank's leading position as measured by its balance sheets. Obviously, the banks were not the stimulus: it was a typical example of Joan Robinson's dictum 'where output leads, finance follows' (Prast, 2001, p. 188).

Based on the Bank Act 1863, a nation-wide network of branches, or agencies, and correspondents of the Bank was established from 1864 onwards. Within a decade, the agencies in total attracted more business than the head office in Amsterdam. One of the activities of the agencies was discounting accommodation bills (*kredietpapier*). For this they needed a good knowledge of the customers, that is, the corporate sector (Jonker, 1996). When the private banking sector gradually took over the credit function of the Bank, this monitoring activity came to be concentrated on the newly founded commercial banks and mutual credit unions rather than on private sector entrepreneurs. With hindsight, these were the first, albeit informal, supervisory activities undertaken by the Bank. An outstanding example of this are the ups and downs of the Zuid-Hollandsche Crediet-Vereeniging in the late 1880s. This mutual credit union was one of the largest clients of the Bank's agency at The Hague. Based on documents sent in every month, the Bank detected that the credit union's business policy was dangerous for its solvency. So it asked the managing board to change its policy. During the following course of events it became clear to the Bank that mismanagement and fraudulent behaviour had caused severe losses. In order to rescue this credit union, Bank President Pierson initiated a reorganization and demanded the dismissal of the directors and the commissioners. Their successors were appointed only after Pierson had given his consent (Kymmell, 1996; Van Maarseveen, 1992).

The Bank Act adopted in 1903 confirmed that the Bank was allowed to act as bank of issue, and its banknotes were given the status of legal tender. No mention is made in this Bank Act of any responsibility for macroeconomic stability or of a supervisory function. And although the Bank was in fact the lender of last resort, this was not explicitly laid down in the law.[1] Supervision was realized through persuasion, as is clear from the terminology used at the time, 'paternal supervision' (De Vries, 1994). During the first decades of the twentieth century, the Bank gained importance as a banker's bank (Vanthoor, 1994). Its focus was on the creditworthiness of the banks as borrowers, not as key institutions in the system of payments and financial intermediation. However, as the Bank was adviser to the government it had, albeit informally, a public duty, and De Vries (1992) stresses its role in those days as an 'economic watchtower'.

Meanwhile, the banking sector in the Netherlands showed a marked degree of expansion in the first decade of the twentieth century.[2] In this period, banks were growing both in size and in number: in the period 1894–1910 more than 100 new banks were established. New communication technology – telephony – enabled the banks to serve large areas, and business growth led to an increase in demand for larger funds. Not all new banks were successful, however; by 1913, 42 banks had disappeared, 38 of which through liquidation. Unfortunately, no further information about these bankruptcies is available. But the mere fact that this large number of banks was allowed to go bankrupt and, perhaps more importantly, that this did not lead to a financial crisis, is an indication of the relatively minor role of banks in the economy at that time. In so far as the Bank felt responsible for both stability and efficiency of the banking system, it was not forced to choose between the two: the less efficient banks could be allowed to disappear without having to worry about systemic implications and financial panic.[3]

The outbreak of the First World War – the Netherlands remained neutral – led to a turbulent situation in the financial sector, but had no dramatic implications for the commercial banks in the Netherlands. One reason may be that deposit-taking was still limited in those days, hence bank fragility due to depositor panic was not as serious a problem as it would have been later. During the post-war years, the Dutch economy was booming and so was the profitability of banks. And when the boom turned into a recession, it became obvious that many banks had not diversified enough, had concentrated too much on lending to industries that undertook war-related activities and had failed to screen their borrowers. Lack of experience and integrity added to these factors, as fraud played a role too. This was especially true of the smaller regional banks, although even the large Rotterdamsche Bank Vereeniging – or Robaver – one of the five largest banks, was suspected of irregularities. The result was a banking crisis. Between 1922 and 1927, 61 banks disappeared, 14 of which through bankruptcy.

During this crisis, the Bank developed as lender of last resort, giving liquidity support to individual banks. In the case of Robaver, the Bank went even further, as it organized a consortium with the aim of supporting the price of Robaver stock by acting as a buyer on the Amsterdam Stock Exchange. The purpose of this action was the prevention of a bank run (De Vries, 1994). Apparently, the Robaver was considered 'too big to fail', although this terminology was not used at the time.[4] Another example of a bank in distress was Marx and Company's Bank, which was liquidated in 1922.[5] The rescue attempt of this bank was, however, to be the last case of major emergency assistance by the Bank on the basis of private responsibility and the unwritten task of lender of last resort, before it was nationalized in 1948. In the case of the Amsterdam Bank Associatie, which got into serious trouble in May 1922, a consortium was organized by other Amsterdam banks. This time the Bank displayed a different attitude. It was not only involved in organizing the consortium, but also enforced a stringent regime of financial orthodoxy and supervised this closely. However, it did not give financial support.[6] (De Vries, 1989; Jonker, 1996) At that time, the Bank believed that preventive supervision of a credit institution which was not in need of constant credit support by the Bank, was out of the question. Its only instrument was to refuse to discount particular bills of exchange or to reject specific stocks as collateral (Vanthoor, 2002).

One of the results of the banking crisis was that banks became reluctant – again – to finance the corporate sector, and their activities became concentrated on short-term credit against transferable collateral (Jonker, 1991). Although this flight to safety provoked a credit crunch and certainly did not mitigate the economic depression, it may have helped the banks to survive the macroeconomic crisis years; there was no serious financial distress during the 1930s. The fact that during the preceding financial crisis, the less healthy banks had disappeared, may also have been helpful. It was in these years that the role of banks in the Netherlands – as lenders to firms and as providers of the means of payment – became crucial to economic performance (Prast, 2001). Not only the banking sector faced a severe crisis in the 1920s. The insurance business, especially life insurance, faced a hard time too. Here the problems resulted in insurance supervision being formalized.[7]

Until the 1930s, the Bank's supervision activities had been of a parental and informal nature. Supervisory activities were carried out on an ad hoc basis and were aimed at isolated cases. In the 1930s, however, the first signs of both monetary and prudential supervision – at that time called business supervision – appeared almost simultaneously. In the case of monetary supervision, this was a response to the suspension of the gold standard by the UK in 1931. In order to get information about the development of the balance of payments, the Bank requested the major commercial banks to send in monthly reports of their foreign assets and liabilities, and of their gold reserves. This data flow was formalized by a gentlemen's agreement (1933–37) between the Bank and over 60 banks. The latter agreed to support the guilder by, among other things, limiting the gold trade with the public. They also agreed not to act as counter-parties in currency transactions against the guilder. Furthermore, they agreed to notify the Bank if they observed signs of any developments that might endanger the guilder. After the devaluation of the guilder the agreement had lost its value and was ended at the initiative of the Bank (De Vries, 1994).

A first step towards prudential supervision was taken in 1932, when the Bank requested the banks to send in quarterly balance sheets. In this way it hoped to gain more insight into the development of the credit system. The reporting was intensified after the collapse of the internationally well-known banking house, Mendelssohn & Co. in Amsterdam. This bank had always submitted its quarterly reports, but now it had turned out that this kind of reporting was inadequate if international banking activities were involved. So the quarterly balances were replaced by monthly balances. The banks agreed that the monthly reports would be checked against the books of the banks by the auditors of the Nederlandsche Bank. At the Bank this agreement led to the establishment of an auditing department in the spring of 1940 (De Jong, 1960). Moreover, the banks agreed to inform the Bank about their outstanding loans over 5 per cent of their own funds or above 1 million guilders. Both forms of co-operation by the banks were voluntary. This approach would become a key issue in the future discussion about institutionalizing supervision of the credit system.

Meanwhile, in 1934, the Dutch parliament discussed the role of both the commercial banking sector and the Bank. This debate should be seen against the background of the financial sector's growing economic power and the bankruptcy of Mendelssohn & Co. This bank collapsed shortly after receiving a major loan from the Bank. For this reason, some contemporaries argued that the information was inadequate and did not enable the Bank to make a good judgement of the financial soundness of individual banks (Bosman, 1958). With regard to the growing economic power of the financial sector, it was said, with reference to the views in academic circles, that commercial banks have an important role to play in stabilizing output and employment. At the time, pleas to nationalize the central bank did not win support but, three years later, a parliamentary debate culminated in the establishment of the State Committee for the banking sector (De Jong, 1960; De Vries, 1994).[8] Its task was to investigate the desirability of a legal provision for the supervision of the banking sector, and to assess whether the statutes of the Bank should be changed. The Committee focused on four questions: is the functioning of the banking system adequate; what is the role of the banking system in the business cycle; are solvency and liquidity of commercial banks adequate; and what should be the relationship between the central bank and the commercial banks?[9] The initiative for the State Committee is mainly to be seen as a response to the discussion about the independence of the Bank in respect of the revision of the Bank Act. An incentive was also given by the growing importance of the financial sector for the economy as a whole, as well as by the adoption of regulatory laws in the USA (Prast, 2001).[10] Owing to the Second World War, the State Committee was unable to publish an official report. However, its discussions and preparatory work laid the foundation for the institutional structure of central banking and supervision in the Netherlands from 1948 onwards.

After the Second World War, the Dutch economy was in ruins. Minister of Finance Lieftinck took measures to end the highly explosive monetary situation. He announced a money purge in September 1945, which was successful (Barendregt and Visser, 1997). Another pressing post-war problem was the lack of foreign currency and gold. The country depended on the import of food to feed its impoverished population and on the import of raw materials and fuels to restore its almost collapsed national production system. The government imposed rules to control the allocation of the scarce currency and gold reserves to ensure that the sectors considered to be most vital for economic recovery would be supplied with the necessary financing. The Bank was in charge of the execution of the imposed regulation. It did not yet have a formal responsibility for banking regulation and supervision. Still, the emergency measures gave the Bank a firm grip on the post-war economy in general, and the banking industry in particular.

Meanwhile, steps were taken to ensure that the Bank would receive the information it deemed necessary for its monetary objective. In early 1946 the Bank agreed with 42 commercial banks, and with the two central organizations of the agricultural banks, that they would send in figures on a monthly basis. This would enable the Bank to gain insight into the general course of banking developments.[11] The co-operation was formalized in a gentlemen's agreement. The Bank tested these credit activities against monetary standards only. Its control did not cover the solvency of the banks, but was purely motivated by monetary objectives. An example is the Bank's policy in the autumn of 1946. A rapid increase in bank credit alarmed the Bank, which was pursuing a strict monetary policy (DNB, *Annual Report*, 1946; 1947). The post-war emergency measures gave the Bank the power to send a general warning to the Association of Commercial Banks requesting the banks to apply a strict standard in providing credit.[12]

THE FIRST ACT ON SUPERVISION (1952)

In 1948, the Dutch Parliament adopted a new Bank Act, which implied nationalization of the Bank. This Bank Act 1948 gave the Bank explicit responsibilities for both macroeconomic stability and the stability of the financial system.[13] Yet, the supervision of the credit system was to be laid down in greater detail in a separate Act on the Supervision of the Credit System (Wet Toezicht Kredietwezen), which came into effect on 16 May 1952.[14] In parliament there had been a difference of opinion about whether or not supervision of the credit system ought to become permanent. The outcome of this debate was a compromise: the Act was given a temporary character and would expire on 1 January 1955. By then, however, the duration had been extended by two more years. Soon the bill for a final settlement of banking supervision was submitted, which illustrates that in this brief period Dutch authorities had become aware of the need for banking supervision on a legal basis. Table 2.1 illustrates the landmarks in the history of Dutch supervision. It clearly shows how the pace of supervisory changes has accelerated over time, especially since 1990.

In the 1952 Act on Supervision a distinction was made between monetary supervision, aimed at supporting monetary policy, business supervision (which was to be called prudential supervision at a later stage, see fifth section in this chapter), aimed at safeguarding the interests of the creditors, and structural supervision, aimed at creating the conditions for a healthy and efficient banking sector (Klompé, 1990). The Bank itself was to decide how to act in case of conflicts between these goals. In 1949 the Bank had already started to exchange views on an informal basis with the banking sector. These regular meetings were given a legal basis by the 1952 Act. Still, the Act met with opposition from the banking sector, employers' organizations and politicians. The representatives of the banking sector were offended by the fact that the Minister of Finance had not consulted them. Their criticism, which focused primarily on monetary supervision and to a lesser degree on business supervision, can be explained by unfamiliarity with the academic views on quantitative credit control as a means of monetary policy (Bosman, 1967).

Monetary supervision was based on the task entrusted to the Bank in section nine of the Bank Act 1948, as described above. It was, in fact, closely related to post-war monetary policy. Monetary supervision will therefore only be discussed here indirectly and only in so far as it interfaced with

Table 2.1   Landmarks in the history of supervision

1814	Establishment of De Nederlandsche Bank
1948	Bank Act
1952	Act on the Supervision of the Credit System
1956	Amendment of the Act on the Supervision of the Credit System
1978	New Act on the Supervision of the Credit System
1988	Basle Capital Accord I
1990	Protocol on the Supervision of Financial Conglomerates
1992	New Act on the Supervision of the Credit System
1993	Revised Protocol on the Supervision of Financial Conglomerates
1994	Exchange Offices Act
	Unusual Transactions Act
	Amendment to 1992 Act with Regard to Supervision of Financial Conglomerates
1995	Amendment to 1992 Act with Regard to Deposit Insurance
1996	Amendment to 1992 Act Regarding Exchange of Information Between Supervisors
1998	New Bank Act with Respect to EMU
1999	Council of Financial Supervisors
	Amendment to 1992 Act with Respect to the Provision of Information to the Public
2002	New Institutional Structure of Financial Supervision
	Covenant Between Prudential and Conduct-of-business Supervisors

business supervision as executed by the Bank after the Act on Supervision of the Credit System of 1952.

Supervision in general was based on the principle of consultation. The Bank could not give a general instruction without consulting the representative organizations first.[15] All 'general instructions, as well as the amendment, withdrawal and prolongation of the same', were subject to approval by the Crown.[16] If no agreement could be reached or if individual institutions would not act in accordance with the agreed course of conduct, the Bank could issue general or special directives. The legislation largely reflected the practice of consultation that had been in vogue ever since the days of paternal supervision.

During the first years, banking supervision was dominated by monetary supervision. In 1954, two arrangements were made to control the still distressed Dutch monetary situation. The first general directive imposed on the commercial banks and all agricultural credit institutions was a potential obligation to hold a monetary cover – in the form of liquid resources in proportion to deposits. This arrangement could come into effect whenever the Bank considered it to be necessary. This, however, never happened and therefore this arrangement came to be known as the *IJskastregeling* (mothballed regulation).

The second general directive of 1954 provided for credit ceilings. The Bank came to a gentlemen's agreement with the commercial and agricultural banks on cash reserve requirements. The banks agreed to hold cash reserves at the Bank if their deposits exceeded 10 million guilders. It was agreed that the required proportion would, as a rule, not exceed 5 per cent but, if money market conditions should make it desirable, the percentage could, at the discretion of the Bank, be raised to ten.

As for business supervision, the 1952 Act on Supervision regulated the powers of the Bank in the field of control of the banking system. Subject to Bank supervision were the commercial banks and central credit institutions, agricultural credit banks and general savings banks. A Royal Decree in 1954 stipulated that stockbrokers who made it their principal business to act as intermediaries in security dealings on the stock exchange and were also engaged in accepting money on deposit or in current account were to be treated as a separate section of securities credit institutions, and were hence under supervision by the Bank. Stockbrokers who did not meet these criteria were removed from the Register of credit institutions (hereafter the Register).[17]

As supervision of registered credit institutions was the core of the Act, much effort was put into making a register. Under the new Act, it became prohibited in the Netherlands to operate as a credit institution without a licence from the Bank. In order to get a licence, the commercial banks needed to fulfil minimum solvency requirements, with the required amount of own resources to be determined by the Minister of Finance.[18] After formal approval by the Bank a credit institution was entered in the public Register. It should be stressed that at the time no requirements were introduced as to the professional abilities and integrity of high-level bank officials.

As for business supervision, the reporting by the credit institutions in order to monitor their solvency and liquidity was intensified in the 1950s. The process started with laying down lines for uniform annual and monthly statements. Between 1954 and 1956, the first directives containing provisions regarding liquidity and solvency were given to the registered banks. The 1952 Act gave the Bank the means to intervene in banking activities concerning the reduction of issued or paid-up capital, the permanent participation in, or taking over of, other credit institutions, the merger with other enterprises or institutions and financial reorganization. In all these cases, a declaration of no objection by the Bank was required. Besides, the Bank could give credit institutions a notification if it detected signs of a development which it thought was or could jeopardize the solvency or liquidity of a particular bank.

As a rule, neither the name of the financial institution concerned nor an indication of its actual financial situation was revealed. It was believed that supervision should not harm the market position of individual credit institutions.

In view of the special character of the agricultural credit banks and the savings banks, the Bank made use of the legal provision to delegate the execution of business supervision in whole or in part to other organizations. Actually, the supervision of the liquidity and solvency of the member co-operative agricultural credit institutions was delegated to their two central organizations (see note 15).[19] The business supervision of the independent registered saving banks was delegated to the Netherlands Association of Savings Banks.[20] In fact most co-operative agricultural credit institutions and the savings banks had been subjected to supervision by their own central institutions for several decades (Bosman, 1958). All three of the above organizations had to carry out their prudential supervision tasks in accordance with the instructions of the Nederlandsche Bank.

THE 1956 AMENDMENT

Even though much value was attached to the voluntarily arrangements, it was decided that a legal structure of banking supervision was inevitable. The general feeling was that because of the large number of banks, it was almost impossible to rely on gentlemen's agreements only (Bosman, 1958). So, based on the experiences of executing supervision, the original Act was amended and sent to parliament. In fact, 1956 can be regarded as the final settlement of the 1952 Act. This time, the Minister of Finance had consulted the banking sector about the content of the amendment and the bill passed through parliament without any opposition. Subsequently, on 15 August 1956, the Amendment of the Act on the Supervision of the Credit System came into force. The revised Act strengthened the Bank's position as a supervisor of the credit system.[21] Commercial banks which did not possess the required minimum amount of resources determined by the Minister of Finance were no longer allowed to act as a credit institution. Small banks were not forbidden, but were not subjected to supervision by the Bank either and, hence, did not require authorization. This would become impossible under the 1978 Act.

In respect of monetary supervision, the original 1952 Act stipulated consultation between the Bank and the representative organizations before the former could give a directive. In the revised Act, this was only one phase in the process towards a directive. From now on it was stipulated that if no agreement was reached, the Bank could give a general directive which had to be submitted within three months to parliament for consent. If agreement was reached, the Bank obtained the power to give specific directives to institutions that refused to follow the agreed course of conduct. As for business supervision, the general instructions on solvency and liquidity did get the status of guiding principles for the conduct of the credit institutions' business. If an institution did not comply, the Bank's only weapon was the procedure provided for in Article 17 of the Act on Supervision. This article enabled the supervisor to give an unwilling registered credit institution a notification. If necessary, this could be accompanied by an instruction and a specified statement of reasons. If the situation did not improve, the Bank's ultimate weapon was that of publishing the instruction and – at the credit institution's request – at the same time publishing the correspondence between the Bank and the credit institution regarding the given instruction. With this procedure, supervision had become more transparent in general, but remained confidential in every individual case.

Meanwhile, the financial landscape in the Netherlands was changing considerably. Unlike in Belgium and Germany, the links between industrial firms and the banking system were traditionally rather weak in the Netherlands. This pattern did not immediately change in the 1950s, when firms financed their expansion largely (for over 70 per cent) with internal funds. But it did change dramatically in the 1960s. Corporate lending increased considerably thanks to economic growth. At the same time, demand for deposits boomed as a result of the increase in household wealth and the progress made in payment technology. An explosion of retail banking ensued. With an average yearly production growth of 8 per cent during the period 1963–73, the banking system grew more rapidly than any other sector (Van Zanden and Griffiths, 1989). This expansion was accompanied by concentration, most likely as a combined result of large-scale credit demand by the industrial sector, international competition and the high cost of new technologies which could only be borne by large-scale banks.

During the 1950s and 1960s, credit ceilings were an important instrument in creating monetary stability. By imposing quantitative limits on credit growth, the Bank intended to influence aggregate liquidity.[22] In the 1950s and 1960s, the credit ceilings were repeatedly imposed with the aim of preventing liquidity from getting 'out of hand'. However, they clearly had the potential of distorting financial sector efficiency: Not only did the credit ceilings limit the growth of the banking sector as a whole, they also prevented individual banks from growing at an above-average speed, thus distorting competition. The Bank preferred credit ceilings over an indirect method of credit control, as it feared that in the latter case competition would push interest rates up to unacceptably high levels. During the 1960s, the system of credit ceilings was criticized by the government because of its paralysing effect on the banking sector. In response the system was adapted to make it more flexible, for example by allowing credit growth above the ceilings under certain conditions. However, the Nederlandsche Bank did not abolish it until March 1972.[23]

Despite the limitations imposed on individual banks, the financial sector changed considerably during this period due to the two major mergers that resulted in the establishment of two large banks, ABN and Amro. In 1964 the ABN was created by a merger of Twentsche Bank and Nederlandsche Handel-Maatschappij, and Amro bank by a merger of Amsterdamsche Bank and Rotterdamsche Bank. The announcement of the mergers took the Bank by surprise. Its responsibility for structural supervision had given the Bank the power to refuse a declaration of no objection if in its opinion a merger would 'lead to an undesirable development of the credit system'. In their request for approval, the banks mentioned cost efficiency, adaptation to the growth of their clients and, last but not least, the need for the banking system to strengthen its position in the international financial playing field (Van der Werf, 1999). It was especially the latter argument that convinced the Bank that it could not refuse its approval, despite the risk that the new institutions would gain too much market power. With the takeover of HBU in 1968, the ABN gained access to Latin America and became the first 'global player' among the banks in the Netherlands.

The Bank faced a huge increase of applications for bank licences in the 1960s, of which most had to do with mergers. Banks traditionally could be categorized by their specific activities, for example commercial banks, mortgage banks, savings banks and agricultural banks. By the 1970s this division gradually disappeared as banks started to expand their range of activities. The co-operative agricultural banks which were traditionally focused on financing agricultural activities had began to diversify their banking activities in order to attract a new clientele. In December 1972, finally, the two agricultural banking co-operations merged into RABO-bank.

Between 1954 and 1966 the Bank had given a total of 34 cautionary recommendations to credit institutions after having detected signs of a development which, in its opinion, endangered or might endanger the solvency or liquidity of a particular credit institution. This is what happened in 1966 with Gebr. Teixeira de Mattos, a small bank that ran into difficulties due to its risky credit policy. In the end, suspension of payment and publication were inescapable. It subsequently appeared that the bank had misled the Bank, which had no instruments to prevent this kind of deceptive conduct (Fase, 2000). This incident got much attention in the newspapers during the summer of 1966. One of the reasons was that many small depositors suffered financial consequences because of this bank failure. Another reason was the general belief, at that time, that banking supervision could and indeed should prevent bank failures.

The Teixeira incident led to parliamentary questions to the Minister of Finance about the role of the Dutch central bank. The minister replied that the Bank had warned Teixeira more than once. He also stressed that legislation could never prevent false representation, nor guarantee that problems would be brought into the open in time for creditors to take action. Nevertheless, this bankruptcy would influence the future Act on Supervision, which was already in preparation, although it would take more than 12 years before it was passed. The protection of the interests of depositors was to receive more attention. Furthermore, emergency regulations were to be introduced.

The main characteristic of business supervision up to the 1970s was that, in essence, it was based on the figures submitted by the registered banks. Furthermore, up to then each of the four categories of credit institutions, namely, commercial banks, agricultural banks, securities credit institutions and general savings banks, faced their own set of directives. The need to change this was already felt in the late 1960s as a result of the changing financial environment. It was one of the main reasons for revising the 1956 Act on Supervision, a process which started in 1965. Another reason for revision was the tendency to harmonize business supervision according to European Community regulations. It would, however, take until 1979 before the new Act came into force.

THE 1978 ACT

With the 1978 Act, the emphasis of banking supervision shifted from monetary towards prudential supervision. The collapse of the Bretton Woods system in 1973, and the liberalization of international capital markets that would take place in later years, implied that monetary policy would ultimately become directed at pegging the exchange rate of the guilder to the Deutsche Mark (De Greef, Hilbers and Hoogduin, 1998). At the same time, the growing importance of the banking sector called for more detailed prudential supervision. For that matter, banking supervision in some European Economic Community (EEC) countries was studied at the Bank. Special attention was paid to elements like deposit insurance, business licensing conditions, security funds and solvency requirements. Later on, the US system of deposit insurance was examined as well.[24] Another aspect of consideration were mergers. In most other countries, regulations on mergers existed at that time. In 1964, confronted with the mergers of four large banks, the Bank had stipulated, as a condition, that it would judge every participation of 5 per cent or more on its admissibility. Ways of incorporating this in new legislation were now explored. The revision of the Act as well as the process of consultation was finished by the end of 1970.

In addition, the bill for revised supervision of the credit system together with an explanatory memorandum was sent to parliament. Due to a lengthy and rather complicated decision process, the new Act on Supervision, together with a number of decrees and orders for its implementation, did not enter into force until 1 January 1979.[25] At first glance it is perhaps surprising that it took such a long time. However, during the entire process the bill was adjusted to the latest developments, keeping it up to date. So, the Act on Supervision of 1978 met the first EEC directive with regard to the co-ordination of banking legislation (DNB, 1979).

In the Act on Supervision 1978, the expression 'prudential control' replaced the old expression of 'business supervision' or 'supervision over solvency and liquidity'. Apart from this modernization, the former three directions under which supervision on the credit system was carried out remained the same. Now they were referred to as 'monetary supervision', 'prudential control' and 'structural supervision'. On the whole, the Act on Supervision was broader, more detailed and provided the Bank with more instruments. It reflected a firmer grip on the business of banking in the Netherlands. In general it broadened the scope of supervision. The definition of credit institutions was widened to embrace all credit institutions whose business comprised receiving funds repayable at less than two years' notice, and of granting credits and making investments on their own account. Additionally, supervision was extended to other categories of institutions like capital market institutions and near-banks. So industrial and non-banking enterprises which contributed to liquidity creation were subjected to monetary supervision. From then on supervision also included mortgage banks,[26] Bank for Netherlands Municipalities (Bank voor Nederlandsche Gemeenten NV) (in 1981), the National Investment Bank (De Nationale Investerings Bank NV[27]) (in 1981) and the Postal Cheque and Giro Services (Postcheque-en Girodienst) as well as the Post Office Savings Bank (Rijkspostspaarbank) (from 1986 onwards The Postbank).

As to monetary supervision, the old instruments based on the Exchange Control Decree were now incorporated in the new Act. The possibility of imposing regulations on the net external position of banks became one of the two 'structural' instruments of the 1978 Act. Furthermore, the Bank could prescribe a structural cash reserve in proportion to the liabilities of the financial institutions.

One of the most fundamental changes was the introduction of a system with licence requirements. Among other things, it was laid down that the day-to-day policy should be determined by at least two people, that a credit institution which is a public company or private company with limited liability should have a supervisory board of at least three members, that credit institutions should have a certain minimum amount of available own resources and that each credit institution should submit its annual accounts – balance sheet and profit and loss account – accompanied by an explanatory report and certified by a registered accountant to the Bank in accordance with the model laid down by the Bank, within six months of the end of the year.

Other novelties were the prerequisites on expert knowledge of one or more persons who determine the day-to day policy of the credit institution and on the reliability of the persons who determine or co-determine the policy of the credit institution. If the Bank considered them inadequate or was of the opinion that the interests of the creditors might seriously be at risk, it could refuse to grant a licence. Furthermore, these conditions applied to both new institutions and existing ones. A licence could be revoked if a credit institution no longer fulfilled the requirements. Under the 1978 Act a company without a licence was not allowed to act as a financial institution and legally was no longer allowed to call itself a 'bank' from 1 January 1980. Under the old Act, the Bank had no legal means to interfere if a financial institution did not meet the criteria required for a licence. In addition, the Bank acquired the power according to the amended Bankruptcy Act to request suspension of payment for an investigated non-registered institution if it, in the opinion of the Bank, was unable to continue paying its due debts. This could be used if the Bank, having made inquiries based on the 1978 Act, had the impression that such an institution was unable to continue paying its due debts.

As for structural supervision, the 1978 Act stated that a declaration of no objection was needed for, among other things, participation (over 5 per cent) by credit institutions in other institutions and the exercise (by anyone) of voting rights in respect of shareholdings of more than 5 per cent in credit institutions. These declarations were given by the Minister of Finance after consulting the Bank or in special cases by the Bank on behalf of the Minister. The Act did not explicitly forbid credit institutions to merge with other enterprises or institutions. However, through the system of declarations of no objection the structural policy could be executed. This policy aimed at avoiding financial concentration. Futhermore, it was meant to discourage the coming about of so-called 'banque d'affaires'. The rationale was to prevent concentration of power or developments which might be against the general interest.

As far as protecting the interests of creditors was concerned, the new Act introduced deposit insurance and emergency regulations. The main objective of deposit insurance, which guarantees bank depositors a repayment of their deposits, usually up to a maximum amount, is that it prevents bank panic and runs on healthy banks, as these runs would lead to illiquidity followed by insolvency.[28] If a registered credit institution went bankrupt or was in need of provisions, the newly introduced Implementing Body (Uitvoerend Orgaan) would pay up to a fixed maximum sum to each affected creditor as soon as possible.[29] In doing so, the Implementing Body took over the creditors' claims on the credit institution. It was laid down that the Bank would act as the Implementing Body and was to be assisted by an advisory body.[30]

As noted before, emergency regulations were introduced. They were designed for situations when the solvency or liquidity of a credit institution showed signs of a dangerous trend and no improvement in this trend could reasonably be expected. In those cases the Court could, at the Bank's request, declare 'the credit institution to be in a position requiring special measures in the interest of all creditors' (sections 31 and 32). Under the new Act on Supervision, legal provisions regarding the suspension of payment were not applicable to credit institutions.

With the new Act that came into force in January 1979, the Bank had become the supervisor of mortgage banks in the interest of their solvency and liquidity, a sector which thus far had been, like the savings banks and the agricultural credit banks, characterized by self-regulation. Credit institutions were granted a period of three years in which to adapt their organization and operations to the new legislation. But shortly after the introduction of the new Act, the mortgage banking sector was confronted with serious difficulties, partly as a result of macroeconomic developments. The 1970s had been a period of double-digit inflation and high nominal interest rates. Real rates were low and this elicited a boom in the real estate market. By the end of the decade this bubble burst. Inflation fell, real rates rose and the real estate market in the Netherlands collapsed. Banks with large mortgage portfolios experienced serious difficulties. In fact, in 1982 the Tilburgsche Hypotheek Bank (Tilburgh Mortgage Bank) went bankrupt as a result of serious losses on its debt portfolio. These were for a large part related to developments in the commercial real estate market. It should also be kept in mind that the difficulties arose at a time when not all the changes for adapting to the new Act had been made. Thus, Tilburgh Mortgage Bank had not yet applied the 'four-eyes principle'. It became the first mortgage bank to which the 'emergency regulation', introduced with the 1978 Act and described in the previous section, was applied.[31]

During the period preceding the collapse of the Tilburgh Mortgage Bank, an attempt was made to rescue this mortgage bank. Three other large mortgage banks did, in co-ordination with the Bank, try to prevent the failure, but this attempt was unsuccessful. Two other regional mortgage banks, Westland-Utrecht Hypotheekbank (in 1983) and Friesch-Groningsche Hypotheekbank (in 1985), got into difficulties as well. However, they survived with the help of two major insurance companies, Nationale Nederlanden and Aegon, and Postbank. This operation was facilitated by the statement by the Minister of Finance in 1981 that, if banks and insurance companies wished to increase the solvency of mortgage banks, a declaration of no objection under Article 25 of the Supervision Act would not be automatically refused. With hindsight, the Minister's statement can be seen as a first step towards the lifting of the prohibition on cross-sector mergers that was to take place in 1990.

THE 1990S: TOWARDS A NEW STRUCTURE OF FINANCIAL SUPERVISION

The final decades of the twentieth century saw a distinct change in the financial landscape in the Netherlands. Globalization, conglomeration, the blurring of distinctions between banking, insurance and securities activities, the single market for financial services in the European Union, the birth of the euro and a growing awareness of the importance of financial integrity and consumer protection were challenging regulatory and supervisory policy and affected the institutional structure of financial supervision in the Netherlands in various ways. This section will describe the interplay between these trends and banking supervision. The changing financial environment did call for closer co-operation between the different financial supervisors within the Netherlands and it implied that banking regulation would become subject to international agreements.

The liberalization of capital markets in the 1980s legalized cross-border activities for financial institutions. The subsequent developments in information and communication technology made these activities economically profitable. In order to be successful players in a global financial market, the banks in the Netherlands had to grow. The lifting in 1990 of the prohibition on combining banking and insurance activities in one financial institution, helped them by paving the way for mergers between banks and insurance companies into large financial conglomerates. Immediately after the lifting, a process of mergers and acquisitions ensued (Van der Zwet, 1999). In fact, the Netherlands was one of the pioneers in the area of 'bancassurance'. By 2000, 10 of the 15 largest banks in the Netherlands had become part of a financial conglomerate. Growth was not only realized cross-sector but also cross-border (Fortis), and by expanding international activities, as ABN Amro did in the USA.

The lifting of the prohibition on combining banking and insurance activities was an important change in structural supervision. It also marked the beginning of a process of co-operation between the financial supervision authorities in the Netherlands. The emergence of financial conglomerates called for co-ordination between the banking and insurance authorities. In 1990 the Bank and the insurance supervisor (Verzekeringskamer) concluded a protocol in order to ensure adequate supervision of financial conglomerates. The basic idea of the protocol was that the banking and insurance branches of a financial conglomerate should each be supervised by their respective authorities. The protocol established rules for the conditions to be fulfilled by conglomerates in order to be granted an authorization (a declaration of no objection for holding a bank and an insurance company) and obliged the supervisors to exchange information. Depending on whether the conglomerate is primarily engaged in banking or in insurance, it was to be the banking or the insurance supervisor, respectively, that decided upon minimum solvency requirements at the holding company level, but the holding company had to inform both supervisors about its financial position on a consolidated basis.[32] In response to the rapid developments in the creation of financial conglomerates, the new Act on the Supervision of the Credit System in 1992, and an evaluation of the 1990 protocol, the latter was revised and given a legal basis in 1994.

Meanwhile, the internationalization trend had prompted supervisors worldwide to intensify their contacts and co-operation. This implied that, although banking supervision remained a national responsibility, banking supervision in the Netherlands became more and more constrained by international agreements and regulations. As a rule, the international agreements provided minimum standards and left further regulation at the discretion of national supervisors. Some agreements were to cover the European Union (EU), others applied to industrialized countries worldwide. An example of the latter is the Basle Capital Accord of 1988, which established common international minimum solvency standards for banks. It was drawn up by the Basle Committee on Banking Supervision, which consists of representatives of the banking supervisors and central banks of the Group-of-Ten countries (plus Switzerland, Luxembourg and Spain since 2001).[33] The Basle Accord was inspired by the desire to create an international level playing field for banks. As far as the EU is concerned, the creation of the single market for financial services in 1992 was an important step forward in the financial integration in Europe. Banks, insurance firms and investment firms authorized by one member state of the EU are allowed to establish branches or provide cross-border services in other member states. Within this single market, supervision is the responsibility of national authorities and it is thus the home country authority that supervises cross-border activities. The single market policy, based as it is on mutual recognition of national regulations, requires a considerable degree of harmonization of financial regulation. The harmonized directives are important instruments in this respect. They are legally binding and are designed to prevent regulatory arbitrage and to create a level playing field. The legislation in the EU obliges the supervisors to co-operate with each other and to exchange information. One way that this co-operation takes shape is through a web of consultative and decision-making bodies, such as the Banking Supervision Committee, the Groupe de Contact and the Banking Advisory Committee. Further co-operation is reflected in, mostly bilateral, Memoranda of Understanding between member states.

In 1992 a new Act on the Supervision of the Credit System was drawn up in order to adapt national legislation to the demands of the single market for financial services in the EU. Since the late 1980s, various EU directives had indicated how Dutch legislation relating to diverse banking activities and (prudential) supervision should be modelled. As far as prudential supervision was concerned, they were largely based on recommendations by the Basle Committee on Banking Supervision. The 1992 Act legalized the principle of home country control (only within the EU). It also widened supervision to the administrative organization of credit institutions. From now on, recommendations and general directives could be given concerning the way credit institutions are conducting their business. An additional adjustment to the Act was made in July 1995 when the Deposit Insurance Scheme had to be revised according to the EC directive on this matter of May 1994.

During this decade, financial integrity became an increasingly important issue in the discussion about financial market regulation and supervision. This was in part a reaction to developments at the Amsterdam Exchanges, with suspicions of insider trading provoking a debate about the importance of integrity of financial market participants. This would lead to a stronger role for the financial markets authority. For the banking sector, the authorization requirements for bank management were sharpened. As to the prerequisites on expert knowledge of persons who determine the day-to-day policy of the credit institution and on the trustworthiness of the persons who (co-)determine this policy, the Act was far more detailed. It was stipulated that the Bank shall authorize unless (among other things) it is of the opinion that the expertise of persons who determine the day-to-day policy 'is insufficient in connection with the pursuit of the business of a credit institution' and 'in view of the interests of the creditors or future creditors of the enterprise or institution, the trustworthiness of one or more persons who determine or co-determine the policy of the enterprise or institution, is not beyond doubt' (Section 8). The expertise is tested prior to the appointment on the grounds of education, professional experience and references. The trustworthiness is tested both on the basis of the references given and on the information available to the Bank or other supervisors in the financial sector. In addition, police records may be consulted. Furthermore, on applying for authorization the applicant should give detailed information about the number, the names and the past history of the persons who determine the day-to-day policy of the institution.

Since 1992, the Act on Supervision and the rules based on it have been adjusted several times. This is an ongoing process. The Act has been amended as a result of regulations concerning the supervision of financial conglomerates (1994), the exchange of information with other supervisory authorities (1996) and the provision of information to the public (1999). During this decade, financial supervision was broadened, as more financial intermediaries were brought under supervision regarding their conduct of business. In 1994 two new, separate Acts entered into force – the Unusual Transactions Notification Act and the Identification Financial Services Act – aimed at preventing the financial system from being used for money laundering. This was followed by the Exchange Offices Act, which entered into force on 1 January 1995. From then on exchange offices had to be registered by the Bank and were subject to prudential supervision, which in their case focused on integrity and the administrative organization.

In view of the establishment of the Economic and Monetary Union and the single currency on 1 January 1999, a new Bank Act was adopted in the Netherlands in 1998. With this Act, the right for the government to give directives to the Bank was abolished, making the Bank independent with regard to monetary policy. The supervisory task is laid down in section 4 of the Act, which states that: 'The Bank shall have the task of supervising financial institutions in pursuance of the relevant statutory regulation.' The same section (4.2) gave the Bank for the first time the explicit task of 'promoting the smooth operation of the payment system'. The establishment of the European Central Bank (ECB) implied that emergency liquidity support by the Bank should not interfere with monetary policy by the ECB. To the extent that this support would have an overall effect that would be relevant for monetary policy or have a financial stability implication for the euro area, the Eurosystem would be actively involved. However, the lender-of-last-resort function is not explicitly defined, as maintaining 'constructive ambiguity' may help to reduce the moral hazard associated with a safety net (Padoa-Schioppa, 1999). As far as banking supervision is concerned, the Maastricht Treaty gives the Eurosystem the task to 'contribute to the smooth conduct of policies pursued by competent authorities relating to the prudential supervision of credit institutions and the stability of the financial system' (Maastricht Treaty, 1992, Article 105 (5)), while keeping the primary responsibilities in these areas at the national level.

Over time, it became clear that the blurring of distinctions between banking, insurance and securities activities in the Netherlands called for a further reflection on the optimal institutional structure of supervision. This need was not only evidenced by mergers and acquisitions, and therefore the birth of financial conglomerates, but also by the characteristics of the new, increasingly complicated financial products.

In some countries, developments in the financial environment had prompted the authorities to create a single supervisor for the various financial sectors (Lannoo, 2000). In those countries the reorganization was sometimes triggered by bank failures and the ensuing discussion about the question whether supervision and regulation were adequately designed. Initially, the Netherlands did preserve the existing institutional set-up, with regulation and supervision of the banking system entrusted to the central bank, and with insurance and securities firms having separate supervisors. The choice in the Netherlands to maintain a structure in which the central bank is responsible for the prudential supervision of banks has to do with stability considerations. In view of the high degree of concentration of the banking sector, systemic and prudential supervision are appropriately placed close at hand to the central bank (Brouwer, 2002).

Still, the blurring of distinctions between different types of financial firms and products called for more co-operation between the three supervisors. In 1999 a council of the banking, insurance and securities supervisors was established.[34] The aim of this Council of Financial Supervisors (Raad Financiële Toezichthouders) was to give an additional impulse to cross-sector co-operation between the financial supervisors. The Council is not a decision-making body on supervisory and regulatory issues, but should be viewed as a forum for discussion and further co-operation in the field of cross-sector regulatory and supervisory issues. One of the prominent issues on the agenda of the Council was financial integrity and consumer protection. As more small amateur investors entered the markets and increasingly complicated financial products became available, the protection of consumers of financial products became more important. Also, society became more aware of the potential adverse effects of a lack of integrity in financial markets. The Bank and the securities and insurance supervisors, for example, recognized the need for regulation of the quality of the information offered by suppliers of financial products. Their co-operation resulted in the requirement, as of 1 July 2002, that financial products be accompanied by standardized minimum information about their key features.

In anticipation of the reorganization of supervision that was to take place in 2002, the Bank and the Pensions and Insurance Supervisory Authority established close links between their Boards of Directors, with cross-board appointments at executive and non-executive levels. In 2002, a major change took place in the institutional structure of financial supervision in the Netherlands. In the new model, financial supervision is organized not by industry, with each sector having its own supervisor, but on a cross-sector basis in line with its main objectives: systemic stability, prudential supervision and conduct-of-business supervision.

The reorganization of the model of financial supervision is based on the philosophy that financial supervision should meet three criteria. It should be effective, market-orientated and efficient. Effectiveness implies that supervision should meet the objectives of systemic supervision, soundness of financial institutions and proper conduct of business, including market transparency. Market-orientated implies that markets should be as undistorted as possible, and that institutions can compete on a level-playing field. Efficiency requires that the overlap between the tasks of the different supervisors should be kept to a minimum and that the administrative burden of the supervised institutions should be restricted.

In the new set-up, the Bank remains responsible for systemic stability. The responsibility for prudential supervision is taken care of by both the Bank and the Pensions and Insurance Supervisory Authority. As a separate supervisor, the STE, which changed its name to the Netherlands Authority for the Financial Markets (Autoriteit Financiële Markten) is responsible for conduct-of-business supervision on a cross-sector basis. It should be stressed that despite the institutional separation, co-operation between the prudential supervisors on the one hand and the conduct-of-business-supervisor on the other is important, as some issues, for example financial integrity, have both prudential and conduct-of-business dimensions. Thus, the Council of Financial Supervisors will remain as a consultative platform for common issues. A Covenant between the three supervisors, which entered into force in September 2002, established further rules for their co-operation and co-ordination, within the legal framework (De Nederlandsche Bank et al., 2002). Thus, the Bank and the Pensions and Insurance Supervisory Authority are jointly responsible for authorizations to banks and insurance companies, whereas the Authority for the Financial Markets holds this responsibility with regard to securities.

CONCLUSION

The role of the Bank as an informal financial supervisor can be traced back to the nineteenth century. Since 1814, when the Bank was established, it has evolved from a privately owned commercial bank into a central bank responsible for monetary policy, prudential supervision and systemic stability. The increasing importance of banks for the economy and the changing views on the role of the state in the inter-war years led to the nationalization of the Bank in 1948 and to the adoption of the 1952 Act on the Supervision of the Credit System. Since the adoption of the latter, the financial environment in which the Bank operates has changed considerably. This influenced the way banking supervision was formalized. The first Act still reflects the old spirit of gentlemen's agreements. Later amendments and new Acts provided for more codification and, as time went on, for more detailed formalization.

In the 1950s and 1960s the focus of banking supervision in the Netherlands was on monetary supervision. This changed with the liberalization of capital markets and with the shift in monetary policy. From the late 1970s, prudential supervision and consumer protection became more significant, and from the 1990s financial integrity and conduct-of-business supervision gained importance. Over time, supervision was broadened, first, because more institutions were brought under the definition of credit institution, and hence became subject to solvency and liquidity requirements, and secondly, because conduct-of-business supervision was applied not only to credit institutions, but also to other financial intermediaries.

Over the past 50 years, the pace at which supervision in the Netherlands changed has increased considerably. The 1956 Act on the Supervision of the Credit System survived for 22 years, its 1978 successor for 14 years and, since 1990, there has been a rapid succession of major changes both in the legal framework and in the institutional structure of supervision. Although the 1978 and 1992 Acts on Supervision reflected the lessons learned from the failures of individual banks, the changes in financial supervision in the Netherlands have been primarily inspired by the evolving role of banks and by changes in the structure of the financial sector rather than by banking crises. The cross-sector basis of the new model of financial supervision clearly reflects the continuing integration of financial institutions in the Netherlands and is therefore expected to provide a solid supervisory structure for the future.

NOTES

1. However, this is not exceptional. As a rule, the lender of last resort function is not made explicit in Bank laws out of fear that the explicit mention of a safety net might induce moral hazard behaviour by banks. See Hartmann and Carletti (2002).
2. Still, the banks did not stimulate the industrial revolution that took place around the turn of the century (Van Zanden and Griffiths, 1989; De Vries, 1994). Rather, they benefited from it. From 1880 through to 1913, yearly average per capita growth in the Netherlands was 0.9 per cent. This was low compared to economic growth in other European countries (De Vries, 1994, table 1).
3. Recent views stress, however, that there is hardly a trade off between efficiency and stability in the banking sector. See Hartmann and Carletti (2002).
4. The initiative for the rescue operation was taken by the government, which gave the Nederlandsche Bank a guarantee for an amount up to 60 million guilders after Robaver's top official had visited Prime Minister Colijn.
5. The liquidity support resulted in a loss to the Nederlandsche Bank of 26.9 million guilders, the lion's share of its total loss in connection with the banking crisis, which amounted to 31.1 million guilders. It comes therefore as no surprise that the Bank was heavily criticized for its support, as Marx and Company's doubtful position was common knowledge since 1916 (Jonker, 1991).
6. The Amsterdam Bank Associatie was liquidated in 1937. Parts of it were taken over by the Incasso-Bank.
7. Partly due to the threat of war, the business of life insurance was booming. As a result, in 1919 the total sum insured by Dutch life insurance companies was 50 per cent higher than in 1914. This post-war boom ended in an insurance crisis in the early 1920s. Two life insurance companies, the Algemeene Maatschappij van Levensverzekering en Lijfrente (General Life Insurance and Annuity Company) and Kromos, had to be liquidated as they

no longer could meet their obligations. Decades before, policy-makers already had agreed on the importance of a sound functioning of the insurance business to the economy. As for the banking industry, confidence is crucial for the good functioning of the insurance sector. Pleas by some politicians to nationalize the insurance sector did not gain general support. The crisis of the early 1920s, however, called for a legal provision for supervision of the insurance sector and speeded up the realization of the Act on the Life Insurance Business. This Act provided for the foundation of the Verzekeringskamer (Insurance Board) in 1923 (De Wijs, 1998). In the beginning the execution of the Insurance Supervision covered only the life insurance companies and saving banks (spaarkassen). After the Second World War, insurance supervision was extended to the building societies and various forms of pension funds and property insurance companies.

8. According to De Vries (1994), the timing of the establishment of the Committee is surprising, given that the banks in the Netherlands had managed quite well during the then recent depression years. It is likely that the developments in the academic world and in US legislation had their impact only after a lag.

9. Some members stressed the 'vocation' of the banking sector and its crucial role in macroeconomic performance. Others argued that banks, if left to themselves, could not be expected to focus their strategy on the public interest

10. The Glass-Steagall Act of 1933, which created a separation between banking and securities activities, and the Regulation Q which forbade interest payments on deposits.

11. In 1951 the number of financial institutions reporting monthly to the central bank had risen from 42 to 117 due to the increase of credit restrictions.

12. This was laid down in Article 19 of the so-termed Deblocking Decree 1945 together with General Licence No. 40.

13. The tasks have been laid down in section 9:
    1. It shall be the duty of the Bank to regulate the value of the Nederlands monetary unit in such a manner as will be most conducive to the nation's prosperity and welfare, and in so doing to keep the value as stable as possible.
    2. It shall supply bank notes for circulation in the Netherlands, and facilitate domestic and external money transfers
    3. It shall supervise the credit system in pursuance of the Act on the Supervision of the Credit System (De Nederlandsche Bank, 1994).

14. Until 1952, the business of banking in the Netherlands could be conducted under commercial and civil law.

15. Nederlands Bankers' Association (Nederlandse Bankiersvereniging) was designated by the Minister of Finance as representative organization of the commercial banks; the Co-operative Central Farmers' Credit Bank (Coöperatieve Centrale Raiffeisenbank) and the (Co-operative Central Agricultural Credit Bank (Coöperatieve Centrale Boerenleenbank) as the representative organizations agricultural credit banks; Netherlands Association of Savings Banks (Nederlandse Spaarbankbond) as the representative of the general savings banks.

16. Article 10.

17. At the same time, the Minister of Finance designated the Stock Exchange Association (Vereniging voor De Effectenhandel) as the stockbrokers' representative organization in the field of credit.

18. The required amount could not exceed 100 000 guilders. Article 3.2 of the 1952 Act. As a transitory measure, it was laid down that commercial banks which did not possess the required minimum amount of own resources could be temporarily registered, but they had to meet the criterion within two years. This transitory measure was not included in the Amendment of 1956.

19. Royal Decree, 28 October 1953, Staatsblad, No. 486.

20. Royal Decree, 30 August 1954, Staatsblad, No. 390.

21. In the new Act some adjustments were made regarding stockbrokers. Originally they were defined as enterprises and institutions which operated mainly as intermediaries in connection with security dealings on the stock exchange. It had turned out that a large group of them neither granted credit nor accept deposits to a large extent. Since the scope of

supervision was restricted to the credit system, the Bank no longer subjected stockbrokers not meeting the legal definition of security credit institution to supervision. The others, however, were now regarded as a separate collective subject to the Supervision Act, i.e. securities credit institutions.

22. These ceilings were imposed on the credit granted by each individual bank during a certain month, calculated as a percentage of total credit granted during the 12 months preceding the restriction.

23. In 1977 credit ceilings were reinstalled. Hilbers and Hoogduin (1996) give an overview of post-war instruments of credit control in the Netherlands.

24. Deposit insurance was introduced in the USA in 1934, after the country had faced a banking crisis in the years before. However, it is of much earlier origin, according to Calomiris and White (2000)

25. In June 1975 the Minister of Finance submitted his Memorandum in Reply (Memorie van Antwoord) accompanied by a revised bill to parliament. This enabled the Standing Committee on Finance of the Second Chamber of Parliament to resume discussion of the bill, after an interval of more than four years since the Interim Report of April 1971. After some alterations, parliamentary debate took place in February 1977. That same month the further amended bill was presented to the First Chamber of Parliament. When the government resigned, discussions were postponed. After the new government took office the Standing Committee on Finance of the First Chamber handed over its Interim Report in January 1978 (DNB, *Annual Reports*, 1975–78).

26. By Decree of the Minister of Finance of 29 December 1978, the Netherlands Association of Mortgage Banks (Nederlandse Vereniging van Hypotheekbanken) was designated as representative organization of the mortgage banks.

27. As a result of business developments the National Investment Bank was registered as a universal bank from 1 January 1988 (Coljé, 1988).

28. By Royal Decree of 29 June 1978 the Bank was authorized to perform the required activities in connection with the administration of the collective guarantee scheme referred to in section 44, 1 of the Act on Supervision of 1978. In the USA during the Great Depression, deposit insurance was introduced to prevent bank runs. Although this may have contributed to preventing bank runs, it may also have created moral hazard behaviour on the part of the insured institutions. In 1980s the large number of bankruptcies and the resulting deficits in the guarantee fund gave rise to a discussion about the pros and cons of deposit insurance. As for the Netherlands, there is no guarantee fund. Bikker and Prast (2001) give a survey of the discussion in the Netherlands.

29. The maximum amount was index linked and would be revised every three years.

30. By Royal Decree of 21 December 1978 the Nederlandsche Bank was authorized to act as such. The six members of the latter were appointed by the representative organizations.

31. A year before, the emergency regulation was used for the first time in the case of the failure of Amsterdam American Bank N.V.

32. In 1992 the Insurance Board was separated from the Ministry of Finance and became an independent public institution.

33. The Basle Committee was established in 1975 at the initiative of the central bank governors of the G-10 countries in response to the well-known Herstatt crisis, which made clear the need for information exchange and co-ordination between national banking supervisors.

34. As for the securities industry, the sector itself (Amsterdam Exchanges and the Options Exchange) had established its own Authority (Stichting Toezicht Effectenverkeer [STE]) in 1988. This self-regulation was gradually transformed, between 1988 and 1997, into a public institution (though financed by the sector and not through public funding). This transformation was motivated by a growing awareness of the importance of integrity in financial markets, by suspicions about insider trading and by international competition and regulation abroad. At a later stage, the STE would become responsible for conduct of business supervision of the financial sector.

REFERENCES

Barendregt, J. and H. Visser (1997), 'Towards a new maturity 1940–1990', in M. 't Hart, J. Jonker and J.L. van Zanden (eds), *A Financial History of the Netherlands*, Cambridge: Cambridge University Press, pp. 152–94.

Bikker, J.A. and H.M. Prast (2001), 'De depositoverzekering tegen het licht' ('Deposit insurance in perspective'), *Economisch-Statistische Berichten*, 26 October, 820–22.

Bosman, H.W.J. (1958), *De Wet toezicht kredietwezen* (*The Act on the Supervision of the Credit System*), Leiden: Stenfert Kroese.

Bosman, H.W.J. (1967), 'Het toezicht op het bankwezen in het tijdperk-Holtrop' ('Supervision on banking in the Holtrop era'), *Orbis economicus*, September, pp. 69–82.

Brouwer, H. (2002), 'Regulatory challenges for European financial markets', speech delivered at the CEPR/ESI-conferentie, Vienna, 20–21 September.

Calomiris, C.W. and E.N. White (2000), 'The origins of federal deposit insurance', in C.W. Calomiris (ed.), *U.S. Bank Deregulation in Historical Perspective*, Cambridge: Cambridge University Press, pp. 164–211.

Coljé, H. (1988), *Het toezicht op banken in Nederland* (*Banking Supervision in the Netherlands*), Serie Bank- en Effectenbedrijf nr 24, Amsterdam: NIBE.

De Greef, I.J.M., P.L.C. Hilbers and L.H. Hoogduin (1998), *Moderate Monetarism: A Brief Survey of Dutch Monetary Policy in the Post-war Period*, DNB Staff Reports, Amsterdam.

De Jong, A.M. (1960), *De wetgeving nopens de Nederlandsche Bank 1914–1958. Een historische studie* (*The Legislation with Respect to the Nederlandsche Bank 1914–1958. A Historical Study*), The Hague: Martinus Nijhoff.

De Nederlandsche Bank (DNB), *Annual Report*, various years, Amsterdam: De Nederlandsche Bank.

De Nederlandsche Bank (DNB) (1978), *Act on the Supervision of the Credit System and Credit System Supervision Manual*, Amsterdam: De Nederlandsche Bank.

De Nederlandsche Bank (DNB) (1979), *De herziene Wet Toezicht Kredietwezen* (*The Revised Act on Supervision of the Credit System*), Amsterdam: De Nederlandsche Bank.

De Nederlandsche Bank (DNB) (1992), *Wet Toezicht Kredietwezen* (*The Act on the Supervision of the Credit System 1992*), Amsterdam: De Nederlandsche Bank.

De Nederlandsche Bank (DNB) (1993), *Act on the Supervision of the Credit System and Credit System Supervision Manual*, Amsterdam: De Nederlandsche Bank.

De Nederlandsche Bank (DNB) (1994), *Bank Act 1948 and Articles of Association*, Amsterdam: De Nederlandsche Bank.

De Nederlandsche Bank, Stichting Autoriteit Financiële Markten, Stichting Pensioen- en Verzekeringskamer (2002), *Convenant inzake de coördinatie van het toezicht* (*Covenant Regarding the Co-ordination of Supervision*), September, Amsterdam: De Nederlandsche Bank.

De Vries, J. (1989), *Geschiedenis van de Nederlandsche Bank. Vijfde deel (1). De Nederlandsche Bank van 1914 tot 1948* (*History of the Nederlandsche Bank. Vol. 5 (1). The Nederlandsche Bank from 1914 through 1948*), Amsterdam: NIBE.

De Vries, J. (1992), 'Het Nederlandse financiële imperium, schets van de geschiedenis van het Nederlandse bankwezen' ('The Dutch financial empire, sketch of the banking system in the Netherlands'), in *Bankwezen. Een geschiedenis en bronnenoverzicht*, Amsterdam: NEHA.

De Vries, J. (1994), *Geschiedenis van de Nederlandsche Bank. Vijfde deel (2). De Nederlandsche Bank van 1914 tot 1948* (*History of the Nederlandsche Bank. Vol. 5 (2). The Nederlandsche Bank from 1914 through 1948*), Amsterdam: NIBE.
De Wijs, C. (ed.) (1998), *'Toezien of toekijken?': Verzekeringskamer 75 jaar, 1923–1998* (*'Supervising or watching?': Insurance Board 75 Years*), Apeldoorn: Stichting Verzekeringskamer.
ECB (2002), *The Monetary Policy of the ECB*, Frankfurt: ECB.
Fase, M.M.G. (2000), *Geschiedenis van de Nederlandsche Bank. Zesde deel. Tussen behoud en vernieuwing: Geschiedenis van de Nederlandsche Bank 1948–1973* (*History of the Nederlandsche Bank. Vol. 6. Between Maintenance and Modernization. History of the Nederlandsche Bank 1948–1973*), The Hague: SdU Uitgevers.
Hartmann, P. and E. Carletti (2002), 'Competition and stability: what's special about banking?', *ECB Working Paper*, no. 146, May.
Hilbers, P.L.C. and L.H. Hoogduin (1996), *Monetair beleid in vogelvlucht. Ontwikkelingen in de Nederlandse monetaire politiek na de Tweede Wereldoorlog* (*A Brief Survey of Monetary Policy. Developments in Dutch Monetary Politics after the Second World War*), Financiële & Monetaire Studies, Groningen: Wolters-Noordhoff.
Jonker, J. (1991), 'Sinecures or sinews of power? Interlocking directorships and bank–industry relations in the Netherlands, 1910–1940', in J.L. van Zanden (ed.), *The Economic Development of The Netherlands since 1870. Economic Development of Modern Europe since 1870. Vol. VII*, Aldershot: Edward Elgar, pp. 160–72.
Jonker, J. (1996), 'Between private responsibility and public duty. The origins of bank monitoring in the Netherlands, 1860–1930', *Financial History Review*, **3**, 139–52.
Klompé, M.E.J. (1990), 'Zestig Jaar Bankentoezicht: van vrijwillige samenwerking tot Tweede bankenrichtlijn' ('Sixty years of banking supervision: from voluntary co-operation to second banking directive'), *De Naamloze Vennootschap*, November–December, 262–8.
Kymmell, J. (1996), *Geschiedenis van de algemene banken in Nederland 1860–1914* (*History of the Universal Banks in the Netherlands 1860–1914*), Vol. IIb, Amsterdam: NIBE.
Lannoo, K. (2000), *Challenges to the Structure of Financial Supervision in the EU*, Brussels: Centre for European Policy Studies.
Maarseveen, J.G.S.J. van (1992), *Briefwisseling van Nicolaas Gerard Pierson 1839–1909* (*Correspondence of Nicolaas Gerard Pierson 1839–1909*), Vol. II, 1885–87, Amsterdam: NIBE.
Maastricht Treaty (Treaty on European Union) (1992), Luxembourg: Council and Commission of the European Communities.
Padoa Schioppa, T. (1999), 'EMU and banking supervision', Lecture at the London School of Economics, February.
Prast, H.M. (2001), 'Financial stability and efficiency in the twentieth century: the Netherlands', *Journal of European Economic History*, March, 185–213.
Vanthoor, W.F.V. (1994), 'De Nederlandsche Bank', in M. Pohl and S. Freitag (eds), *Handbook on the History of European Banks*, Aldershot: Edward Elgar, pp. 743–8.
Vanthoor, W.F.V. (2002), 'Centrale bank in een bewogen tijdvak:1914–1948' ('Central bank in an eventful era'), De Nederlandsche Bank, Onderzoeksrapport WO nr 702, October.
Van Zanden, J.L. and R.T. Griffiths (1989), *Economische geschiedenis van Nederland in de 20ᵉ eeuw* (*Economic History of the Netherlands in the Twentieth Century*), Utrecht: Het Spectrum.

Van der Werf, D.C.J. (1999), *Banken, bankiers en hun fusies* ('Banks, Bankers and their Mergers'), Amsterdam: NIBE.
Van der Zwet, A. (1999), *Toezicht op banken* (*Supervision of Banks*), serie Bank- en Effectenbedrijf nr 43, Amsterdam: NIBE.

PART II

Convergence of Supervisory Practices

3.   Opening remarks

Nout Wellink

The Dutch Act on the Supervision of the Credit System that was enacted 50
years ago formalized the supervisory task of De Nederlandsche Bank. It was
a response to the major changes in the financial and economic environment
that took place between the two world wars. The banking crises of the 1920s,
the Glass Steagall Act in the USA and the growing role of the banking sector
in the economy all made it clear that a sound functioning of the banking
system was too important to be arranged informally. In this respect it is
noteworthy that supervision of the insurance sector was formalized even
further back in time and has existed almost 80 years now. But, of course, in
the decades that have passed since then the financial environment has kept on
changing, and with it the challenges that supervisors face. Two trends have
been particularly prominent in the past decades. The first is the enormous
increase in cross-border activities made possible by the liberalization of
capital markets. The second is the blurring of the boundaries between banking, insurance and securities activities. These fundamental developments are
the driving force behind the increasing need for convergence of supervisory
practices across borders and sectors.

Let me illustrate this by looking at our experiences in the Netherlands. The
international dimension of our major financial institutions has increased dramatically. As a result, in some cases nowadays more than half of assets and
profits are related to activities in foreign countries. There are no signs that the
internationalization of the financial industry will slow down, rather the contrary. In a world where national financial systems and institutions are
increasingly dependent upon one another, it is obviously crucial for financial
stability that high and comparable supervisory standards are maintained every-
where.

This has long been recognized in the field of banking regulation. Indeed, it
was reflected in the establishment and the work of the Basle Committee, as
well as in the work of the European committees in this field. Importantly, as
part of Basle 2, there is wide recognition that besides having convergence in
regulation, it is equally important that supervisory practices (the implementation of the rules!) converge. The creation of the Accord Implementation

Group by the Basle Committee, and the work being done by the Groupe de Contact in Europe reflect this understanding.

It is important to keep in mind that the importance of cross-border convergence is not confined to the banking industry. It applies equally to other parts of the financial sector, such as insurance. This brings me to the other main trend that I mentioned, the blurring of the boundaries between banking, insurance and securities activities.

Here, too, the development in this country is a case in point. We have been front-runners when it comes to financial conglomerates or bank assurance, institutions that combine banking, insurance and securities activities. As is well known, the Netherlands is home to several of the world's major internationally active financial institutions. Most of the major Dutch banks currently combine banking, insurance and securities activities. The emergence of these conglomerates was made possible by the lifting, in 1990, of the prohibition on combining banking and insurance activities in a single financial institution.

As the importance of cross-sectoral financial activity increases, so does the need of the supervisory response. The main challenge in this field is to achieve a consistent approach in the supervision at group level as well as at the level of the entities within the conglomerate. Consistency does not imply that the approaches should be identical. It should be interpreted as avoiding the potential for regulatory arbitrage as well as regulatory overlap.

Again, we try to take the lead in the way we organize supervision in the Netherlands. Co-operation between bank and insurance supervisors dates back to the early 1990s and has performed well. Nevertheless, in anticipation of a continuation of the trend that I have described, we have come to the conclusion that a cross-sectoral approach to supervision is the right way forward. In this approach we make a clear distinction between prudential and conduct-of-business supervision. It assigns the responsibility for these inherently different objectives to separate authorities.

This is not to say that this is the only way to address this challenge. It depends on the specific characteristics of the financial sector in a country as to which design is best suited. In our case, for instance, we have a highly concentrated financial sector with institutions that are, almost by definition, systemically relevant. As a consequence we considered it essential to link prudential banking supervision with the central bank and its other functions such as oversight of the payment system and providing lender-of-last-resort facilities. But as I said, circumstances and the solutions chosen will vary from country to country. This is fine, as long as the approaches have at least one thing in common: they should be designed with the aim of ensuring consistency – consistency not only in regulation, but also in supervisory practice. This is an important precondition for achieving a level playing field for the international financial industry.

Let me add, as a final observation, that in achieving this goal, there is an important complementary role to be played by market discipline. Meaningful disclosure by financial institutions is a potentially powerful tool in furthering the cause of a level playing field between countries and across institutions.

Looking back in history, we are now far from where we were 50 years ago, when our predecessors introduced formal banking supervision in the Netherlands. Looking forward into the future, I am pretty sure that our successors will not be celebrating the centenary of the Act on the Supervision of the Credit System, or even the centenary of insurance supervision 20 years from now. We will have entered a cross-sectoral world long before then! And as to the topic they will be discussing, that could well depend on the turning we take on the crossroads that we are at now.

4. A functional approach to fifty years of banking supervision

Kees van Dijkhuizen[1]

INTRODUCTION

For a long time, economists have been trained to analyse topics of public policy in terms of objectives and instruments. Since the first Act on the Supervision of the Credit System was introduced in 1952, legislative reforms of the Act have largely focused on the instruments of supervision. At present, the supervisory system is being reformed again. This time, the reform also focuses on the institutional structure for achieving the objectives of supervision.

Against this background, the fiftieth anniversary of the Dutch Act on the Supervision of the Credit System provides a good opportunity to take a closer look at the objectives of supervision. The first section of this chapter briefly reviews developments in 50 years of banking supervision from the viewpoint of the objective of prudential supervision. The second section explains the new Dutch model in a long-term perspective, elaborating why banking supervision is at the crossroads. The third section will take a brief look at the future: how might financial integration affect the supervisory objectives for which De Nederlandsche Bank (DNB) is responsible, that is, prudential and systemic supervision?

FIFTY YEARS OF BANKING SUPERVISION

This section will review the development of the banking sector from the point of view of the objective of prudential supervision, which is to protect the creditors of banks and thereby contribute to financial stability. At some points, developments in the financial sector will be linked to the development of the Act on the Supervision of the Credit System, since the fiftieth anniversary of this Act is the central theme of this book.

A Short History of Banking Stability

Evidently, the history of financial stability in the Netherlands did not start 50 years ago with the first Act on the Supervision of the Credit System. The 1920s seem to provide an acceptable starting point of the analysis. At that time the Dutch banking sector experienced a crisis and DNB acted as a lender of last resort, although it did not yet have a formal supervisory task.[2] The Dutch economy had been booming following the years after the First World War, as had the profitability of banks. When the boom turned into a recession, many banks faced difficulties since they had diversified too little and failed to screen their borrowers. Fraud, as well as a lack of experience and integrity added to these factors. Between 1922 and 1927, 61 banks disappeared, 14 of which through failure. The losses by banks as a result of defaulted loans in the years 1920 through 1922 have been estimated at about 1.5 per cent of annual gross domestic product (GDP). De Nederlandsche Bank acted as a lender of last resort during this period, with total losses on the loans amounting to 31.1 million guilders. This period also provides an example of government support to the financial sector, when the government gave DNB a guarantee for an amount of up to 60 million guilders to rescue the Robaver bank.

The banking sector did not experience significant problems of financial instability in the 1930s. The disappearance of less healthy banks during the 1920s may have been helpful in this respect, just as the flight to quality by banks may have added to the economic depression of the time. The debate on the role of DNB shifted more towards crisis prevention. The role of DNB as a supervisory authority became more visible. The first voluntary agreement between DNB and the banks was signed and reporting requirements for banks were extended. In 1937, a State Committee for the banking sector was established to investigate whether the supervisory role of DNB needed a formal legal basis. In 1940 this Committee reached a positive conclusion, but the Second World War hindered the follow-up. In 1946, DNB and the banks signed a gentleman's agreement, similar to the one that had existed before the war. Finally, in 1952, the first Act on the Supervision of the Credit System was adopted, a few years after the adoption of the Bank Act in 1948 which implied the nationalization of DNB and gave DNB formal responsibilities in the field of the stability of the financial system. The main argument for introducing formal legislation was that banks did not always follow directions given by DNB and that smaller banks did not participate in the gentleman's agreement.

The following decades until the early 1970s can be characterized as years of stability and development. With an average yearly production growth of 8 per cent during the period 1963–73, the banking system grew faster than any other sector in the economy. In 1966, however, an influential incident took place. In that year, the small Teixeira de Mattos Bank collapsed. This was the starting point for a major reform of the Act on the Supervision of the Credit System. In the new Act, the supervisory instruments for DNB were extended. One of the reasons for the reform was the blurring of boundaries between different kinds of banks. Furthermore, new developments in Europe also had an influence. The first steps towards harmonization of banking regulation were taken. The result was the first EU co-ordination directive on the supervision of banks. The full reform was finally completed by Minister Duisenberg in 1978, 12 years after the start of the reform and two years after members of parliament had noted that less frequent changes of government might have contributed to a quicker process of adapting the Act on the Supervision of the Credit System.

At the beginning of the 1980s, incidents at Dutch banks occurred when one mortgage bank filed for bankruptcy and two were taken over by other financial institutions. Finally, the last major review of the Act on the Supervision of the Credit System was completed in 1992. At that time the second EU co-ordination directive on the supervision of banks was implemented. The single market was created based on the principle of home country control and a single license for financial institutions.

Assessment

So how did DNB perform with regard to the objectives of supervision? The objective is to protect the creditors of financial institutions and thereby contribute to financial stability. There have been some incidents with individual banks, but there has been no significant crisis. This is in line with the principle that supervision cannot prevent the failure of a single bank.

It might be interesting to put these results into an international perspective. General figures on the costs of banking crises show that since the 1970s there have been over 100 banking crises, about 20 of which resulted in negative worth of failed banks in excess of 10 per cent of GDP.[3] Table 4.1 contains a list of industrialized countries, based on a survey by the International Monetary Fund.[4] Of the 30 members of the Organization for Economic Co-operation and Development (OECD), 23 experienced significant banking problems or a crisis since 1980.

In the category of 'significant banking problems', there are countries such as Denmark, France, Germany and the USA. About the USA, for example, the survey notes that: 'during the period of 1980 until 1992, 1142 savings and loans associations and 1395 banks were closed; 4.1 per cent of commercial bank loans were nonperforming in 1987' (p. 34). Problems have been even worse in countries of the category 'banking crisis'. This includes countries

Table 4.1 Banking problems in the OECD, 1980–2002

No significant banking problems	Significant banking problems	Banking crisis
Austria	Australia	Finland
Belgium	Canada	Japan
Luxembourg	Czech Republic	Korea
Netherlands	Denmark	Mexico
Portugal	France	Norway
Switzerland	Germany	Spain
United Kingdom	Greece	Sweden
	Hungary	Turkey
	Iceland	
	Ireland	
	Italy	
	New Zealand	
	Poland	
	Slovakia	
	United States	

such as Japan, Finland, Norway, Spain and Sweden. On Finland, for example, the survey states: 'nonperforming loans and credit losses reached 13 per cent of total exposure at their peak in 1992; there was a liquidity crisis in 1991' (p. 25).

In spite of some problems with mortgage banks in the early 1980s, the Netherlands was ranked as a country with 'no significant problems'. It might not be justified to attribute this result completely to the performance of DNB. Supervision is a necessary but not a sufficient condition for financial stability. Furthermore, some may argue that the stable countries in Table 4.1 are the ones with a concentrated financial sector and that their relative stability could be related to the 'too big to fail' effect. However, as is shown by the brief historic overview above, there is no history of public support to the financial industry in the Netherlands. Moreover, some countries ranked in the other two categories ('significant problems' and 'banking crisis') also have a concentrated financial sector (Sweden, for example). In sum, both a comparison of the period before and after 1952 in the Netherlands and an international comparison show that DNB has performed well as regards it's legislative objective concerning prudential supervision since 1952.

BANKING SUPERVISION AT THE CROSSROADS

In the course of 2002, the Dutch supervisory model was reformed from a sectoral model to a functional model. This section explains the new Dutch model from a long-term perspective, elaborating why banking supervision is at the crossroads.

Supervisory Structure Follows Market Developments

The main driving force behind the reform is the continuing market integration. Following the liberalization of structural policies in the early 1990s, financial conglomerates have become the dominant players in the Netherlands. Financial conglomerates account for a market share of 86 per cent of banking, 73 per cent of insurance and 57 per cent of securities business. These conglomerates come in many different shapes and sizes, and seek synergies in various ways, for example in product development, reputation/branding, risk management and financing.[5] Within the large conglomerates, firm-wide risk measurement and management techniques are evolving rapidly. It is impossible to classify these conglomerates according to traditional sectoral boundaries. What can be said, however, is that conglomerates are financial institutions that perform financial market functions.[6] Therefore, a functional approach may be more suited than a sectoral approach to guide the structure of financial supervision.

Key Elements of the Dutch Supervisory Model

The Dutch model envisages a two-pillar system: prudential supervision combined with systemic stability (closely associated with the central bank) and conduct-of-business supervision under a separate supervisor. The model is organized along the main objectives of supervision: systemic stability, prudential supervision and conduct of business (Table 4.2).

As regards the role of DNB, Table 4.2 points out that the focal point of supervision has shifted from the banking sector to the objectives of systemic stability and prudential supervision, while broadening its scope of application to the whole of the financial sector. Systemic supervision relates to the traditional central bank task of overviewing the financial system as a whole, with the aim of identifying vulnerabilities and acting when necessary. More formally, the objective is to prevent problems at a single institution or in the payment system spreading to other institutions and markets. Both the descriptions of banking problems in the Netherlands during the 1920s (when DNB acted as a lender of last resort) in an earlier section of this chapter, as well as the examples of 'banking crises' in Table 4.1 illustrate the importance of this part of supervision.

Table 4.2 *The structure of supervision in the Netherlands*

	Systemic stability	Prudential		Conduct of business
		Sectoral	Cross-sector	
Banks/investment funds	DNB	DNB	DNB/PVK	AFM
Securities firms				
Insurance companies		PVK		

Notes: DNB = De Nederlandsche Bank; PVK = Pension and Insurance Supervisory Authority (Pensioen- en Verzekeringskamer); DNB and PVK are integrated through cross-board appointments; AFM = Netherlands Authority for the Financial Markets (successor to STE).

As mentioned before, the objective of prudential supervision is to protect the creditors of financial institutions and, thereby, to contribute to financial stability. Prudential concerns do not differentiate between different types of financial institutions such as banks and insurance companies. That is why DNB and the Pension and Insurance Supervisory Authority (PVK) share the objective of prudential supervision in the new model, covering the whole range of financial institutions. DNB and PVK are integrating their cross-sector activities through cross-board appointments and through joint teams and practices for prudential supervision of financial conglomerates.

The financial sector of the Netherlands is dominated by large financial institutions. As a result it is important that prudential supervision and systemic supervision are closely linked. This can be achieved by combining both types of supervision within one institution: DNB.

The first section of this chapter showed that the history of banking supervision and regulation is one of continuous change. Incidents at financial institutions, developments in the sector (such as the blurring of different types of banks in the 1970s) and international developments have always been among the main factors to influence supervisory instruments and structure. It is part of the everyday task of supervision and regulation to adapt to the dynamics of the market. In this respect, the current reform can be seen as another example of successful adaptation to market developments.

What is new about the current reform is that the organizational structure of supervision has rotated from sectors to objectives. This required a reorganization of supervisory tasks, which precedes a reform of legislation. The objectives of supervision themselves, however, have not changed. Objectives are more stable than the institutional characteristics of the financial sector and, therefore, provide better guidance on which to base the organizational and legislative structure. To illustrate this point: in 1952, the main objective[7] of the Act on the Supervision of the Credit System was to maintain the solvency and liquidity of banks in order to protect the interests of creditors. This is similar to the objective of prudential supervision today. Moreover, the supplementary note to the first Act on the Supervision of the Credit System even contained a section on the linkages between banking and insurance supervision: 'This objective (that is, of prudential supervision) is generally the same as the objective of statute-based supervision on life insurance, for which the Insurance Board is responsible.'

THE INTERNATIONAL STRUCTURE OF FINANCIAL SUPERVISION

The days that financial supervision was a purely national affair have long been gone. Financial markets within the European Union are in a state of transformation from 15 national financial markets to a single integrated EU-wide financial market. The internal market programme, the introduction of the euro and the financial services action plan (with the aim of harmonizing and modernizing financial services regulation within the EU) have all contributed to the integration of financial markets within the EU, but the process is not yet complete.[8]

As indicated, financial market developments have always influenced the supervisory structure and will continue to do so in the future. From an international perspective, it is financial integration that matters, both within the EU and globally. The integration of international financial markets will (again) change the institutional characteristics of financial markets. In the same vein, the functions of financial markets and the objectives of financial supervision will again remain more stable, so these provide for a better starting point of analysis. The challenge for public policy is to accommodate financial integration as much as possible, since a growing body of empirical evidence supports the notion that financial integration leads to a better performance of the functions of the financial system and hence a better economic performance.[9] Therefore, this section contains some preliminary thoughts on future developments: how might financial integration affect the supervisory objectives for which DNB is responsible, that is prudential and systemic supervision? This requires a forward-looking analysis. Consequently, the purpose of this section is not to give clear answers, but rather to identify some of the challenges for the future.

Prudential Supervision: Regulation

Financial integration, as well as advances in technology and risk management techniques, have a strong impact on the contents of prudential supervision. The challenge for the legislative process within the EU is to keep up with these market developments and to modernize financial regulation in response. This is no easy task, since experience shows long lead times for EU directives. The average time taken for a co-decision procedure from the Commission's proposal to final agreement in co-decision is over two years – and in the financial service area, the average time is even longer.[10] As a consequence, the legislative process often lags behind changes in the market. An example might illustrate the impact on the effectiveness of prudential supervision. In 1996, US banks were allowed to calculate their 'market risks' on the basis of sophisticated models and became subject to more accurate and lower capital requirements. In the EU, two and a half years were needed to introduce the necessary amendments to the directives before banks in the EU could operate under equivalent conditions.

A particular challenge for the next few years will be the transposition of the forthcoming new Basle capital accord into EU directives. This accord will be far more complex than anything we have seen before in this area, giving rise to numerous issues of interpretation and transposition. It will probably also need frequent revisions as a result of its complexity and unforeseen effects. Discussions on the necessary adaptations to the legislative process within the EU have intensified during the last year, since a faster legislative process will be crucial for safeguarding the effectiveness of financial supervision.

Execution of Prudential Supervision

Financial integration implies that international competition will intensify further and that cross- border business of financial institutions – either through physical presence in other countries or cross-border supply – will increase. Two issues arise from this. First, harmonization of regulation and an even execution of supervision across the EU need to go hand in hand, in order to establish a level playing field across the EU. Second, the efficiency of the international supervisory framework becomes a relevant factor: how to maintain the effectiveness of supervision while minimizing the supervisory burden for financial institutions? In this respect, there have already been calls from the industry that in the future supervisors should devote more efforts to the consistency of rulebooks, the standardization of reporting requirements and the standardization and harmonization of supervisory practice.[11] Summarizing, further convergence of supervisory practices is needed, both to maintain a level playing field[12] and to reduce the administrative burden.

Systemic Supervision

It is not entirely clear what the impact of financial integration will be on contagion and systemic risk. On the one hand, financial integration increases the opportunities for risk-sharing and might therefore lower systemic risk. On the other hand, linkages between financial markets and institutions will intensify and systemic risk might therefore increase. What is clear, however, is that it has become almost impossible to analyse the issue of systemic risk in a purely national context. Payment systems and clearing and settlement systems for securities transactions show a strong international consolidation. Large financial groups are present all over the world. By now, the largest financial groups are far larger than the largest financial institution that has ever been wound down. The implication is that the effectiveness of systemic supervision will become more dependent on the ability to co-operate and co-ordinate with other actors involved, such as supervisors, central banks and ministries of finance.

SUMMARY AND CONCLUSIONS

The common theme of this chapter is that the objectives of financial supervision are more stable than the institutional characteristics of financial markets. Financial markets change, but the objectives of financial supervision largely remain the same.

Such an objective-based approach to the history of banking stability in the Netherlands shows that there have been incidents at individual institutions, which is in line with the principle that supervision cannot prevent the failure of a single bank. The bottom line is that the performance of DNB with regard to its legislative objective has been good, both in a national and an international perspective.

A long-term perspective on the new objective-based (or functional) approach of the new Dutch supervisory model shows that, indeed, the objectives of financial supervision by DNB have been more stable than the institutional characteristics of the financial sector. The history of banking supervision is one of continuous response to market developments, but the objective of prudential banking supervision is the same today, as it was 50 years ago.

The functional approach to financial supervision is equally relevant for analysing challenges that result from the internationalization of the financial sector. In particular, three challenges are identified that are crucial for maintaining the effectiveness of financial supervision in the years to come. First, a faster legislative process is needed within the EU, in order to keep up with market developments. Second, further international convergence of supervisory practices is needed, both to maintain a level playing field and to lower the administrative burden for financial institutions. Third, the effectiveness of systemic supervision will become more dependent on international co-ordination with other actors involved.

NOTES

1. With many thanks to Peter Wierts for his contribution to this chapter.
2. The parts on the history of financial stability in the Netherlands in this section (including the figures) are based on H.M. Prast (2001), 'Financial stability and efficiency in the twentieth century: the Netherlands', *Journal of European Economic History*, Banca di

Roma, Special Issue, 185–213. Some parts on the development of the Act on the Supervision of the Credit System draw on M.E.J. Klompé and J.W.J.M. van de Vossen (1990), 'Zestig jaar bankentoezicht: van vrijwillige samenwerking tot Tweede Bankenrichtlijn', *De Naamloze Vennootschap*, November–December, 262–8.

3. See, for example, C. Calomiris (2002), 'Interview', *Financial Regulator*, **7** (1), June, 18.
4. M.J. Lindgren, G. Garcia and C.-J. Saal (1996), *Bank Soundness and Macroeconomic Policy*, Washington, DC: IMF. The figures have been updated on the basis of *Experiences with the Resolution of Weak Financial Institutions in the OECD Area*, Paris: OECD, 2001.
5. For a more extended description of the new Dutch model, see A. Jonk, J.J.M. Kremers and D. Schoenmaker (2001) 'A new Dutch model', *Financial Regulator*, **6** (3), December, 35–8.
6. For an elaboration of the functional approach to the financial sector, see R.C. Merton and Z. Bodie (1995), 'A conceptual framework for analysing the financial environment', in D.B. Crane (ed.), *The Global Financial System*, Cambridge, MA: Harvard University Press.
7. The other objectives of the first Act on the Supervision of the Credit System are those of monetary supervision and structural supervision. These are outside the scope of this chapter.
8. The analysis in this section is restricted to arrangements within the European Union, although financial integration is a global phenomenon.
9. M. Thiel (2001), 'Finance and economic growth – a review of theory and the available evidence', DG EcFin Economic Paper No. 158, Brussels: Commission of the European Communities.
10. The figures and examples in this paragraph are based on P.J. Pearson (2003), 'Comments on financial integration across borders and sectors: implications for regulatory structures', in J.J.M. Kremers, D. Schoenmaker and P.J. Wierts (eds), *Financial Supervision in Europe*, Cheltenham: Edward Elgar.
11. F. Heinemann and M. Jopp (2002), 'The benefits of a working European retail market for financial services', report to the European financial services round table, Berlin: Institut für Europäische Politik.
12. Report on Financial Stability, prepared by the ad hoc working group of the Economic and Financial Committee, European Commission, Economic Papers No. 143, May 2000.

5. The new single regulator in Germany

Jochen Sanio

The conference is aptly titled 'Banking supervision at the crossroads', as our profession has clearly reached a crucial juncture at which important decisions are to be taken that could go one way or another, and I may contribute that Germany has just decided to realign the course of national financial supervision.

It is interesting to compare the new German approach with the recently approved Dutch model of a cross-sector structure for financial supervision. From precisely the same reasons that in Germany made persuasively the case for a single regulator – strengthening systemic stability, prudential supervision and conduct of business – a rather different conclusion was drawn by the Dutch legislator. De Nederlandsche Bank shall remain responsible for systemic stability and for prudential supervision of banks; the Pensions and Insurance Supervisory Authority remains in charge for the prudential supervision of financial conglomerates and insurance companies. By giving market supervision to a separate supervisor, the Authority for Financial Markets, the Netherlands have committed themselves to the doctrine of the separation of supervisory powers, a clear-cut division, on a cross-sectoral basis, between prudential supervision and conduct-of-business supervision. It will be interesting to see how the different strategies pursued in the Netherlands and Germany will work out in the end, judged against the degree to which they provide stability to the financial system and contain the risk of systemic failure.

The new German model of integrated financial supervision, which I am reviewing today, obviously differs quite considerably from the latest Dutch approach in terms of how far supervision is integrated. Germany has embarked on full cross-sectoral supervision combining both prudential and market aspects. So, its new approach may fairly be described as a single regulator model, even though the new regime has its particularities which have been tailored to meet the specific German needs, which are, as you may have heard, often very complex.

As you are well aware of the pros and cons of the single regulator concept, I will not try your patience by repeating the arguments over and over again. In the end, the decision on the structural make-up of supervision is a political one. And that is just what happened in Germany: a long-simmering, sometimes heated policy debate, which had often been conducted to extremes, came to a sudden end on 22 March when the bill on restructuring financial supervision was finally passed. Due to the law on a single financial services supervisory authority (Gesetz über die integrierte Finanzdienst-leistungsaufsicht), the new financial services supervisory authority (Bundesanstalt für Finanzdienstleistungsaufsicht [BaFin]) will start operating from 1 May – that is within exactly one week from today.

The objective of the law is to create a new Federal Authority for Financial Services Supervision with responsibility for the supervision of credit institutions, insurance companies, investment firms and other financial institutions. The new supervisory authority is the result of a full merger of the hitherto existing sectoral authorities – the Federal Banking Supervisory Office and the Federal Insurance Supervisory Office, both based in Bonn, and the Federal Securities Supervisory Office which is based in Frankfurt. The powers of the new integrated authority cover, from a prudential point of view, the supervision of the widest range of financial institutions. On the market supervision side, consumer protection, market transparency and market integrity are the BaFin's pre-eminent goals, which have to be accomplished by formerly separated solvency regulators now working hand in hand. What we do not want to see is the outbreak of a 'Kulturkampf', a cultural struggle between different types of supervisors who have to live under one roof. I would prefer to make the famous motto from Alexandre Dumas' novel, *The Three Musketeers*, the campaign slogan for building the new institution: 'All for one, one for all.' What is needed is a concerted effort to make sure that the single regulator will converge as soon as possible on common rules that impose uniformly high standards of behaviour on the regulated firms and persons. The way to achieve this goal, to which all must pledge their support, is relatively easy in theory, yet quite difficult in practice, particularly in Germany where much regulation is enshrined in law and change is slow.

As you have heard about the wide array of responsibilities for a single regulator before – you only need to think of the British FSA – you may ask yourself: what is so special about the new German approach? The answer, of course, is the significant role the Bundesbank will play in banking supervision, and that is the reason, why I would like to call the new BaFin a 'modified' single regulator as compared to the British Financial Services Authority (FSA), for example. The Bundesbank is – to adopt the words of Dumas – the fourth musketeer, to whom specific statutory duties are assigned. To help prevent financial supervision from being afflicted with differing ambitions a special arrangement should be created that defines how BaFin and the Bundesbank join forces when carrying out their tasks.

Let me illustrate the German institutional structure in this regard somewhat more extensively. The new law introduces a new article 7(1) of the Banking Act, a provision whose wording caused a sharply polarized debate in the legislative procedure. The new provision maintains the general principle which from the very beginning has been part of the existing structure in German banking supervision: the BaFin remains, as was the Federal Banking Supervisory Office, the only decision-making authority within the supervision of credit institutions, investment firms and other financial institutions regulated by the Banking Act. The Bundesbank's involvement in the field of prudential supervision, however, is laid down in more detail. In practice, most of this involvement applies to the day-to-day supervision of credit institutions, investment firms and other financial institutions where you will see a close co-operation between the BaFin and the former *Land* central banks (*Landeszentralbanken*), which now, after the restructuring of the Bundesbank, continue as administrative offices (*Hauptverwaltungen*) of the Bundesbank. The second sentence of article 7(1) of the new Banking Act clarifies the operational involvement of the Bundesbank in the ongoing supervision of banks and financial institutions. To the extent legally possible, the BaFin is now enabled to base its supervisory decisions on the assessments and findings by the Bundesbank. In this regard, the BaFin will continue to commission either certified public accountants or Bundesbank staff as auditors when ordering special or regular audits under Article 44 of the Banking Act. The BaFin will participate in most of the Bundesbank audits in order to gauge the situation within the banks at first hand. All in all, the new law will increase the effectiveness of day-to-day banking supervision while continuing to provide legal certainty with regard to supervisory measures taken under the Banking Act.

In matters relating to the stability of the German financial system, the new law provides the legal basis for co-ordination and co-operation between the BaFin and the Bundesbank by formalizing the meetings between high-ranking representatives from both institutions. The already existing Financial Markets Regulation Forum (Forum für Finanzmarktaufsicht), created some time ago by a Memorandum of Understanding (MoU), will now be a legal body under Article 3 of section 1 of the new law. The forum, which represents both institutions, the BaFin and the Bundesbank, shall co-ordinate the ongoing work in the two institutions concerning regulatory and supervisory matters, including those with a bearing on financial stability. By establishing such a forum, the BaFin and the Bundesbank are acknowledged as the authorities jointly responsible for the stability of the financial system.

Coming back to the BaFin, formidable challenges will confront us next week when we start laying the foundations for unified financial supervision in Germany. There is not enough time to enter into a discussion of how to play the complex game of integrated financial supervision today. I might note in an aside that no one really knows which strategies will eventually carry the day. But I suppose I should say at least a word or two about our most pressing problem. In a very short time we have to develop a new internal organizational structure that will allow us to create the largest possible synergy from our merger while maintaining, for the time being, the ongoing day-to-day supervision in the existing three pillars of banking, insurance and market supervision. Our combined efforts must be stronger than the sum of what has been delivered until now by the hitherto non-integrated parts of German financial supervision.

We have identified a number of issues that have to be addressed on a cross-sectoral basis, and at its initial stage the BaFin will most likely have three or four cross-sectoral departments in addition to the three pillars. One of these departments will deal with cross-sectoral policy related to financial markets, research and economic analysis, financial conglomerates and international affairs and co-ordination. A second department will probably be responsible for deposit insurance, consumer protection and pension funds as well as legal affairs. And the third department could tackle international financial crime, illegal, notably unlicensed financial businesses and money laundering. Not all details are fully worked out at this juncture because the passage of the bill on financial supervision a month ago came as a surprise to everyone.

Let me emphasize, however, in closing that at a time when the German financial market has to change more profoundly than was imaginable just a few years ago, born-again financial supervisors in my country are bristling with energy and will not throw away the chance to create a coherent and efficient regulatory system that is fit to keep up with the increasing evolution of the financial markets.

6. The role of the Eurosystem in prudential supervision

Wim Duisenberg

The law on banking supervision enacted 50 years ago formalized the role of De Nederlandsche Bank in banking supervision. These duties had to some extent developed 'organically', through the history of the Bank, out of its original function as provider of liquidity to commercial banks and its gathering of statistical data from them. The supervisory system in the Netherlands has been undeniably successful. Dutch banks – like the financial system as a whole – have prospered and steadily improved their efficiency, and the stability of the system as a whole has generally withstood structural changes and episodes of financial market turbulence.

The fact that we are celebrating a supervisory law, which was established so long ago, might give an image of a static regulatory and supervisory system. Some sceptical observers even take the general view that supervisory structures are rigid and are only discussed critically after major disruptions in the financial system.

As we know, this image does not correspond to reality. In the Netherlands, many adjustments have been introduced over time in response to market developments rather than crisis events. For instance, co-operation mechanisms between the authorities in charge of supervising banks, securities firms and insurance companies were established – in the form of the Council of Financial Supervisors – in reaction to the growing importance of financial conglomerates and the development of close links between different financial products. Moreover, the Dutch Ministry of Finance proposed last year – with subsequent approval by parliament – to strengthen the role of the central bank in the prudential supervision of banks and financial conglomerates and to establish even closer links with the prudential supervision of insurance companies.

These responsibilities are separate from the tasks of overseeing the conduct-of-business and consumer protection aspects. Among other things, this model honours the close links between the systemic stability interests of central banks and the prudential supervision of financial institutions. Financial stability is always in the direct interest of central banks, because of its importance for the successful conduct of the basic central banking tasks in the fields of monetary policy and payment systems. Although one should always be cautious when exporting national institutional structures to other countries, the Dutch model might provide useful insights to others.

The current supervisory landscape in other European Union countries, as well as at the Community level, is also far from being static. Discussions of the appropriate institutional structures and mechanisms have intensified both at the national and European level. These debates are very healthy and demonstrate an active response by policy-makers to the development of cross-sectoral links in the financial industry, as well as to the changes brought about by the euro and financial integration.

I would like to review briefly these national and European discussions. As the issues are manifold, I would like to concentrate on the role of the national central banks and the Eurosystem in prudential supervision. The role of the Eurosystem is rooted in the Maastricht Treaty, which gives it the task of contributing to prudential supervision and financial stability, while keeping the primary responsibilities in these areas at the national level.

Let me first turn to national developments. Following the creation of the Financial Services Authority in the UK, proposals have been put forward in a number of European countries, for instance in Austria, Germany and Ireland, to set up a single supervisory authority in charge of all financial institutions. In some cases – unlike here in the Netherlands – the proposals have also included a reduced role for the central bank in prudential supervision, while increasing the responsibilities of the separate supervisory agency. In 10 out of 12 euro area countries, the central bank is still either directly responsible or otherwise closely involved in the operational conduct of supervisory duties. Only in Luxembourg and Belgium is this not the case, and in the latter a reform is being proposed that increases significantly the involvement of the central bank.

As we have often said, the Eurosystem strongly supports a continued involvement of national central banks in prudential supervision, although the institutional set-up of financial supervision needs to be tailored to the structure of the respective national financial system. Any solution other than direct responsibility should be coupled with close co-operation and operational involvement of central banks in order to allow the potential synergies between central banking and prudential supervision to be exploited. Central banks' knowledge of the overall economy and financial system, and their information from payment and settlement systems and monetary policy operations, are valuable for the performance of the supervisory tasks. Conversely, for central banks, supervisory information can play an important role in the oversight of payment and settlement systems and of market infrastructures, and in managing liquidity crises.

Strong comments have been made against this view. The most often used arguments against central bank involvement in supervision have been the increasing importance of financial conglomerates and the blurring of the distinction between the three segments of the financial sector. These developments would call for the establishment of a single financial supervisor which should not be the central bank, the argument runs, since this would worsen conflicts of interest between central banking and prudential supervision and would lead to a concentration of power. In my view, one should not be too dogmatic about these arguments. Situations in which such conflicts of interest would arise are very rare in practice and central banks, like all other public bodies, are subject to accountability procedures. In any case, these concerns are dispelled in the euro area setting by the fact that decision-making takes place at different levels: euro area wide for monetary policy, national for prudential supervision.

The arguments for keeping central banks closely involved in prudential supervision are even reinforced in the context of Monetary Union. More integrated financial markets can absorb shocks more easily than in the past, which is a very beneficial outcome. However, if shocks do occur, they are likely to have a wider impact across borders through wholesale banking and capital market links – or through payment and settlement systems. Thus, the contribution of the Eurosystem to monitoring vulnerabilities in the financial system on an euro area-wide basis will be greater if the central banks are extensively involved in prudential supervision.

Let me move on to the European debate. The Economic and Financial Committee has already assessed the adequacy of the existing arrangements for prudential supervision and the safeguarding of financial stability in the European Union in the two reports produced under the chairmanship of Henk Brouwer from De Nederlandsche Bank. The outcome of this analysis was that the current institutional system based on national responsibility is appropriate, but there is a need to strengthen cross-border and cross-sectoral co-operation between supervisors, to enhance convergence in supervisory practices and to reinforce collaboration between supervisory and central banking functions. The Eurosystem supports these conclusions. There are clear benefits in keeping supervision close to the institutions being overseen at the national level, while financial integration requires co-operation between the relevant authorities to be stepped up.

In my view, positive developments have already occurred in the implementation of these recommendations. For example, the Banking Supervision Committee of the European System of Central Banks (ESCB) – chaired by Deutsche Bundesbank Directorate member Edgar Meister – has enhanced and continues to develop its regular monitoring of the soundness of the European Union banking system as a whole, as well as its analysis of

structural banking and financial developments. These activities rely extensively on the close and constructive co-operation established within the
Committee between central banks and banking supervisory authorities. Indeed, the Eurosystem regards the promotion of co-operation between central
banks and supervisory authorities as one of its main contributions in the
field of prudential supervision. However, the full implementation of the
'Brouwer recommendations' requires additional work in order to establish
an effective information exchange – both in times of calm and in times of
crisis – and to achieve further convergence in supervisory practices.

In addition to the financial stability considerations, the issue of supervisory
co-operation also needs to be looked at from the angle of the efficiency of the
financial system. Indeed, policy-makers and market participants are paying
increasing attention to the remaining inefficiencies in the financial sector and
the residual obstacles to financial integration. For instance, the recent
'Gyllenhammar report' drew attention to the need for greater standardization
of supervisory compliance requirements and practices because of the cost
burden on financial institutions developing cross-border businesses. These
conclusions were further reinforced in the recent report by the Economic and
Financial Committee under the chairmanship of Kees van Dijkhuizen, the
Dutch Treasurer-General.

In a similar quest for greater efficiency, considerable attention has also
been paid to the Community regulatory process, with emphasis on the need to
achieve swift rule-making and consistent implementation in different member states. The recent institutional agreement achieved on the implementation
of the 'Lamfalussy procedures' represents a major step forward in the field of
securities regulation. It removes the burden of detailed and cumbersome
regulation at the Community level by delegating rule-making powers to a
committee of regulators and by promoting consistent implementation at the
national level through a committee of supervisors. Extending such a mechanism to banking and insurance would probably also produce tangible benefits,
though differences existing between the three sectors should be taken into
account. As we know, a particularly important regulatory exercise is ahead in
the transposition of the new Basle Capital Accord into the EU regulatory
framework, in which the European Commission will play a key role.

All in all, there are strong reasons to continue deepening supervisory co-
operation at the EU level. The current debate on how to achieve this objective
is intense, and not yet finished. I perceive the part played by the Eurosystem
in nurturing this debate not, as it has been suggested, as an attempt to
enhance the supervisory role of the ECB but, instead, as a constructive
contribution to setting up a comprehensive architecture for an effective multi
lateral supervisory co-operation. The latter, I believe, is a common goal of
central banks, supervisory authorities and ministries of finance.

In the banking sector, the Eurosystem feels – in line with what I highlighted earlier – that there is a need for continued involvement of central banks in multilateral supervisory co-operation, along the lines of the work of the Basle Committee on Banking Supervision. I would definitely not welcome a solution that would alter the current situation by excluding central banks without supervisory responsibilities from supervisory co-operation. Firewalls should not be unnecessarily created between central banks and supervisory bodies. The Banking Supervision Committee of the ESCB is an existing EU forum catering for co-operation between central banks and supervisory authorities. In principle, it could also be suitable as a forum for co-operation between banking supervisors, provided that it operated in a setting, which ensured an adequate degree of autonomy for this activity.

I would like to conclude that De Nederlandsche Bank, as well as the Dutch Ministry of Finance, have contributed constructively to the recent European and global developments in supervision and regulation.

7. Convergence in supervision: a commercial banker's perspective

Tom de Swaan

I would like to use this opportunity to say a couple of things on Basle 2, because in my opinion this is the most important crossroads the supervisors and the financial institutions have to cope with in the coming years. I think that the agreements that will eventually be reached in Basle will fundamentally influence the conduct of supervisory institutions and the conduct and the development of markets. One of the interesting things of Basle 2 is that it is increasingly attracting international political attention. Consequently, the risks that the negotiations might collapse, and I am convinced that this is very remote but nevertheless we have to look at that, have become more serious, given a global political arena characterized by increased tensions. We have been supporting the efforts of the Bank for International Settlements (BIS). The Basle Committee's progress over the last two and a half years is a reflection of the shared interest we have as commercial banks, as supervised institutions, with the supervisors. A key condition for us is confidence and stability of the financial system and that is something we share with the supervisor. This has shown to be a very fruitful basis for co-operation between the supervisors and banks, and I think that the increased dialogue we had with the Basle Committee will prove to be a good example of what I would call a 'learning organization'. Why is it so important? ABN AMRO is one of the most globalized banks in the world. We have operations in 60 countries and as all of you know that does not mean you have 60 supervisors; you have a multitude of them and for us it is of vital importance to have international transparent rules. In that respect, a potential failure of the internationally harmonized capital reform would represent to us a 'nightmare scenario'. In such a scenario, countries would have to look at alternatives and could opt for different 'stand-alone' solutions. And this would undoubtedly lead to price distortions, an enormous increase in compliance costs and, even more importantly, would substantially heighten systemic risk. I think that these arguments should strongly motivate you as members of the Basle Committee and the political arena to reach agreement as soon as possible. I said I would use this opportunity to highlight two issues that are of concern to us, if you do not mind. The first one is the level playing field; the other one may be less obvious, but is very important none the less, namely, the issue of how project finance is treated under the new proposals, not only from my perspective, being one of the major players in the project finance area, but also because of the importance of the project financing in the development of the emerging markets, where both the market and the participants are issuers of product finance and the sponsors of those projects play a major role.

The first item with regard to the level playing field is the perceived legal foundation of the BIS rules. We all know that, officially, the BIS does not have legislative power. National authorities are responsible for integrating the BIS agreement into national legislation. This has resulted, and will result again, in potential problems. The BIS agreement covers all internationally active banks but, as far as I know, we still do not have an official definition of an internationally active bank. This also means that the BIS agreement has to be integrated into European legislation. That will mean in European Directives, which point to all banks, and even to investment firms/security houses, while other countries outside Europe can make exceptions for local banks and can decide not to apply these rules to investment firms. That can lead, and does lead today, to unfair competition between those internationally active banks that are subject to the Basle agreement and European legislation versus local banks and those banks that are not subject to these rules.

The second item is much more topical as far as the level playing field issue is concerned. I fully support the basic principle that capital adequacy calculated under Pillar I cannot replace sound banking practices, and I also see certain potential risks stemming from differing interpretations. However, the main issue concerns the discretionary powers for supervisors under Pillar II. We, within the industry, have little idea of how Pillar II will work, nor the areas in which it will be brought to bear. There is suspicion as to the extent that it will barely be used as a device to, what I would call, 'claw back' capital changes under Pillar I. The positive possibilities of Pillar II enabling less complex regulation are not widely understood or believed in actually. For example, national supervisors are allowed to impose additional capital requirements on an individual bank, if in their view, the credit portfolio includes an extreme concentration of credit risk in industry or countries. The fact that this is not defined or quantified by Basle introduces, in my opinion, potential competitive distortion. And the source of these potential problems lies in the large differences in supervising practices across countries. National supervisors differ in size, legal structure, culture, tradition and operational approach. Despite gradual moves towards international convergence, significant differences remain and must be addressed internationally. In this respect, I would also like to address my own callings in the financial sector. The limited understanding of Pillar II has led to the situation that the industry has prima-rily focused on Pillar I issues. And, given the efforts to create a level playing field on the one hand and to produce the minimum burden of regulatory capital on the other hand, the focus on Pillar I has produced and continues to produce significant complexity and has increased the costs of implementation with little if any risk management gains.

My second reason for concern is the treatment of project finance. As I said, this concern emanates on the one hand from our position in that market, but also from the important influence the treatment of project finance will have on the willingness of the markets to finance major infrastructural projects in emerging markets. The committee has come up with proposals based on the premise that project finance is by nature more risky than corporate lending. I think that the committee has taken an extremely conservative approach here. Given the broad range of project loans, one can argue whether the probability of default for project finance is higher or lower than for corporate loans. However, for all well-structured project financing the average loss-given-default is much better than for normal corporate loans. In order to give our view an empirical foundation, we have pooled our data with three other major global finance players and I am pleased to know that the Basle Committee is prepared to look at the data we have produced for them.

I started my brief introduction by underlining the importance of an interna-tional agreement on capital adequacy, not only for internationally active banks such as ABN AMRO, but also for other parties such as supervisors, our clients and our shareholders. Banks and supervisors alike are interested in a sound global financial system, which is the basis of a fruitful co-operation. I would like to end by saying that the new Basle 2 agreement is expected to have a broad and deep impact on the banking industry and the markets, which can hardly be underestimated.

PART III

Issues in the Theory of Banking Supervision

8. The optimal regulatory environment

David Llewellyn

INTRODUCTION AND ISSUES

Financial systems are changing substantially and to an extent that undermines traditional approaches to regulation and most especially the balance between regulation and official supervision on the one hand, and the role of market discipline on the other. In particular, globalization, the pace of financial innovation and the creation of new financial instruments, the blurring of traditional distinctions between different types of financial firm, the speed with which portfolios can change through banks trading in derivatives and so on, and the increased complexity of banking business, create a fundamentally new environment in which regulation and supervision are undertaken.

The theme and title of this conference is 'Bank supervision at the crossroads'. Given that a major change to the regulation and supervision of banks for capital adequacy purposes is currently being discussed (the proposed Basle 2 Capital Accord), the topic is very timely and De Nederlandsche Bank is to be congratulated on such a timely theme. But what is the nature of the 'crossroads'? This conjures up an image that we have arrived at a point in the road where a decision has to be made about in which direction to turn or even whether we should turn back. A central theme of this chapter is that this may be an unfortunate terminology as it presupposes that we must choose one direction. The theme to be developed is precisely the opposite: that we need to proceed in several directions simultaneously by optimizing the combination of the several components of, what a previous paper (Llewellyn, 2000) termed, the Regulatory Regime. In particular, the various components of the regime are not to be regarded as alternatives. Rather, regulatory strategy should focus on how the various components are combined to create an optimal regulatory environment. It is difficult to imagine what the road analogy would be: certainly not a roundabout, that would imply that we keep going around in circles!

The objective of the earlier chapter was to draw lessons from recent banking crises with respect to the design of optimum regulatory arrangements. A central theme was that just as the causes of banking crises are multidimensional, so the principles of an effective regulatory regime also need to incorporate a wider range of issues than externally imposed rules on bank behaviour. Strategies to sustain systemic stability and the safety and soundness of banks also need to be multidimensional involving a wider set of issues than official regulation and supervision and including all elements of the regulatory regime such as official monitoring and supervision, incentive structures, market discipline, corporate governance arrangements, intervention in the event of bank distress, and the accountability mechanisms of regulatory agencies.

The current chapter develops the argument for a holistic approach to achieving the objective of financial stability and relates this to the proposed Basle 2 Capital Accord. The discussion is set within the regulatory regime context, which is wider than the rules, and monitoring conducted by regulatory agencies. The focus is on how the components of a regulatory regime need to be combined to produce an optimal regulatory strategy. In essence, and in relation to the title of the chapter, optimum regulatory arrangements incorporate all components of the regulatory regime rather than focus myopically on regulation and official supervision. This follows on the tradition of Lindgren, Garcia and Saal (1996) who emphasize the three key strands of governance: internal to the firm, the discipline of the market, and regulation and supervision by official agencies. This chapter takes that paradigm further and considers a holistic approach to regulation and supervision. As noted by Summer (2002), comparatively little analysis has been undertaken into the co-ordination between the different components of the regime.

The proposed Basle 2 Accord represents a radical new approach to capital adequacy regulation. Our theme is that, while a great deal of attention has been given to refining the many and very detailed capital adequacy rules (refinement of risk weights, and so on) the real challenge lies not so much in these refinements but in how the three proposed pillars (minimum capital requirements, the supervisory review process and market discipline requirements) are related and are to be co-ordinated. In particular, it is likely that Pillars II and III will prove to be more important and significant than the details of capital adequacy rules in Pillar I. The real significance of the Basle 2 proposals is the setting of regulation within the wider context of the regulatory regime with a clear recognition that mechanisms other than rules are important in sustaining the safety and soundness of banks and systemic stability. This is likely to be its most powerful benefit.

As bank failures involve avoidable costs that can be significant (see Hoggarth and Saporta, 2001), there is a welfare benefit to be derived from lowering the probability of bank failures, and reducing the cost of bank failures that do occur. In what follows, these are the twin objectives of the regulatory regime. Both need to be considered and are related, as arrangements to lower the cost of bank failures may impact on the incentive structure faced by banks and hence on the probability of bank failure. There is some confusion between the safety and soundness of banks, on the one hand, and systemic stability, on the other, as the objective of regulation. This dichotomy is discussed by Summer (2002) who argues that supervisory practice that focuses bank by bank is flawed because it fails in this way to detect the risk position of the banking system as a whole. On this basis

> A regulator with a system's perspective would not entirely concentrate on the supervision of single institutions but would want to know the exposure of the bankingsystem as a whole … Supervision that is able to detect hidden aggregate exposure must face a major reorientation from practice that proceeds institution by institution to a system perspective. What this practically means in terms of reporting and measurement remains up to now an important open question. (Summer, 2002, p. 14)

This issue is also addressed in Hellwig (1995; 2000) and Dow (2000).

When a particular regulatory problem emerges, the instinct of a regulator is often to respond by creating new rules. This implies an incremental approach to regulation by focusing upon the rules component of the regulatory regime. The chapter argues that there are potentially serious problems with such an incremental rules approach in that it may blunt the power of the other mechanisms in the regime and may, in the process, reduce the overall effectiveness of the regime.

Although there is considerable academic debate about whether or not banks should be regulated at all, this issue is not addressed here. The general economic rationale for financial regulation has been outlined elsewhere (Llewellyn, 1999). For the purposes of the present chapter, the economic rationale for regulation is taken as given. While this ground will not be repeated, two observations are nevertheless entered at the outset. First, the presence of an economic rationale for regulation does not justify everything that a regulator does. Secondly, the case for regulation does not exclude a powerful role for other mechanisms to achieve the objectives of systemic stability. On the contrary, the central theme of the chapter is to emphasize that the various components of the regulatory regime need to be combined and that, while all are necessary, none are sufficient. There is always a potential danger that the regulation component, if pressed too far, will blunt the other mechanisms. The theme is that regulation is an important, but only one, component of a regime designed to achieve the twin objectives.

In practice, regulatory agencies have many choices in the construction of regulatory strategies, and in four dimensions in particular: (1) over the degree of regulatory intensity and the degree of prescription and intervention; (2) over the choice and combination of regulatory instruments; (3) with respect to the degree of uniformity or differentiation between different regulated firms, and (4) with respect to the combination and emphasis to be given to the key components of a regulatory regime and, in particular, the extent to which emphasis is given to detailed and precise rules. This all amounts to emphasizing a 'regulatory strategy' rather than focusing on regulation per se. Giving too much emphasis to regulation carries the danger that the importance of the other components is downplayed, or even marginalized.

The structure of the chapter is as follows. The next section outlines the concept of the regulatory regime and the trade-offs that can exist between its components. This is followed in the third section by a brief discussion of each of the seven components of the regime. The fourth section discusses the concept of what is termed *contract regulation* whereby regulated firms are able to self-select regulatory contracts. The penultimate section considers the proposed Basle 2 Accord in the context of the regulatory regime and suggests a set of criteria by which to judge any capital adequacy regime. A brief overall assessment is offered in the final section.

THE CONCEPT OF A REGULATORY REGIME

The concept of a regulatory regime is wider than the prevailing set of rules established by regulatory agencies. External regulation has a positive role in fostering a safe and sound financial system and consumer protection. However, this role, while important, is limited and insufficient in itself. Equally, and increasingly important, are the other components of the regime and most especially the incentive structures faced by financial firms, and the efficiency of the necessary monitoring and supervision by official agencies and the market.

Optimal regulatory arrangements are viewed in terms of the seven core components of the regulatory regime:

- the rules established by regulatory agencies (the regulation component);
- monitoring and supervision by official agencies;
- the incentive structures faced by regulatory agencies, consumers and, most especially, banks;
- the role of market discipline and monitoring;
- intervention arrangements in the event of bank failures;
- the role of internal corporate governance arrangements within banks; and
- the disciplining and accountability arrangements applied to regulatory agencies.

Regulatory strategy is not solely about the rules and supervision of regulatory agencies. In some respects the debate about regulation is often too narrow because it tends to focus almost exclusively on the first component of the regime and views the components of the regime as alternatives. The debate should be about how to optimize the combination of the seven components of the regime. Strategy should focus on optimizing the overall regulatory regime rather than any one component. This is a difficult and demanding mandate, and to the regulator the more effective approach in the short-run might appear to be imposing more rules. The danger is of thinking in terms of incremental change to regulation, rather than strategically with respect to the overall regime. The objective is to move towards an optimal mix of the seven components. Thus, it is not a question of choosing between either regulation or market discipline.

There are several reasons why emphasis is given to the overall regulatory regime rather than myopically to regulation and official supervision:

- Prescriptive regulation is not invariably effective in achieving the twin objectives: reducing the probability of bank failures and the costs of those that do occur.
- Regulation may not be the most effective way of securing these objectives.
- Regulation is itself costly both in terms of its direct costs and unwarranted distortions that may arise (for example, via inaccurate risk weights applied in capital adequacy arrangements) when regulation is inefficiently constructed.
- Regulation may not be the most efficient mechanism for achieving financial stability objectives in that alternative routes may achieve the same degree of effectiveness at lower cost.
- Regulation tends to be inflexible and insufficiently differentiated.
- There are inherent potential dangers arising from a monopolist regulator.
- Regulation may impair the effectiveness and efficiency of other mechanisms for achieving the objective of financial stability, that is, there may be trade-offs within the regime.

In current conditions it would be a mistake to rely wholly, or even predominantly, on external regulation, monitoring and supervision by the official sector. The world of banking and finance is too complex and volatile to warrant dependence on a single set of prescriptive rules for prudent behaviour. The central role of incentive structures in particular needs to be constantly emphasized as there are many reasons why incentive structures within financial firms may not be aligned with regulatory objectives (Llewellyn, 1999).

This means that a central consideration for the regulator is the impact its own rules have on regulated firms' incentive structures, whether they might have perverse effects and what regulation can do to improve incentives. Incentive structures are central to all aspects of regulation because, if these are wrong, it is unlikely that the other mechanisms in the regime will achieve the regulatory objectives. It is necessary, therefore, to consider not only how the various components of the regime impact directly on regulatory objectives, but also how they operate indirectly through their impact on the incentives of regulated firms and others. Incentive structures are at the heart of the regulatory process. And yet remarkably little is known about the incentives faced by bank managers.

Trade-offs within the Regime

The optimizing strategy needs to be set in the context of trade-offs between the various components of the regime. Trade-offs emerge at two levels. In terms of regulatory strategy, a choice has to be made between the balance of the various components and the relative weight to be assigned to each. For instance, a powerful role for official regulation with little weight assigned to market discipline might be chosen, or alternatively a relatively light touch of regulation but with heavy reliance on the other components. A given degree of effectiveness can be provided by different combinations of rules, supervision, market discipline, and so on, and with various degrees of discretion applied by the regulator.

The second form of trade-off relates to how the different components of the regime may be causally related. In some circumstances, the more emphasis that is given to one of the components (regulation, for example) the less powerful becomes one or more of the others (market discipline on banks, for example), and to an extent that may reduce overall effectiveness. Thus, while regulation may be viewed as a response to market failures, weak market discipline and inadequate corporate governance arrangements, causation may also operate in the other direction with regulation weakening these other mechanisms. For instance, the more emphasis that is given to detailed, extensive and prescriptive rules, the weaker might be the role of incentive structures, market discipline and corporate governance arrangements within financial firms. Simpson (2000, p. 15) has put this as follows: 'In a market, which is heavily regulated for internal standards of integrity, the incentives to fair dealing diminish. Within the company culture, such norms of fair dealing as "the way we do things around here" would eventually be replaced by "It's OK if we can get away with it".'

Similarly, an excessive focus on detailed and prescriptive rules may blunt the incentive of others to monitor and control the behaviour of banks. Weakness in corporate governance mechanisms may also be a reflection of banks being monitored, regulated and supervised by official agencies. In addition, the way intervention is conducted in the event of bank distress (whether forbearance is practised for example) may also have adverse incentive effects on the behaviour of banks and the willingness of markets to monitor and control banks' risk-taking.

The public policy objective is to optimize the outcome of a regulatory strategy in terms of mixing the components of the regime, bearing in mind the possibility of negative trade-offs. The key to optimizing overall effectiveness is the mix of the components. The skill lies in devising a regulatory strategy that combines the various components in the regime.

COMPONENTS OF A REGULATORY REGIME

Having established the overall framework and the nature of the regulatory regime, this section briefly considers some of the issues related to each of the components with particular reference to regulatory strategy designed to optimize the overall effect of the regime as a whole rather than any of the components.

Regulation

A former US regulator has noted that:

> Financial services regulation has traditionally tended towards a style that is command-and-control, dictating precisely what a regulated entity can do and how it should do it ... generally, they focus on the specific steps needed to accomplish a certain regulatory task and specify with detail the actions to be taken by the regulated firm. (Wallman, 1999, p. 81)

This experience of the USA also suggests that the interaction of the interests of the regulator and the regulated may tend towards a high degree of prescription in the regulatory process. Regulators tend to look for standards they can easily monitor and enforce, while the regulated seek standards they can comply with. The result is that regulators seek precision and detail in their requirements, while the regulated look for certainty and firm guidance on what they are to do. Wallman (1999, p. 8) suggests that: 'The result is specific and detailed guidance, not the kind of pronouncements that reflect fundamental concepts and allow the market to develop on its own.'

Although precise rules have their attractions for both regulators and regulated firms, there are several problems with a highly prescriptive approach to regulation:

- An excessive degree of prescription may bring regulation into disrepute if it is perceived by the industry as being excessive, with many redundant or unrealistic rules.
- Risks are often too complex to be covered by simple rules.
- Balance sheet rules reflect the position of an institution only at a particular point in time, and its position can change substantially within a short period.
- An inflexible approach based on a detailed rulebook has the effect of impeding firms from choosing their own least-cost way of meeting regulatory objectives.
- Detailed and extensive rules may stifle innovation.
- A prescriptive regime tends to focus upon firms' processes rather than outcomes and the ultimate objectives of regulation. The rules may become the focus of compliance rather than the objectives they are designed to achieve. In this regard, it can give rise to a perverse culture of 'box-ticking' by regulated firms. The letter of the regulation may be obeyed but not the spirit or intention.
- A prescriptive approach is inclined towards 'rules escalation' whereby rules are added over time, but few are withdrawn.
- A highly prescriptive approach may create a confrontational relationship between the regulator and regulated firms, or cause firms to overreact and engage in excessive efforts at internal compliance out of fear of being challenged by the regulator. In this sense, regulation may become more prescriptive and detailed than is intended by the regulator because of the culture that a rules-based approach generates.
- In the interests of 'competitive neutrality', rules may be applied equally to all firms, although they may be sufficiently heterogeneous to warrant different approaches. A highly prescriptive approach to regulation reduces the scope for legitimate differentiation. Treating as equal firms that in practice are not equal is not competitive neutrality.
- A prescriptive rules approach may in practice prove to be inflexible and not sufficiently responsive to market conditions.
- A potential moral hazard arises in that firms may assume that, if something is not explicitly covered by regulation, there is no regulatory dimension to the issue.
- Detailed rules may also have perverse effects if they are regarded as actual standards to be adopted rather than minimum standards, with the result that, in some cases, actual behaviour of regulated firms may be of a lower standard than without rules. This is most especially the case if each firm assumes its competitors will adopt the minimum regulatory standard.

There is a further danger that, in situations of uncertainty with respect to optimum rules of behaviour, the precision of rules may create the illusion of accuracy. This is discussed further in the context of the risk weights applied in the proposed Basle 2 Accord in a later section.

Monitoring and Supervision

In practice, in countries that have recently experienced banking crises 'some form of supervisory failure was a factor in almost all the sample countries' (Lindgren, Garcia and Saal, 1996, p. 60). In many countries supervisory agencies did not enforce compliance with regulations (Reisen, 1998).

In many crisis countries there has often been a lack of political will on the part of supervisory agencies to exercise strong supervision. This may have been associated with adverse incentive structures faced by politicians and others who may gain from imprudent banking (Fink and Haiss, 2000). While prudent banking is a public good, hazardous behaviour can be beneficial to some stakeholders. Others have noted the lack of political will to exercise strong supervision in the transitional economies of Eastern Europe (Baer and Gray, 1996).

Because of the nature of financial contracts between financial firms and their customers, continuous monitoring of behaviour is needed. The question is, who is to undertake the necessary monitoring: customers, shareholders, rating agencies, and so on? In practice, there can be only a limited monitoring role for retail depositors due to major information asymmetries that cannot easily be rectified, and because depositors face the less costly option of withdrawal of deposits. Saunders and Wilson (1996) review the empirical evidence on the role of informed depositors. The funding structure of a bank may also militate against effective monitoring in that, unlike with non-financial companies, creditors tend to be numerous with a small stake for each. Several analysts have considered the potentially hazardous incentive structures associated with deposit insurance (see, for instance, Garcia, 1999) who, in particular, analyses the trade-off between systemic stability and moral hazard (Garcia, 1996).

As most (especially retail) customers cannot in practice undertake monitoring, and in the presence of deposit insurance they may have no incentive to do so, an important role of regulatory agencies is to monitor the behaviour of banks on behalf of consumers. In effect, consumers delegate the task of monitoring to a regulatory agency. There are strong efficiency reasons (economies of scale, expertise, free-rider problems, and so on) for consumers to delegate monitoring and supervision to a specialist agency to act on their behalf, as the transactions costs for the consumer are lowered by such delegation (Llewellyn, 1999). However, this is not to argue that a regulatory agency should become a monopolist monitor and supervisor of financial firms.

Incentive Structures

A maintained theme is that the incentive structures and moral hazards faced by decision-makers (bank owners and managers, lenders to banks, borrowers and regulators) are central in the regulatory regime. Within the regulatory regime paradigm, a central role for regulation is to create appropriate incentives within regulated firms so that the incentives faced by decision-makers are consistent with the safety and soundness of financial institutions and systemic stability. At the same time, regulation needs to avoid the danger of blunting the incentives of other agents (rating agencies, depositors, shareholders and debtholders, for example) that have a disciplining role with banks. The position has been put well by Schinasi, Drees and Lee (1999, p. 6): 'Policymakers are therefore faced with the difficult challenge of balancing efforts to manage systemic risk against efforts to ensure that market participants bear the costs of imprudent risk taking and have incentives to behave prudently.' They argue that banks have complex incentive structures. The presence of regulation and official supervision overlays the structure of incentives faced by bank decision-makers.

If incentive structures are hazardous, regulation will always face formidable obstacles. There are several dimensions to this in the case of banks: the extent to which reward structures are based on the volume of business undertaken; the extent to which the risk characteristics of decisions are incorporated into management reward structures; the nature of internal control systems within banks; internal monitoring of the decision-making of loan officers; the nature of profit-sharing schemes and the extent to which decision-makers also share in losses, and so on. Reward systems based on short-term profits can also be hazardous, as they may induce managers to pay less attention to the longer-term risk characteristics of their decisions. High staff turnover, and the speed with which officers are moved within the bank, may also create incentives for excessive risk-taking. A similar effect can arise through the herd behaviour that is common in banking. In the case of the Barings collapse, managers who were supposedly monitoring the trading activity of Leeson also benefited through bonuses derived from the profits he was making for the bank.

It is clear that some incentive structures may lead to dysfunctional behaviour (Prendergast, 1993). This may often emerge when incentives within regulated firms relate to volume, which create a clear bias towards writing business. Bank managers may be rewarded by the volume of loans, not by their risk-adjusted profitability. Many cases of bank distress have been associated with inappropriate incentive structures creating a bias in favour of balance sheet growth, and with moral hazard created by anticipated lender-of-last-resort actions (Llewellyn, 2000). Dale (1996) suggests that profit-related bonuses were an important feature in the collapse of Barings Bank.

Laws, regulations, and supervisory actions provide incentives for regulated firms to adjust their actions and behaviour, and to control their own risks internally. Within this framework, regulation involves a process of creating incentive compatible contracts so that regulated firms have an incentive to act consistently with the objectives of financial stability. Well-designed incentive contracts induce appropriate behaviour by regulated firms. Conversely, if they are badly constructed and improperly designed, they might fail to reduce systemic risk (and other hazards that regulation is designed to avoid) or have undesirable side effects on the process of financial intermediation (impose high costs, for example). At centre stage is the issue of whether all parties have the right incentives to act in a way that satisfies the objectives of regulation.

Given that incentives for individuals can never be fully aligned with the objectives of the bank, there need to be external pressures on managers to encourage adequate internal control systems to be established. Several procedures, processes and structures can, for instance, reinforce internal risk control mechanisms. These include internal auditors, internal audit committees, procedures for reporting to senior management (and, perhaps, to the supervisors) and making a named board member of financial firms responsible for compliance and risk analysis and management systems. In some countries the incentive on bank managers has been strengthened by a policy of increased personal liability for bank directors, and bank directors are personally liable in cases involving disclosure of incomplete or erroneous information.

The form and intensity of supervision can differentiate between regulated institutions according to their relative risk and the efficiency of their internal control mechanisms (Goodhart et al., 1998). Supervisors can strengthen incentives by, for instance, relating the frequency and intensity of their supervision and inspection visits (and, possibly, rules) to the perceived adequacy of the internal risk control procedures, and compliance arrangements. In addition, regulators can create appropriate incentives by calibrating the external burden of regulation (for example, number of inspection visits, allowable business and so on) to the quality of management and the efficiency of internal incentives.

With respect to prudential issues, capital requirements should be structured so as to create incentives for the correct pricing of absolute and relative risk. In this area in particular, the potential for regulation to create perverse incentives and moral hazard is well established. If regulatory capital requirements do not accurately map risk, banks are encouraged to engage in regulatory arbitrage. If differential capital requirements are set against different types of assets, and the risk weights are incorrectly specified, perverse incentives may be created for banks because the implied capital requirements are either more or less than justified by true relative risk calculations. A critique of the current Basle capital arrangements is that risk weights bear little relation to the relative risk characteristics of different assets, and the loan book largely carries a uniform risk weight even though the risk characteristics of different loans within a bank's portfolio vary considerably.

Market Discipline

The fourth component of the regulatory regime relates to the arrangements for market discipline on banks. The central theme is that regulation can never be an alternative to market discipline. On the contrary, market discipline needs to be reinforced within the regime, as suggested in Pillar III of the proposed Basle 2 Accord Monitoring is not only conducted by official agencies whose specialist task it is. In well-developed regimes, the market has incentives to monitor the behaviour of financial firms. The disciplines imposed by the market can be as powerful as any sanctions imposed by official agencies. The disciplining role of the markets (including the inter-bank market) was weak in the crisis countries of South East Asia in the 1990s. This was due predominantly to the lack of disclosure and transparency of banks, and to the fact that little reliance could be placed on the quality of accountancy data provided in bank accounts. This is not an issue for less developed countries alone. For instance, Nakaso et al. (2000) argue that market discipline did not operate efficiently in Japan due largely to insufficient financial infrastructure (weak accountancy rules, inadequate disclosure, and so on).

Market discipline works effectively only on the basis of full and accurate information disclosure and transparency. Good quality, timely and relevant information needs to be available to all market participants and regulators so that asset quality, creditworthiness and the condition of financial institutions can be adequately assessed.

Several parties are potentially able to monitor the management of banks and other financial firms: owners, bank depositors and customers, rating agencies, official agencies (the central bank or other regulatory body for example) and other banks in the market. In practice, excessive emphasis has been given to official agencies. The danger in this is that a monopoly monitor is established with many of the standard problems associated with monopoly power. There may even be adverse incentive effects in that, given that regulatory agencies conduct monitoring and supervision on a delegated basis, the incentive for others to conduct monitoring may be weakened.

The role of all potential monitors (and notably the market) needs to be strengthened, with greater incentives for other parties to monitor financial firms in parallel with official agencies. The merit of increasing the role of market discipline is that large, well-informed creditors (including other banks) have the resources, expertise, market knowledge and incentives to conduct monitoring and to impose market discipline. A further advantage of having agents other than official supervisory bodies monitor banks is that it removes the inherent danger of having monitoring and supervision conducted by a monopolist with less than perfect and complete information with the result that inevitably mistakes will be made. A monopolist supervisor may also have a different agenda than purely the maintenance of financial stability. It has been noted that:

> Broader approaches to bank supervision reach beyond the issues of defining capital and accounting standards, and envisage co-opting other market participants by giving them a greater stake in bank survival. This approach increases the likelihood that problems will be detected earlier … [it involves] broadening the number of those who are directly concerned about keeping the banks safe and sound. (Caprio and Honohan, 1999, p. 60)

Some analysts (Calomiris, 1997, for example) are sceptical about the power of official supervisory agencies to identify the risk characteristics of banks compared with the power and incentives of markets. Several analysts (see Evanoff and Wall, 2000, for a survey) argue the case for banks being required to issue a minimum amount of subordinated and uninsured debt as part of the capital base. Holders of subordinated debt have an incentive to monitor the risk-taking of banks (see also Benink, 2002). As noted by Lang and Robertson (2000), discipline can be imposed through three routes: the cost of raising funds, market signals as expressed in risk premia implicit in the price of subordinated debt, and through supervisors themselves responding to market signals. In particular, because of the nature of the debt contract, holders of a bank's subordinated debt do not share in the potential upside gain through the bank's risk-taking, but stand to lose if the bank fails. They therefore have a particular incentive to monitor the bank's risk profile compared with shareholders that, under some circumstances, have an incentive to support a high-risk profile.

However, while there is a potentially powerful role for market discipline to operate through the pricing of subordinated debt, the interests of holders of such debt do not necessarily precisely coincide with those of depositors or the public interest more generally (Dewatripont and Tirole, 1994). It is not, therefore, a substitute for official monitoring. It is intended as an extension of the role of market monitoring.

While market discipline is potentially powerful, it has its limitations and Bliss and Flannery (2000) argue that there is no strong evidence that equity and debtholders do in fact affect managerial decisions. This means that, in practice, it is unlikely to be an effective complete alternative to the role of official regulatory and supervisory agencies:

- Markets are concerned with the private costs of a bank failure and reflect the risk of this in market prices. The social cost of bank failures, on the other hand, may exceed the private cost (Llewellyn, 1999) and hence the total cost of a bank failure may not be fully reflected in market prices.
- The cost of private monitoring and information collection may exceed the benefits.
- Market disciplines are not effective in monitoring and disciplining public sector banks.
- 'Free-rider' problems may emerge.
- The market is able to efficiently price bank securities and inter-bank loans only to the extent that relevant information is available, and in many cases the necessary information is not available. Disclosure requirements are, therefore, an integral part of the market disciplining process.
- It is not self-evident that market participants always have the necessary expertise to make risk assessment of complex, and sometimes opaque, banks. In addition, there are some areas within a bank (its risk analysis and control systems for example) where disclosure is not feasible.
- In some countries, the market in debt of all kinds (including securities and debt issued by banks) is limited, inefficient and cartelized, although market discipline can also operate through inter-bank and swaps markets.
- When debt issues are very small it is not always economic for rating agencies to conduct a full credit rating on a bank.

The theme being developed is not that market monitoring and discipline can effectively replace official supervision, but that it has a powerful role, which should be strengthened within the overall regulatory regime. In addition, Caprio (1997) argues that broadening the number of those who are directly concerned about the safety and soundness of banks reduces the extent to which insider political pressure can be brought to bear on bank regulation and supervision. As neither the market nor regulatory agencies are perfect, the obvious solution is to utilize both with neither having a monopoly of wisdom and good judgement.

Intervention

A key component of the regulatory regime is the nature, timing and form of intervention by regulatory agencies in the event of financial distress with banks. A key dimension is the impact rescue interventions have on future incentive structures of banks and their appetite for risk. As put by Summer (2002, p. 63): 'rescue policies for distressed banks are an important tool of crisis management. Despite its detrimental effect on ex ante incentives of bank owners, ex post interventions are relatively frequent'. He cites the recent experience of Argentina, Indonesia, Chile, Thailand, South Korea, Malaysia, Venezuela, Japan, Czech Republic, Finland, Hungary, Brazil, Russia and Sweden. A different dimension to the same problem is given by Acharya (2000) who argues that uniform capital requirements applied to all countries, but where different countries have different intervention policies, can have the effect of increasing systemic risk.

The closure of an insolvent or, under a Structured Early Intervention and Resolution (SEIR) regime, a near-insolvent bank, can impose a powerful discipline on the future behaviour of banks. Such 'creative destruction' has a positive dimension. Intervention arrangements are important not least because they have incentive and moral hazard effects which potentially influence future behaviour by banks and their customers. These arrangements may also have important implications for the total cost of intervention (for example, initial forbearance often has the effect of raising the eventual cost of subsequent intervention) and the distribution of those costs between taxpayers and other agents.

The key issue is when intervention is to be made. The experience of banking crises in both developed and developing countries indicates that a well-defined strategy for responding to the possible insolvency of financial institutions is needed. A response strategy in the event of bank distress has three key components:

- taking prompt corrective action to address financial problems before they reach critical proportions;
- being prepared to close insolvent financial institutions while nevertheless not destroying what value remains; and
- closing of unviable institutions, and vigorously monitoring weak and/ or restructured institutions.

A central issue relates to rules versus discretion in the event of bank distress: the extent to which intervention should be circumscribed by clearly defined rules (so that intervention agencies have no discretion about whether, how and when to act), or whether there should always be discretion. The obvious prima facie advantage for allowing discretion is that it is impossible to foresee all future circumstances and conditions for when a bank might become distressed and close to (or actually) insolvent. It might be judged that it is not always the right policy to close a bank in such circumstances.

There are, nevertheless, strong arguments against allowing such discretion and in favour of a rules approach to intervention. First, it enhances the credibility of the intervention agency in that market participants, including banks, have a high degree of certainty that action will be taken. Secondly, allowing discretion may increase the probability of forbearance, which usually eventually leads to higher costs when intervention is finally made. Kane (2000), for instance, argues that officials may forbear because they face different incentives from those of the market: their own welfare, the interests of the agency they represent, political interests, reputation, future employment prospects, and so on. Perhaps less plausibly, he also argues that, under some circumstances, the present generation of taxpayers may believe they can shift the cost of resolution to future generations. In the same way, a rules discipline guards against hazards associated with risk-averse regulators who themselves might be disinclined to take action for fear that it will be interpreted as a regulatory failure, and the temptation to allow a firm to trade out of its difficulty. This amounts to the regulator also 'gambling for resurrection'. Thirdly, and this was relevant in some countries which recently experienced banking distress, it removes the danger of undue political interference in the disciplining of banks and regulated firms. Experience in many countries indicates that supervisory authorities face substantial pressure to delay action and intervention. Fourthly, and related to the first, a rules approach to intervention is likely to have a beneficial impact on *ex ante* behaviour of financial firms. A rules-based approach, by removing any prospect that a hazardous bank might be treated leniently, has the advantage of enhancing the incentives for bank managers to manage their banks prudently so as to reduce the probability of insolvency (Glaessner and Mas, 1995).

Put another way, time-inconsistency and credibility problems can be addressed through pre-commitments and graduated responses with the possibility of override. Many analysts have advocated various forms of predetermined intervention through a general policy of SEIR. The case for a graduated-response approach is that there is no magical capital ratio below which an institution is in danger and above which it is safe, as potential danger gradually increases as the capital ratio declines. An example of the rules-based approach is to be found in the Prompt Corrective Action (PCA) rules in the USA. These specify graduated intervention by the regulators with predetermined responses triggered by capital thresholds. In fact, several countries have such rules of intervention (Basle Committee, 1999a). The SEIR strategies can, therefore, act as a powerful incentive for prudent behaviour.

The need to maintain the credibility of supervisory agencies creates a strong case against forbearance. The overall conclusion is that there should be a clear bias (though not a bar) against forbearance when a bank is in difficulty. While there should be a strong presumption against forbearance, and that this is best secured through having clearly defined rules, there will always be exceptional circumstances when it might be warranted in the interests of systemic stability. However, when forbearance is exercised the regulatory agency should, in some way or another, be made accountable for its actions.

Corporate Governance

In the final analysis, all aspects of the management of financial firms (including compliance) are ultimately corporate governance issues. This means that, while shareholders may at times have an incentive to take high risks, if a financial firm behaves hazardously, it is, to some extent, a symptom of weak corporate governance. This may include, for instance, a hazardous corporate structure for the financial firm, inter-connected lending within a closely related group of companies, lack of internal control systems, weak surveillance by (especially non-executive) directors, and ineffective internal audit arrangements which often includes serious under-reporting of problem loans. Corporate governance arrangements were evidently weak and under-developed in banks in many of the countries that have recently experienced bank distress. For a general survey of the relationship between regulation and corporate governance arrangements see Harm (2002).

There are several reasons why corporate governance arrangements operate differently in the case of banks than with other types of firms. First, banks are subject to regulation that adds an additional dimension to corporate governance arrangements. Secondly, banks are also subject to continuous supervision and monitoring by official agencies. This has two immediate implications for private corporate governance: shareholders and official agencies are to some extent duplicating monitoring activity, and the actions of official agencies may have an impact on the incentives faced by other monitors, such as shareholders and even depositors. However, official and market monitoring are not perfectly substitutable. Thirdly, banks have a fiduciary relationship with their customers (for example, they are holding the wealth of depositors) which is rare with other types of firm. This creates additional principal–agent relationships (and potentially agency costs) with banks that generally do not exist with non-financial firms.

While there are significant differences between banks and other firms, corporate governance issues in banks have received remarkably little attention. A key issue noted by Flannery (1998) is that little is known about how the two governance systems (regulation and private) interact with each other and, in particular, the extent to which they are complementary or offsetting. An interesting possibility is of a moral hazard associated with official regulation and supervision: a further negative trade-off within the regulatory regime. It could be that the assumption that regulatory authorities impose regulation and monitor banks reduces the incentive for non-executive directors, shareholders and, even, the market to do so. The presumption may be that regulators have more information than do non-executive directors, shareholders and market participants, and that their own monitoring would only be wastefully duplicating that being conducted by official supervisors.

Corporate governance arrangements need to provide for effective monitoring and supervision of the risk-taking profile of banks. These arrangements need to provide for, *inter alia*, a management structure with clear lines of accountability, independent non-executive directors on the board, independent audit committees, the four-eyes principle for important decisions involving the risk profile of the bank, a transparent ownership structure, internal structures that enable the risk profile of the firm to be clear, transparent and managed, and the creation and monitoring of risk analysis and management systems. Some bank ownership structures also produce ineffective corporate governance. Particular corporate structures (for example, when banks are part of larger conglomerates) may encourage connected lending and weak risk analysis of borrowers. This was the case in a significant number of bank failures in the countries of South East Asia and Latin America. Some corporate structures also make it comparatively easy for banks to conceal their losses and unsound financial position.

The Basle Committee has appropriately argued that effective oversight by a bank's board of directors and senior management is critical. It suggests that the board should approve overall policies of the bank and its internal systems. It argues in particular that: 'lack of adequate corporate governance in the banks seems to have been an important contributory factor in the Asian crisis. The boards of directors and management committees of the banks did not play the role they were expected to play' (Basle Committee, 1999b, p. 78).

Disciplines on the Regulator

Four perspectives reinforce the case for regulatory authorities to be subject to strong disciplining and accountability measures: (1) there is an ever-present potential for over-regulation as it may be both over-demanded and over-supplied (Goodhart et al., 1998); (2) regulatory agencies have considerable power over both consumers and regulated firms; (3) the regulator is often supplying regulatory services as a monopolist although, in the USA, there is scope for banks to switch regulators, and (4) the regulator is not subject to the normal disciplines of the market in the supply of its services.

Several accountability mechanisms have been put in place with respect to the Financial Services Authority (FSA) in the UK. Its objectives have been clearly defined in an Act of Parliament, and the FSA reports directly to Parliament. In addition, there is a formal legislative requirement for the FSA to use its resources in the most efficient way, and to make any regulatory burden proportionate to its benefits. The last mentioned includes a require-ment on the FSA to conduct cost–benefit analyses on its regulation. The Act also outlines a strong set of accountability mechanisms including the scope for judicial review, public reporting mechanisms to the Treasury, require-ments for consultation, the creation of Consumer and Practitioner Panels, independent review of its rules and decisions including by the Office of Fair Trading, independent investigation of complaints against the FSA, and an independent appeals and enforcement procedure.

Given the power that regulatory agencies have, accountability needs to be wider than merely being held accountable for the particular decisions it makes. In a broader context they need to be judged and monitored for effec-tiveness (whether mandated objectives are achieved), efficiency (the manner in which internal resources are employed) and economy of its regulation and supervision. The last mentioned relates to the wider economic impact that regulation has on, for instance, competition, and fostering a climate of inno-vation in the financial sector, and to the proportionality of regulation as indicated, for example, by Regulatory Impact Analysis and, where possible, cost–benefit analysis. It also covers the question of whether the same degree of regulatory effectiveness could be achieved at less cost to both consumers and regulated firms.

There is a strong case for all regulation to be subject to Regulatory Impact Analysis (RIA). Despite its long history and extensive application, it is often the case that remarkably little is known about the impact of regulation. Regula-tory measures may be proposed and implemented on the basis of views that are vague, impressionistic, without analytical foundation and uncoordinated. Al-though perfect insight will never be possible, RIA can improve on this situation and can reduce areas of uncertainty by identifying how regulation impacts on financial firms, consumers and the financial system generally.

There are several specific advantages to the application of RIA to financial regulation with respect to both new regulatory measures and existing regula-tion:

- A systematic approach to identifying the impact, costs and benefits of regulation will always be more valuable than casual ad hoc investiga-tion.

- Regulators can learn a great deal about regulation simply through the discipline of conducting RIAs and this informs future regulatory strategy. In this sense, RIA is part of the continuing learning process and contributes to building up corporate understanding.
- The common methodology implied in a clearly defined RIA model means that it can readily and easily be applied to all regulatory interventions. This also enables investigation to be consistent across the full range of financial regulation.
- A good RIA model imposes a valuable discipline on decision-makers at all levels in the decision-making process and avoids the danger of regulation being based exclusively on simple intuition.
- Equally, it forces decision-makers to consider a wide range of impacts, costs and potential benefits of proposed regulatory measures, and in the process reduces the risk of focusing upon a narrow set of criteria.
- There is a clear trend within the European Union (EU) to make regulators more accountable. RIA is a powerful tool of accountability and enables regulatory agencies to demonstrate why particular regulatory measures have been proposed or adopted. This advantage is likely to increase over time, as accountability becomes more demanding.
- Equally, and following Lamfalussy, regulators will be increasingly required to consult on proposed regulatory measures.
- Regulatory Impact Analysis exercises, most especially when they involve consultation with regulated firms, often have the effect of lowering scepticism and antagonism in regulated firms as it enhances the scientific basis of regulation and contributes to eroding the perception amongst those firms that regulation is often an arbitrary and ill-thought-out process. In this regard, it also serves as a vehicle for regulators to explain to those to whom regulation is applied what is trying to be achieved.

One way of viewing the benefits of RIA is in terms of insurance. Badly constructed regulation has the capacity to do harm and to impose avoidable costs: both compliance costs – those imposed on regulated firms – and economic costs – those imposed on the economy as a whole. There is always a risk that such costs are imposed. An advantage of RIA is that, by forcing a systematic consideration of all dimensions of the impact of a proposed intervention (including those that may not be intended), the risks are reduced. In this sense the costs of applying RIA can be viewed as an insurance premium to be paid to guard against the imposition of avoidable costs. It is never known *ex ante* whether we start with a full appreciation of the impact and the costs and benefits involved.

CONTRACT REGULATION

A given degree of regulatory intensity does not in itself imply anything about the degree of prescription or detail. Even within the regulation component of the regime a wide range of options is available, and in particular with respect to the degree of discretion exercised by the regulator. At the risk of oversimplification, two alternative approaches may be identified. At one end of the spectrum, the regulator lays down precise regulatory requirements that are applied to all banks. While there may be limited differentiation within the rules, the presumption is for a high degree of uniformity. At the other end of the spectrum (in what might be termed *Contract Regulation*) the regulator establishes objectives and general principles. It is then for each regulated firm to demonstrate to the regulator how these objectives and principles are to be satisfied by its own chosen procedures.

A detailed and prescriptive rulebook approach may add to compliance costs without commensurate benefit in terms of meeting the objectives of regulation. If the objectives can be achieved by an alternative regime that is less costly for banks to operate with lower compliance costs, there would be advantage in reducing the deadweight costs. It may, for instance, be possible to achieve the same objectives in a way that allows firms more scope to choose the manner in which they satisfy the regulator's requirements and, at the same time, minimize their own compliance costs.

Under this regime, the regulator sets clear objectives and general principles. It is then for each bank to demonstrate how these objectives and principles are to be satisfied by its own chosen procedures. In effect, the bank chooses its own regulation but within the strict constraints set by the objectives and principles set by the regulator. Put another way, the firm is able to choose its preferred route to achieving the objectives of regulation. Presumably, each bank would choose its own least-cost way of satisfying the regulator. Once the regulator has agreed with each bank how the objectives and principles are to be satisfied, a contract is established between the regulator and the bank. In other words, what is involved is a regime of 'self-selecting regulatory contracts'. Contract Regulation necessarily implies increased differentiation in the regulatory arrangements between banks. The contract requires the bank to deliver on its agreed standards and procedures, and sanctions apply in the case of non-performance on the contract.

An analogy can be drawn with regulation in other areas. For instance, pollution regulation (say, with respect to factories not contaminating local rivers) is framed in terms of the ultimate objective related to the measurable quality of water. Regulation does not prescribe how the factory is to undertake its production processes in order to meet the objective. It is for each firm to choose its own least-cost way of satisfying water quality standards. Providing the standards are met, the regulator is indifferent about how the standards are achieved or what the production processes are.

Under a regime of Contract Regulation the role of the regulator is fivefold: defining the degree of regulatory intensity, establishing regulatory objectives, approving self-selected contracts, monitoring standards and the performance on agreed contracts, and disciplining infringements of contracts. A by-product advantage is that the regulator would learn more about optimum regulatory arrangements through the experience of the variety of contracts.

While there are clear limits to how far this regime could be taken in practice, in some areas the regulator could offer a menu of contracts to regulated firms requiring them to self-select. Many countries are moving toward a pre-commitment approach to regulation (Kupiec and O'Brien, 1997). In this approach, each bank agrees with the supervisory agency the models and procedures it will use to evaluate their risks, but are subject to penalties if they violate these procedures. There are several advantages to a pre-commitment strategy: it avoids the necessity of detailed and prescriptive regulation, it creates powerful incentives for bank decision-makers (the choice of an excessive amount of capital imposes costs on the bank, while choosing too low a level of capital risks the imposition of penalties) and it is flexible to the extent that it offers scope for each bank to choose a level of capital which is appropriate to its own particular circumstances. On the other hand, Estrella (1998) argues that the precise design of the penalty structure is likely to be complex.

THE BASLE 2 ACCORD PROPOSALS

Having outlined the paradigm, we turn to a consideration of the proposed Basle 2 Accord within this framework. The problems with the current Bank for International Settlements (BIS) capital adequacy regime (the 1988 Accord) are well established. Partly because of these weaknesses, the Basle Committee on Banking Supervision has proposed a new framework for setting capital adequacy requirements (Basle Committee, 1999a). The proposed new approach can be viewed in terms of the regulatory regime paradigm.

Substantial emphasis is to be given to the importance of banks developing their own risk analysis, management and control systems, and it is envisaged that incentives will be strengthened for this. In some cases (those banks with sophisticated risk analysis systems, that is), this will enable banks to apply their own methodologies to calculating risk and the required capital backing.

The Committee's consultative paper stresses the important role of supervision in the overall regulatory process. The Supervisory Review Process will mean that supervisors are to ensure that banks have sound internal risk analysis and management systems to assess capital adequacy. This will require a high standard of sophistication on the part of bank supervisors if they are to be able to assess banks' systems. This in turn has implications for the training and qualifications of bank supervisors. This second pillar of the capital adequacy framework will: 'seek to ensure that a bank's capital position is consistent with its overall risk profile and strategy and, as such, will encourage *early supervisory intervention*' [italics added] (Basle Committee, 199a, p. 80).

In an attempt to bring regulatory capital more into alignment with economic capital, it is proposed to widen the range of risk weights and to introduce weights greater than unity. Risk weights to be applied will be refined by reference to a rating provided by an external credit assessment institution (such as a rating agency) that meets strict standards. One of the central problems of the 1988 Basle Accord is that, as corporate loans are not differentiated with respect to risk and all carry the same risk weight, there has been an incentive, for instance, for banks to securitize low-risk loans (because the imposed capital charge is excessive in relation to true risk) which, perversely, has the effect of raising the average risk of the loan portfolio which does not call forth a higher capital requirement because of the uniform risk-weight attached to all corporate loans.

Two alternative approaches to assessing credit risk for purposes of defining required capital will be applied: a standardized approach (similar to the current arrangement with the addition of more risk weights), and an internal ratings based (IRB) approach (which allows banks to use their own internal models). Although a modified form of the current Accord will remain as the 'standardized' approach, the Committee believes that, for some sophisticated banks, use of internal and external credit ratings should be incorporated, and also that portfolio models of risk could contribute towards aligning economic and regulatory capital requirements. The IRB approach will not rely on predetermined supervisory risk weights. Banks will be able to input their own assessment of the probability of default associated with each borrower. The Committee recognizes that use of internal ratings is likely to incorporate information about customers that is not available either to regulators or external rating agencies. The object is to bring the regulatory process more into line with the way banks undertake risk assessment. The Committee states that, over time, it would like to see more banks moving from the standardized approach to the IRB approach and also that, within the IRB approach, banks will shift from the 'foundation' to the 'advanced' approaches as their risk management capabilities develop.

A major aspect of the proposed new approach is to ask banks what they judge their capital should be. Any use of internal ratings would be subject to supervisory approval: this is an element of what earlier was termed 'contract regulation'.

Allowance is to be made for risk-mitigating factors such as the use of derivative contracts to the extent that they are applied to shift or reduce risk.

The proposals also include the possibility of external credit assessments in determining risk weights for some types of bank assets. This would enhance the role of external rating agencies in the regulatory process. The Committee also suggests there could usefully be greater use of the assessment by credit rating agencies with respect to asset securitizations made by banks.

Greater emphasis is to be given to the role of market discipline, which is the third pillar in the proposed new approach. It will encourage high standards of transparency and disclosure standards, and 'enhance the role of market participants encouraging banks to hold adequate capital' (ibid., p. 40). It is envisaged that market discipline should play a greater role in the monitoring of banks and the creation of appropriate incentives. The Committee recognizes that supervisors have a strong interest in facilitating effective market discipline as a lever to strengthen the safety and soundness of the banking system. It argues: 'market discipline has the potential to reinforce capital regulation and other supervisory efforts to promote safety and soundness in banks and financial systems. Market discipline imposes strong incentives on banks to conduct their business in a safe, sound and efficient manner' (ibid., p. 53). This will require more information disclosure by banks and regulators will specify the precise detail of information disclosure.

The principle is established that supervisors should intervene at an early stage to prevent capital from falling below the minimum levels required to support the risk characteristics of a particular bank.

Emphasis is also given to the important role that shareholders have in monitoring and controlling banks.

Overall, the new approach being proposed envisages more differentiation between banks, a less formal reliance on prescriptive rules, a recognition that incentives for prudential behaviour have an important role in the overall approach, elements of choice for regulated institutions, more emphasis on banks' corporate governance mechanisms, an enhanced role for market discipline, a greater focus on risk analysis and management systems, and some degree of pre-commitment. It also recognizes the need for early intervention is the event of potential bank distress. The new approach would create incentives for banks to improve their risk management methods and to develop their own estimates of economic capital. Equally, there would be powerful incentives for supervisors to develop and enhance their monitoring skills.

In terms of the regulatory regime paradigm, Basle 2 offers more precision in the regulation component and, at the same time, gives emphasis to other mechanisms such as market discipline.

The proposed Basle Accord is certainly more detailed and precise than anything that has gone before. But is this a spurious precision, and is precision being mistaken for accuracy? There are some who would argue that, in a second-best world, where accuracy can never be assured, the optimal strategy might be to revert to a simple set of capital adequacy requirements (with more emphasis on other components of the regulatory regime) rather than to seek yet more precision within the rules component.

Criteria of Assessment

The purpose here is not to look at the proposed new Basle Accord in any detail, but to suggest a framework for assessing it by establishing a set of criteria by which to judge any capital adequacy regime. The following 12 tests are suggested:

- Does it have the effect of aligning *regulatory* and *economic* capital, that is, do the regulatory requirements correspond to the amount of capital a bank needs given the risks in its business? Capital serves as an internal insurance fund to cover risks (most especially credit risks) that cannot be insured externally. It follows that the amount of capital a bank needs to hold is determined by the nature of the risks it faces. The objective of regulation and supervision should, therefore, ultimately be to equate regulatory and economic capital with the latter, incorporating externalities and issues related to systemic stability and not just the safety and soundness of the institution per se.
- Does it create incentives for banks to create effective and efficient risk analysis, management and control mechanisms?
- Does it create appropriate incentives for the correct pricing of risk?
- Does it create incentives for an efficient allocation of capital within the bank across different business areas and different categories of loans and other assets?
- Does it create incentives for regulatory arbitrage: business structures that lower capital requirements without any corresponding reduction in the risk profile of the bank?
- Does it create unwarranted entry barriers?
- Are the capital requirements truly competitively neutral as between countries and competing banks, in that banks with the same risk profile are treated equally but also that banks which are not equal are not treated equally?
- Are the requirements such that the amount of capital is adequate but not excessive for overall portfolio risk (that is, the risk of the bank

overall) as opposed to the sum of project risks (that is, the risks attached to each component of the business)?

- Does it have the effect of impairing competition in banking markets?
- Does it have unwarranted effects on the macroeconomy?
- Is it unnecessarily complicated and prescriptive in that the same effect could be achieved with a simpler and easily applied approach?
- Does it create or reinforce incentives for stakeholders other than official supervisors to monitor the risks of banks and for market discipline to be exercised.

Judged by these criteria there are pluses and minuses in the proposed Basle 2 Accord. The Accord is a welcome move in the direction of a broader approach to bank regulation and a recognition that mechanisms other than regulation (notably an enhanced role for market discipline) are needed.

We next briefly consider some aspects of the Basle 2 proposals in the context of these criteria. In the process, reference is made to several studies contained in SUERF/CSFI (2002).

Alignment of Regulatory and Economic Capital

In an attempt to bring regulatory capital more into alignment with economic capital, it is proposed to widen the range of risk weights and to introduce weights greater than unity. Risk weights to be applied will be refined by reference to a rating provided by an external credit assessment institution (such as a rating agency) that meets strict standards. Some analysts (including Griffiths-Jones and Spratt, 2002) criticize this aspect of Basle 2 with reference to the excessive risk weights applied to loans to some (particularly higher-risk) developing countries. A similar critique has been suggested (including by the German government) with respect to loans to small and medium-sized enterprises (SMEs) though this is currently under review by the Committee.

Risk Analysis, Management and Control Systems

Substantial emphasis is to be given to the importance of banks developing their own risk analysis, management and control systems, and it is envisaged that incentives will be strengthened for this. In some cases (that is, those banks with sophisticated risk analysis systems) this will enable banks to apply their own methodologies to calculate risk and the required capital backing. Davies (2002, p. 57) suggests this will create a dilemma for banks which already have advanced risk analysis and management systems in that: 'many banks already using advanced credit-modelling techniques will divert resources from the development and maintenance of their existing credit-modelling to build a Basle 2 AMA-compliant system'. Under some circumstances a bank might be induced to substitute a Basle-type methodology for what it believes to be its own existing superior model.

Correct Pricing of Risk

The key to this criterion is whether the risk weights applied to different categories of assets are true reflections of absolute and relative risk. If a risk weight applied to a particular class of assets or a particular loan is low relative to true economic risk, there is an incentive for that asset to be underpriced as the full (capital) cost is not incorporated in the pricing structure. The distortion becomes yet more significant if misspecifications of risk weights relative to true risks vary between different classes of assets. In this respect, therefore, the test applied to Basle 2 rests on a judgement about whether the risk categories are correctly defined. Clearly, precision should not be mistaken for accuracy in that, while the proposed capital regime is considerably more precise than its predecessor, this does not in itself make it more accurate. As already noted, in one area (loans to some developing countries) it has been suggested that the proposed weights are too high and that this will reduce the volume of bank lending to such countries.

Internal Allocation of Capital

The same arguments that are relevant to the issue of the correct pricing of risk apply equally to this criterion. This again reinforces the importance of the risk weights being a true reflection of relative risk.

Regulatory Arbitrage

Regulatory arbitrage usually focuses upon the incentive of banks to choose certain categories of assets. The problem arises when relative risk weights are inappropriately set. In emphasizing incentive structures, the European Central Bank (ECB) offers a different dimension to regulatory arbitrage by focusing upon incentive structures as between the choice of methodologies. The issue arises because the range of risk weights is considerably wider in the IRB approach than in the standardized approach. As observed by the ECB: 'banks with a loan portfolio concentrated on lower-risk borrowers may have the strongest incentives to use the IRB approach, as it gives way to a lower capital requirement' (ECB, 2001, p. 47). It goes on to argue that banks with higher-risk loans might opt for the standardized approach. There is also a maturity dimension to this in that, as risk weights can increase with the maturity of loans in the IRB approach whereas there is no such adjustment in the standardized approach, this is an additional incentive to opt for the standardized approach. The bottom line is that, as argued by the ECB, 'those banks that would benefit most from more advanced internal credit risk management techniques could actually have the weakest incentives to develop them' (ECB, 2001, p. 53).

Entry Barriers

That capital, or any other form of regulation, might create entry barriers is not in itself a legitimate critique, as one purpose of regulation and supervision is precisely to exclude hazardous firms. The issue is whether unwarranted or unintended entry barriers are created. Davies (2002) suggests that Basle 2 will create such entry barriers because it ties capital requirements very closely to risk and because it implies a uniform methodology of how risk is calibrated as capital. He also argues that the uniformity of approach to risk analysis and management could increase systemic risks in the event of some shocks. The reduction in diversity of views about credit risk may make the system more at risk. The point is also made that this is in contrast to the approach to market risk, where diversity of strategy and management technique is recognized and not discouraged.

Competitive Neutrality

It is axiomatic that similar banks (in terms of their risk profile and so on) should be treated in the same way, and that particular competitors should not receive competitive subsidies (or pay competitive taxes) through having excess regulatory burdens imposed on them that are not equally applied to all similar institutions.

Non-competitive-neutrality can arise through two routes: the rules themselves are not competitively neutral, or because discretion is allowed and applied in a non-neutral manner. This can arise both within a jurisdiction and, most especially, between jurisdictions. Basle 2 implies substantially more supervisory discretion in assessing banks' capital adequacy than before, and within this there is ample scope for discretion to be applied in different ways in different countries. Monro-Davies (2002, p. 52) emphasizes that in the wide areas of discretion implied in Basle 2:

> given that many of these factors (over which supervisors have discretion) are open to interpretation by individual regulators, there is a significant danger of inconsistencies between different banking systems, even different banks, something which could undermine the Accord's long held objective of creating a level playing field in global financial services.

More controversial is the question of whether different types of institutions (for example, banks versus securities or asset management firms) that are nevertheless conducting the same business should be subject to the same capital and other regulatory requirements. One area of dispute relates to the capital requirements imposed on the securities business of banks and special-ist securities traders. If banks have different systemic implications to those of securities firms, then it is not unreasonable that they should be regulated differently even though they may be conducting business similar to other institutions which are not systemically significant.

Competitive neutrality issues arise between banks and other financial insti-tutions conducting some of the activities conducted by banks. This is especially the case in the EU where the Accord (however it emerges at the end of the consultation process) will be translated into a revised Capital Adequacy Di-rective (CAD). Knight (2002) focuses on the impact of Basle 2 on non-banks (particularly securities firms and fund managers) and is concerned that inap-propriate capital requirements will be imposed on asset management firms within the EU because the EU will apply the CAD to all firms that fall within the Investment Services Directive. There is particular concern that some non-bank financial firms (such as fund managers) may be required to hold capital against operational risk (see Goodhart, 2002b; Knight, 2002). This represents a misplaced concept of 'competitive neutrality': the ultimate rationale of imposing capital requirements on banks is because of the nature of the (debt) contracts they write on both sides of the balance sheet, whereas the contracts of securities (or asset management) firms are different in kind.

However, this is an issue that derives from EU arrangements and the CAD rather than the proposed Basle Accord itself.

Portfolio versus Project Risk

Capital requirements are to take into account the volatility of risks and the extent to which risks are diversified. At the same time, allowance is to be made for risk-mitigating factors such as the use of derivative contracts to the extent that they are applied to reduce or shift risk. Nevertheless, the ECB (2001) has argued that: 'Full recognition of portfolio diversification is not yet present in the new framework'. However, it goes on to argue that: 'the IRB is an "interme-diate step" towards the regulatory acceptance of fully-fledged internal risk models, which explicitly recognise this aspect' (ECB, 2001, p. 59).

Competition

There is a long history in many countries of regulation having the effect of impairing competition. A stronger view is put by, amongst others, Hellwig

(2000) who emphasizes the political economy dimension to regulation where regulators and the banking system share a mutual interest in shielding financial institutions from competition. Davies (2002, p. 52) argues that the single view about risk of different types of assets that is implied in Basle 2 will itself have the effect of reducing competition as 'it will not be as competitive as it otherwise would have been had banks been able to compete on their view of risk'. This, it is argued, is because Basle 2 will limit diversity of view about credit risk and return, and in the process will limit the ability of banks to use advanced credit management as a competitive advantage.

Macroeconomy Effects

Two adverse macroeconomic properties of Basle 2 have been highlighted in public debate: (1) its procyclicality nature and, (2) the impact on lending to developing countries. The former is discussed by Goodhart (2002a) and the latter by Griffiths-Jones and Spratt (2002). The potential for capital adequacy regulation to accentuate economic cycles was first outlined by Blum and Hellwig (1995). Others have focused on credit-crunch phenomena: see, for instance, Drake and Llewellyn (1995), Bernanke and Lown (1991) and Calomiris and Wilson (1998). The procyclicality properties of Basle 2 are particularly serious and derive mainly from the IRB approach where the effect of banks revising their internal ratings over the cycle will have the effect of adjusting bank lending on a procyclical basis. Under some circumstances this can be destabilizing to a degree that could make banks more risky.

The ECB also focuses on the procyclicality nature of the proposed Accord and notes three aspects in particular: the changing risk characteristics of assets over the cycle, some credit risk-mitigating factors (collateral, for example) may also be procyclical, and external ratings can also be volatile over the cycle. The problem arises because risk assessments tend to be based on short-term criteria and particularly the phase of the economic cycle. Goodhart (2002a) also emphasizes that banks, in practice, give too much weight to current conditions when assessing risk.

Complexity

Monro-Davies (2002) argues that Basle 2 undermines one of the key attractions of the original: its simplicity. A key issue is whether Basle 2 is unnecessarily complex in that the objectives could be achieved with a simpler (and less costly) system. As noted by Monro-Davies (2002), complexity is the price of increased sophistication. Lannoo (2002) points to a paradox that, while the proposed new arrangements allow markets to play a bigger role in capital adequacy, the proposed rules component is yet more detailed and precise. It is not clear that these fit well together.

Two immediate issues arise: increased sophistication does not in itself imply increased accuracy, and the same objectives might be achievable with a less complex system and one that is less costly to implement. Again there is a danger of mistaking precision for accuracy. This is hazardous for two reasons: it may impose unnecessary costs, and it may create an image that because the regime is precise it must therefore be accurate. Lannoo also adds that this increased complexity is likely to make the process less transparent and also make the evaluation of capital adequacy more obscure.

The question is whether an equally effective approach would be to have a simple capital adequacy framework (perhaps not greatly different from the current Accord) but bolstered by a considerably more demanding supervisory structure and a yet greater enhanced role for market discipline to operate. Lannoo (2002, p. 42) suggests that:

> Basle should give up the level of complexity that has been developed in the last two years, and should opt instead for a more simple capital standard, which should be as close as possible to the amount of capital that banks would hold in the absence of a government-sponsored safety net. Given that a very detailed, prescriptive and precise set of requirements may be inaccurate (and yet create the false impression that it is accurate), the second-best solution may be to have a simple system with active monitoring and supervision. This would imply a lower role for Pillar I but enhanced role for Pillars II and III. Incentives for the establishment of effective risk analysis and management systems do not require complex formulae.

Milne (2002) hints at a similar approach and argues more fundamentally that the goal of increasing the risk-sensitivity of capital requirements is misplaced. His point is that what matters when it comes to maintaining the safety and soundness of banks is the total level of capital that is held, and that precisely fine-tuning regulatory capital to bank risks is not of huge importance in reducing the overall probability of bank failure. This might be taken to imply that a crude capital-assets ratio might be equally effective in cost–benefit terms. Milne makes the further point that what really matters is the effectiveness of banks' internal risk analysis and management systems and that 'capital regulation is only an adjunct [to this]' (Milne, 2002, p. 48).

Goodhart (2002b, p. 27) also has doubts about the efficacy of the proposed capital charge for Operational risk both in principle and most especially when it would be imposed on the basis of 'coefficients the justification of which is dubious in the extreme': yet again, precision without accuracy.

Market Monitoring and Discipline

Greater emphasis is to be given to the role of market discipline – the third pillar. It should encourage high standards of transparency and disclosure standards and 'enhance the role of market participants encouraging banks to hold adequate capital' (Basle Committee, 1999a, p. 60). It is envisaged that market discipline should play a greater role in the monitoring of banks and the creation of appropriate incentives. The Committee recognizes that supervisors have a strong interest in facilitating effective market discipline as a lever to strengthen the safety and soundness of the banking system. This will require more information disclosure by banks and regulators will specify the precise detail of information disclosure.

A more sceptical note is sounded by Soifer (2002) who argues that there is a degree of circularity in the process. Market participants (such as investment houses who invest in banks) are more focused on whether a bank satisfies the regulator (who in any case has inside information) than on the public information that the regulator might require to be disclosed. In particular, heargues: 'for analysts and fund managers, assessing a bank's capital adequacy and the accuracy of its risk models are of only marginal relevance, at best, to their investment decisions' (ibid., p. 56).

ASSESSMENT

This chapter has developed the concepts of regulatory regime and regulatory strategy. Seven components of the regime have been identified: each is important but none alone is sufficient for achieving the objectives of regulation. They are complementary and not alternatives. Regulatory strategy is ultimately about optimizing the outcome of the overall regime rather than any one of the components. Regulators need to consider that, if regulation is badly constructed or taken too far, there may be negative impacts on other components to the extent that the overall effect is diluted.

The objective is to optimize the outcome of a regulatory strategy in terms of mixing the components of the regime, bearing in mind that negative trade-offs may be encountered. The emphasis is on the combination of mechanisms rather than alternative approaches to achieving the objectives. The skill of the regulator in devising a regulatory strategy lies in how the various components in the regime are combined, and how the various instruments available to the regulator (rules, principles, guidelines, mandatory disclosure requirements, authorization, supervision, intervention, sanctions, redress, and so on) are to be used.

However, there is no presumption for a single optimum combination of the components of the regime. On the contrary, optima will vary between countries at any point in time, over time for all countries, and between different banks within a country at any particular time. The optimum mix of the components of a regulatory regime and of instruments will change over time as financial structures, market conditions and compliance cultures evolve. For instance, the combination of external regulation and market discipline that is most effective and efficient in one set of market circumstances, and one type of financial structure in a country, may become ill suited if the structure changes. Also, if the norms and compliance culture of the industry change, it may be appropriate to rely less on detailed and prescriptive regulation, at least for some banks.

There is no doubt that the proposed Basle 2 Accord is considerably more detailed, sophisticated, prescriptive and precise than its predecessor. However, this in itself is not the point and cannot in itself be the justification for such a radical change. In the final analysis it is a question of its accuracy and, to the extend that it is more accurate, whether this is bought at inordinate cost both to banks and regulatory/supervisory agencies. There are areas of doubt here. Above all, where is the cost–benefit analysis in these proposals, bearing in mind that in many countries (including the Financial Services Authority in the UK) new regulatory requirements are to be subject to at least a rudimentary cost–benefit analysis?

Overall, there could be some doubt, on cost–benefit grounds, as to whether the benefits of a complex set of capital adequacy requirements, designed to make capital requirements more risk sensitive are substantial enough to offset the higher compliance and monitoring costs that they will inevitably entail.

The proposed Basle 2 Accord represents a radical new approach to capital adequacy regulation. Our theme is that, while a great deal of attention has been given to refining the many and very detailed capital adequacy rules (refinement of risk weights and so on), the big challenge lies not so much in these refinements but in how the three proposed pillars are related and are to be co-ordinated. In particular, it is likely that Pillars II and III will prove to be more important and significant than the details of capital adequacy rules in Pillar I. The real significance and benefit of the Basle 2 proposals is the setting of regulation within the wider context of a regulatory regime with a clear recognition that mechanisms other than rules are important in sustaining the safety and soundness of banks and systemic stability. This is likely its most powerful benefit.

REFERENCES

Acharya, V. (2000), 'Is the international convergence of capital adequacy regulation desirable?', mimeo.

Baer, H. and C. Gray (1996), 'Debt as a control device in transitional economies: the experiences of Hungary and Poland', in R. Frydman, C. Gray and A Rapaczynski (eds), *Corporate Governance in Central Europe and Russia*, vol. 1, Budapest: Central European University Press.

Basle Committee (1999a), 'A new capital adequacy framework', consultative paper, Basle Committee on Banking Supervision, BIS, Basle, June.

Basle Committee (1999b), 'Enhancing corporate governance for banking organisations', Basle Committee on Banking Supervision, BIS, Basle.

Benink, H. (2002), 'Broadening the Basle Committee's horizons', in SUERF/CSFI, *Bumps on the Road to Basle: An Anthology of Views on Basle 2*, London: SUERF/CSFI.

Bernanke, B. and C. Lown (1991), 'The credit crunch', *Brookings Papers on Economic Activity*, **2**, 205–48.

Bliss, R. and M. Flannery (2000), 'Market discipline in the governance of US bank holding companies: monitoring vs. influence', Working Paper Series Federal Reserve Bank of Chicago, WP-00-03, Chicago, March.

Blum, J. and M. Hellwig (1995), 'The macroeconomic implications of capital adequacy requirements for banks', *European Economic Review*, **39** (3–40) 739–49.

Calomiris, C. (1997), *The Post-modern Safety Net*, Washington, DC: American Enterprise Institute.

Calomiris, C. and B. Wilson (1998), 'Bank capital and portfolio management: the 1930s 'capital crunch' and scramble to shed risk', NBER Working Paper, 6649.

Caprio, G. (1997), 'Safe and sound banking in developing countries: we're not in Kansas anymore', Policy Research Paper, No. 1739, World Bank, Washington, DC.

Caprio, G. and P. Honohan (1999), 'Restoring banking stability: beyond supervised capital requirements', *Journal of Economic Perspectives*, **13** (4), Fall, 43–64.

Dale, R. (1996), *Risk and Regulation in Global Securities Markets*, London: Wiley.

Davies, B. (2002), 'Basle lags behind the banks', in SUERF/CSFI, *Bumps on the Road to Basle: An Anthology of Views on Basle 2*, London: SUERF/CSFI, January.

Dewatripont, M. and J. Tirole (1994), *The Prudential Regulation of Banks*, Cambridge, MA: MIT Press.

Dow, J. (2000), 'What is systemic risk? Moral hazard, initial shocks and propagation', mimeo.

Drake, L. and D.T. Llewellyn (1995), 'Credit crunch: a British perspective', in F. Capie and G. Wood (eds), *Credit Crunches and the Real Economy*, London: Macmillan.

Estrella, A. (1998), 'Formulas or supervision? Remarks on the future of regulatory capital', *Federal Reserve Bank of New York Economic Policy Review*, October, 80–93.

European Central Bank (ECB) (2001), 'The new capital adequacy regime – the ECB perspective', *Monthly Bulletin*, May, 40–64.

Evanoff, D. and L. Wall (2000), 'Subordinated debt and bank capital reform', paper presented at Western Economic Association International Conference, Vancouver, June.

Fink, G. and P. Haiss (2000), 'Lemming banking: conflict avoidance by herd instinct to eliminate excess capacity', paper to be presented at SUERF Colloquium, Vienna, May.

Flannery, M. (1998), 'Using market information in prudential bank supervision: a review of the US empirical evidence', *Journal of Money, Credit and Banking*, August, 273–305.

Garcia, G.G. (1996), 'Deposit insurance: obtaining the benefits and avoiding the pitfalls', IMF Working Paper, August.

Garcia, G.G. (1999), 'Deposit insurance: obtaining the benefit and avoiding the pitfalls', IMF Working Paper 96/83, Washington, DC: International Monetary Fund.

Glaessner, T. and I. Mas (1995), 'Incentives and the resolution of bank distress', *World Bank Research Observer*, **10** (1), February, 53–73.

Goodhart, C.A.E. (2002a), 'Basle and procyclicality', in SUERF/CSFI, *Bumps on the Road to Basle: An Anthology of Views on Basle 2*, London: SUERF/CSFI, January.

Goodhart, C. (2002b), 'The operational risk issue', in *Bumps on the Road to Basle: An Anthology of Views on Basle 2*, London: SUERF/CSFI, January.

Goodhart, C., P. Hartmann, D.T. Llewellyn, L. Rojas-Suarez and S. Weisbrod (1998), *Financial Regulation: Why, How and Where Now?*, London: Routledge.

Griffiths-Jones, S. and S. Spratt (2002), 'Basle 2 and developing countries', in SUERF/CSFI, *Bumps on the Road to Basle: An Anthology of Views on Basle 2*, London: SUERF/CSFI, January.

Harm, C. (2002), 'Bank management between shareholders and regulators', SUERF study, SUERF, Amsterdam, (forthcoming).

Hellwig, M. (1995), 'Systemic aspects of risk management in banking and finance', *Swiss Journal of Economics and Statistics*, **131** (4/2), 723–37.

Hellwig, M. (2000), 'Banken zwischen politik und markt', *Perspektiven der Wirtschaftspolitik*, **3**, 337–57.

Hoggarth, G. and V. Saporta (2001), 'Costs of banking system instability: some empirical evidence', *Financial Stability Review*, June, 1–32.

Kane, E. (2000), 'Dynamic inconsistency of capital forbearance: long run vs. short run effects of too-big-to-fail policymaking', paper presented to IMF Central Banking Conference, Washington, DC, June.

Knight, A. (2002), 'Collateral damage to European non-banks: the need to unscramble Basle', in SUERF/CSFI, *Bumps on the Road to Basle: An Anthology of Views on Basle 2*, London: SUERF/CSFI, January.

Kupiec, H. and J. O'Brien (1997), 'The pre-commitment approach: using incentives to set market risk capital requirements', Finance and Economics Discussion Series, no. 1997–14, Federal Reserve Board, Washington, DC, March.

Lang, W. and D. Robertson (2000), 'Analysis of proposals for a minimum subordinated debt requirement', paper presented at Western Economic Association International Conference, Vancouver, June.

Lannoo, K. (2002), 'The European policy perspective', in SUERF/CSFI, *Bumps on the Road to Basle: An Anthology of Views on Basle 2*, London: SUERF/CSFI, January.

Lindgren, C.J, G. Garcia and M. Saal (1996), *Bank Soundness and Macroeconomic Policy*, Washington, DC: International Monetary Fund.

Llewellyn, D.T. (1999), 'The economic rationale of financial regulation', Occasional Paper, No. 1, Financial Services Authority, London.

Llewellyn, D.T. (2000), 'Regulatory lessons from recent banking crises', De Nederlandsche Bank Discussion Paper, Amsterdam, May.

Milne, A. (2002), 'Why effective regulatory capital requirements need not be aligned with bank portfolio risk', in SUERF/CSFI, *Bumps on the Road to Basle: An Anthology of Views on Basle 2*, London: SUERF/CSFI, January.

Monro-Davies, R. (2002), 'Complexity is the price of increased sophistication', in SUERF/CSFI, *Bumps on the Road to Basle: An Anthology of Views on Basle 2*, London: SUERF/CSFI, January.

Nakaso, H., M. Hattori, T. Nagae, H. Hamada, T. Kanamori, H. Kamiguchi, T. Dezawa, K. Takahashi, A. Kamimura, T. Suzuki and K. Sumida (2000), 'Changes in bank behaviour during the financial crisis: experiences of the financial crisis in Japan', paper presented to IMF Central Banking Conference, Washington, DC, June.

Prendergast, C. (1993), 'The provision of incentives in firms', *Journal of Economic Literature*, March, 7–63.

Reisen, H. (1998), 'Domestic causes of currency crises: policy lessons for crisis avoidance', OECD Development Centre, Technical Paper 136, Paris.

Saunders, A. and B. Wilson (1996), 'Contagious bank runs: evidence from the 1929–1933 period', *Journal of Financial Intermediation*, **5**, 409–23.

Schinasi, G., B. Drees and W. Lee (1999), 'Managing global finance and risk', *Finance and Development*, December, 14–19.

Simpson, D. (2000), 'Cost benefit analysis and competition', in FSA, *Some Cost Benefit Issues in Financial Regulation*, London: Financial Services Authority.

Summer, M. (2002), 'Banking regulation and systemic risk', Working Paper 57, Oesterreichische Nationalbank, Vienna, January.

Soifer, R. (2002), 'What investors really want to know: thoughts on Pillar three', in SUERF/CSFI, *Bumps on the Road to Basle: An Anthology of Views on Basle 2*, London: SUERF/CSFI, January.

SUERF/CSFI (2002), *Bumps on the Road to Basle: An Anthology of Views on Basle 2*, London: SUERF/CSFI, January.

Wallman, S. (1999), 'Information technology revolution and its impact on regulation and regulatory structure', in R. Littan and A. Santomero (eds), *Brookings-Wharton Papers on Financial Services*, Washington, DC: Brookings Institution Press.

COMMENT ON 'THE OPTIMAL REGULATORY ENVIRONMENT'

Annemarie van der Zwet

It is the task of a discussant to comment on a paper in a more or less critical way. Obviously, weak points identified by the discussant or divergent views between the author and the discussant give more food for discussion than making compliments. I must say that you have given me a tough job, Mr Llewellyn, since I basically agree with all the core messages in your paper. One message is that authorities should place more emphasis on market monitoring and discipline instead of focusing unilaterally on regulation and supervision. I agree, and I am in the good company of at least all members of the Basle Committee; indeed, increasing the role of market discipline is the very reason for dedicating a separate pillar to this important issue in the proposals for a new capital adequacy framework. Another element is that supervisors should improve their accountability. I agree with this suggestion too, and here I am in the good company of the Governing Board of De Nederlandsche Bank. Actually, De Nederlandsche Bank has recently finalized a framework for Regulatory Impact Analysis, which will be applied to all new regulatory instruments in the short term. One final point of your presentation is that the proposed new capital framework is unnecessarily complex and detailed. Although I feel slightly awkward given the active participation of De Nederlandsche Bank in the Basle Committee, I must say that here too I agree with you. The sheer size of the documents containing the new capital adequacy accord is a clear proof of these proposals being very, if not overly, detailed and complex.

However, before we end this conference in total consensus, I would like to elaborate somewhat on the reasons for the size and complexity of the new capital framework. The first reason is that the new capital framework allows banks to use their internal rating systems to calculate solvency requirements. This is the well-known IRB approach. Banks only qualify for this approach if their risk management and control systems meet strict criteria. Therefore, the Basle Committee had to design rules specifying these criteria as well as complementing them by filling in the supervisory review and market discipline. Thus, it is a mistake to think that relying to a larger extent on banks' own risk management systems for solvency requirements reduces the regulatory burden. It is not a matter of fewer rules; it is a matter of different rules.

But this is not the whole story. A large part of the documents on the new capital framework – my guess is around 60 per cent – relates to the simplified version of the IRB approach, namely the foundation IRB approach. This simplification requires much additional regulation: where banks using advanced IRB have to convince supervisors that their computations are prudent, supervisors have to prescribe all separate elements in the foundation IRB. The foundation approach is very useful in practice: it provides a possibility for banks which are not ready yet for advanced IRB, but plan to follow this approach in the future, to gain experience with internal ratings-based management systems.

Besides this positive effect, the introduction of foundation IRB has led to some problems as well. The point is that when an essentially complex method like IRB is simplified, some groups of banks or creditors will inevitably be treated overly favourably and others overly unfavourably. This process politicizes the negotiations, resulting in more regulation to safeguard the level playing field. However, these adjustments cause winners and losers again, requiring even more regulation and so on. Underlying this process is the political desire that the banking system in specific countries or regions is not put at a disadvantage vis-à-vis banks in other countries or regions. The introduction of foundation IRB in itself can be regarded as a result of the political will to give small, and usually less sophisticated banks the same opportunities for reducing their solvency requirements as sophisticated banks. An important precondition is of course, that the risk management systems of these small banks might be less sophisticated, but should meet the same high quality standards. Another well-known example of politics playing an important role in the discussions about a new capital adequacy framework is the treatment of small and medium-sized enterprises. You may recall that at the end of last year Mr Schröder himself threatened that Germany would block the negotiated capital agreement, if the capital accord were to undermine the present treatment of small and medium-sized enterprises by German banks. This political pressure caused additional regulation with regard to collateral and the reduction of the risk sensitivity of the new capital accord.

These examples illustrate that political influences are not the only, but certainly an important, cause of the complexity and the delay of the new capital framework. If negotiating the new capital accord were a purely technical exercise, life would be much easier for supervisors. More importantly, the purpose of fostering the soundness of the banking system and thereby financial stability would be better served as well. Indeed, it makes sense from an economic point of view that in so far as small banks or small and medium-sized enterprises are relatively risky, the corresponding solvency requirements should be higher too. Although I realize that it is impossible to exclude political influences from the negotiations in Basle altogether, I think that the quality of supervision is best served when there is a distance between supervision and politics. In other words, it is important to safeguard the independence of supervisors. This independence is all the more important given the public good of safeguarding financial stability.

The question of how the independence of supervisors can be fostered then arises. One answer can be sought in the institutional structure, or the organization of supervision. I would prefer to leave the debate about the optimal structure of supervision – particularly whether it should be located at the central bank or not – to another conference. In my opinion, the independence of supervisors can be safeguarded within different institutional structures of supervision. Nevertheless, I think that ongoing discussions about the set-up of supervision between supervisors and the national ministries of finance might, in some cases, undermine the independence of supervisors. Furthermore, supervisors should not only be independent of politics, but of the interests of the industry as well. In my view, this risk of industry capture is reduced when supervisors are not financed by levies paid by the industry, but from central bank funds or the general budget.

However, unbalanced independence may open the door to self-interest. This is why Mr Llewellyn rightly draws attention to the importance of proper accountability of supervisors, which can be fostered by instruments like regulatory impact analysis, budgetary accountability, transparency and the formulation of clear objectives. Mr Chairman, when Mr Llewellyn is as much in agreement with my remarks as I am with his paper and presentation, we will have a very short discussion. I therefore hope that you can stimulate the audience to make some critical comments. Thank you.

REPLY

David Llewellyn

I am extremely grateful to Annemarie van de Zwet for her very useful remarks and the valuable perspective she offers on this extremely complex issue. It is evidently the case that we are in large measure of agreement. However, as she implies at the end of her comments, this by no means excludes further debate. As they say in the theatre, this one will 'run and run'.

It is extremely constructive that De Nederlandsche Bank has given a high priority to creating a RIA regime to be applied to its regulation and supervision. As Annemarie says, RIA is a useful component of the accountability process. It may well be that DNB is more advanced in this area of thinking than most, if not all, supervisory agencies. The Bank is to be congratulated in taking this initiative and it is certainly to be commended to other supervisory agencies that might otherwise be taking a more ad hoc approach to considering the impact of their regulation and supervision.

It is when Annemarie gives the background to the reasons for the complexity of Basle 2 that I begin to feel uneasy and I think this reinforces some of the critique outlined in the paper. I certainly agree with her reasoning and she has given us a useful perspective on the practicalities of the process of constructing the Basle 2 proposals. But it is ironic that, as she correctly observes, a large part of the (consultative) documents relates to the simplified version of the IRB approach '*This simplification requires a lot of additional regulation* ... ' [italics added]. She goes on to argue that, in the negotiation process, 'adjustments cause winners and losers again, requiring even more regulation and so on'.

This is precisely my point and what underlies some of my concerns about the 'rules' element in the new accord. It is a classic example of 'rules escalation'. Although she does not say so explicitly, Ms van der Zwet argues that the arrangements have to be complex if they are to be accurate, that is, if they are to achieve what we might term the 'first best' solution. My point is, however, that the risk characteristics of banking are now too complex for a set of rules to be precisely accurate (that is, the 'first best' is probably not achievable), and in the attempt to secure accuracy through rules a degree of complexity and difficulty of implementation is created which in itself has real costs. It is for this reason that there is a case for considering whether a simplified 'second best' solution might be preferable.

I could not agree more with the discussant regarding the danger of politicizing regulation and supervision, and we have seen the dangers of this in several countries that have recently experienced banking crises. I cannot resist the temptation to argue that this danger is more likely when the prescriptions are very detailed simply because, as she hints at, a political bargaining process emerges. I totally endorse her view that 'the quality of supervision is best served when there is ... independence of supervisors'. This is a powerful perspective.

9. The effectiveness of deposit insurance

Gillian G.H. Garcia

INTRODUCTION

This conference, entitled 'Banking supervision at the crossroads', is a celebration of the fiftieth anniversary of the Dutch Act on the Supervision of Credit Systems. My chapter will develop the three themes that this conference pursues. First, it will consider briefly the interplay between bank supervision and deposit insurance. Second, it will examine the effectiveness of deposit protection schemes – as its title suggests it should. Third, the chapter will address the convergence of deposit insurance configurations. In short, the chapter will attempt to relate to all three themes – interrelationships with supervision, effectiveness, and convergence toward good practice.

After this introductory section, the second section of the chapter will examine some interrelationships between banking supervision and deposit insurance. A discussion of the effectiveness of deposit protection schemes will follow in the third section. The fourth section surveys the results of the search by theoreticians, empiricists and practitioners to identify good practices for systems of deposit insurance. Such good practices aim to promote bank soundness and differ from mistaken practices that thwart soundness. The penultimate section will address convergence of deposit insurance practices around the world and in Western Europe toward those judged to constitute good practice for an effective system of deposit protection. Conclusions are offered in the final section.

DEPOSIT INSURANCE AND SUPERVISION

Many deposit insurers like to see themselves as agents of an independent institution/operation but, in fact, deposit insurance and supervision are inextricably linked. For one thing, deposit protection will not be successful unless supervision is effective. This is a major lesson that the USA learned from its savings and loan association debacle in the 1980s. In addition, the initiation of a system of deposit insurance places additional burdens on supervisors (at the very minimum they must communicate and share information with insurers). Finally, the existence of a good system of deposit protection can ease the supervisor's job (for example, when dealing with a failed bank).

This intertwining is a fact. It is true regardless of where the supervisory agency is housed. The supervisor may have responsibility for deposit protection (as in the UK through 2001) or the insurer may be an independent agency (as in Canada and the USA), or the deposit protection system may jointly run by representatives of both the official and private sectors (as in the Netherlands.) In each case, supervision and deposit protection are inexorably mutually dependent.

Prompt Corrective Action

Perhaps prompt corrective action (PCA) is the best example of the importance of good supervision for effective deposit protection. The legislation embodying PCA in the USA was enacted in 1991 in the FDIC (Federal Deposit Insurance Corporation) Improvement Act (FDICIA) following the savings and loans association (S&L) debacle and in the midst of the banking crisis. As a result of banks' problems, the Bank Insurance Fund (BIF) became technically insolvent and was forced to borrow from the Treasury Department in 1991. Prompt corrective action was one of the measures intended to prevent a recurrence of this embarrassment. Henceforth, supervisors would tackle a bank's problems early on, well before it became insolvent. The problem bank would be forced to take remedial actions that would allow it to recover. In fact, PCA in the USA requires the regulator to close the bank when its leverage ratio falls to 2 per cent. Prompt corrective action was intended to reduce the number of failures and lower the cost of resolving unavoidable failures.

While working in the US Senate on the passage of FDICA, I observed that supervisors, in general, resisted PCA during enactment. Nevertheless, those regulators with whom I have spoken recently universally agree that PCA has been a success in the USA. While other factors, such as a strong economic recovery for the 1991 recession, have helped the US banking industry, it has undoubtedly been in a stronger position to withstand the recent recession. In fact, the FDIC recently declared 2001, and the fourth quarter in particular, to be the industry's strongest ever. Nevertheless, some expensive failures have occurred recently in the USA, despite FDICIA. Some in the academic community attribute the costly failures to forbearance by supervisors and they propose that senior supervisors should be held accountable (with their jobs) for costly misjudgements.

Charging Banks for Supervision

But this intertwining can cause a pricing problem and raises the question whether it is possible and efficacious to combine the charges for banks' supervision and insurance coverage. In the USA, the Office of the Comptroller of the Currency (OCC), which oversees nationally chartered banks, makes national banks reimburse the OCC for over 90 per cent of the cost of the inspections that the banks receive. The Federal Reserve and the FDIC, which oversee state chartered banks, do not charge banks for their oversight and cover such costs from other sources. In the FDIC's case, the Bank Insurance Fund foots the bill. This means that a national bank what has already paid directly for its own supervision, indirectly also shares the cost of supervising its state chartered competitors through the premiums it pays to the Bank Insurance Fund. The Comptroller of the Currency has complained about this inequity (Hawke, 2001). Although the dual banking system and the proliferation of financial supervisors is peculiarly American, the issue of risk-basing pricing for supervision and for deposit insurance coverage is more general. I hope to learn how the countries represented at this conference handle this problem.

IDENTIFYING EFFECTIVE SUPERVISION

An effective system of supervision would be one that produces a stable financial system where bank failures are not frequent and where weak banks can be, and usually are, turned around successfully before they fail. In addition, in a successful system, the failures that (inevitably but regrettably) do occur are not disruptive of the system's stability and should not impose heavy costs on the deposit protection system.

Supervisors have been gathering together internationally at the Basle Committee on Banking Supervision (BCBS) to improve the effectiveness of their operations at least since 1974. They had been searching internationally for best practices to keep banks sound for more than 20 years before the BCBS issued its good practice advice in its Core Principles of Banking Supervision in 1997. These supervisory efforts have been effective in causing a convergence towards agreement on the best ways to achieve the soundness of those institutions that take deposits and provide credits, and on ways to put best practices into operation. This is not to suggest that everything that needs to be done in the world of supervision has already been done – new capital standards are still in process – but the progress that has already been made has been substantial and remarkable.

Best practices are also needed for deposit insurance systems. In finding them, a balance needs to be struck between over-insurance and under-insurance. Over-insurance is likely to lead to over-regulation and intrusive supervision in an attempt to curb the moral hazard that attends extensive insurance coverage. Under-insurance hampers failure resolution and leads to delays in closing failed banks, which experience has taught raises the costs of failure to both the public and the private sectors. Finding the right balance for insurance protection can help to encourage an appropriate degree of supervision that protects the system without thwarting competitive markets. We need a Goldilock's world where the insurance/supervisory porridge is not too hot, nor too cold, not too sweet nor too tart, and the insurance/supervisory bed is not too large nor too small, not too soft nor too hard.

How to Evaluate the Effectiveness of Deposit Insurance

The steps necessary to achieve an effective system of deposit insurance are less well understood than those in the path to effective supervision are. Effectiveness could be measured in one of (at least) two ways. First, success could be checked locally against the objectives set for it in any country. A survey of its members conducted by the Financial Stability Forum's Working Group on Deposit Insurance in late 1999, revealed a surprisingly large number of different objectives that officials attributed to their system of deposit protection.[1] But the international community has increasingly come to recognize as unrealistic the full wish list of good things that politicians sometimes express for their system of protection. *Deposit insurance is not a panacea that will solve all banking and economic problems.* Consequently, checking against a long or unrealistic wish list would not be an appropriate way to judge effectiveness of any country's system of protection.

Legitimate Rationales for Deposit Insurance

Rather, it has come to be recognized that there are two principal, legitimate rationales for deposit protection (FSF, 2001). These two rationales are appropriate to any and all countries. They are consumer protection and financial system stability. These two objectives, pursued in moderation can be complementary. Effectively protecting small depositors from loss and inconvenience when their bank fails will convince consumers that there is no need to run from a troubled bank. There will be none of the panic associated with television and press coverage of depositor lines outside bank branches, which can lead to contagion from institution to institution. The financial system will be correspondingly systemically more stable. Consequently, the effectiveness of deposit insurance can be more appropriately checked against its success in protecting small depositors and maintaining financial stability.

I know of no research that has investigated the success of deposit insurance systems around the world in protecting small depositors. But successful protection would need at least two things. First, funds sufficient in amount and liquidity are required to cover the costs of reimbursement of insured depositors' funds (or their transfer to another institution). Second information systems and payment procedures need to be adequate to pay depositors quickly. Consumers who lose access to their funds, especially their transaction balances, will not be happy.

Notice the reference above to pursuing the consumer protection and stability enhancement objectives in moderation. As is well known, a misguided attempt to protect consumers and stabilize the system in the short run by offering unduly high coverage can lead to a severe case of moral hazard, which will destabilize the financial system in the longer run. Attempts to contain the moral hazard that is encouraged by over-insurance will place an unduly onerous burden on the system of bank supervision.

The implication is that the effectiveness of any deposit protection scheme should be judged principally against its success in promoting those two objectives. As mentioned above, that will involve finding the right balance between too little and too much coverage and too little and too much supervision. Theoretical considerations and empirical experience suggest that there are certain good/best practices that will aid in achieving this balance and in successfully pursuing the two legitimate objectives for deposit insurance.

BEST/GOOD PRACTICES FOR DEPOSIT INSURANCE

Some History of the Quest for Good Deposit Insurance Practices

The World Bank and the International Monetary Fund (IMF) have taken the lead in pioneering the concept of best practices for deposit insurance. As a result of their surveillance and technical advisory activities, they have found themselves repeatedly in a position of offering advice to initiate or reform a system of deposit protection. They are, for example, frequently asked to comment on draft deposit insurance legislation. In addition, when a financial crisis occurs in a country, World Bank and IMF staffs ask whether faults in the country's existing guarantee system contributed to its systemic banking problems. It was the IMF that moved forward on the concept of best deposit insurance practices, however, perhaps because it likes to speak with one voice on important topics and to offer consistent advice. The World Bank seems to tolerate more readily internal dissent and divergences in policy opinions and advice.[2]

In any event, in fall 1996 the then IMF Deputy Managing Director, Stanley Fischer, called for an IMF position on best deposit insurance practices. By December the Monetary and Exchange Affairs Department (MAE) had drawn upon its accumulated experience to issue an internal operational paper, 'Deposit Insurance and Crisis Management' (MAE, 1996) that would be used by IMF staff when subsequently offering advice on the design or reform of a system of deposit protection. While this document has not been publicly released, its principles are reflected in the IMF publication, *Toward a Framework for Financial Stability* (Folkerts-Landau and Lindgren, 1998), which summarizes IMF advice. In addition, the IMF has published several more detailed documents on deposit insurance practices by individual authors (for example, Garcia, 1999; 2000; Kyei, 1995).

The European Union (EU) had issued its Directive on Deposit-Guarantee Schemes earlier – at the end of May 1994 – and is currently in the process of revising it. But that event was designed to ensure 'a harmonised minimum level of protection wherever deposits are located in the Community' (European Parliament, 1994) in order to complete a single, unified banking market in the EU. It was less a search for best practices and more a quest for containing competition through preferential deposit insurance provisions. In fact, Professor Maxwell Hall has assessed the effectiveness of the deposit insurance systems and operations in EU countries against IMF best practices and has found the EU's systems somewhat wanting. The EU systems scored an average EU-wide rating of 3.5 on a scale from 1 (low) to 5 (high) (Hall, 2001).

In 1999, the Financial Stability Forum created a Study Group on Deposit Insurance that later became the fully-fledged Working Group on Deposit Insurance.[3] Over the next two years, the working group conducted an intensive and inclusive process by holding meetings for policy-makers, deposit insurers, academics and other interested parties from all parts of the world in Basle, Berlin, Budapest, Buenos Aires, Cancun, Chicago, Kuala Lumpur, Lusaka, Paris, Rome and Washington. The working group criticizes some of the IMF's best practices, arguing that differences among countries' histories, cultures, political and legal systems require more variability in the design of deposit insurance systems than 'IMF' best/good practices decree. It issued general guidance for effective deposit insurance systems in late 2001 (FSF, 2001). The Canadian leaders of the Deposit Insurance Working Group are currently in the process of forming the International Association of Deposit Insurers (IADI) that will hold its first meeting in Basle in May 2002. No doubt the new association will continue to try to identify good practices for effective deposit insurance systems.

Different Approaches to Identifying Good Practices

A number of methods have been used to identify what constitutes good practice for effective deposit insurance design and implementation. The first approach – that of the FSF – is to build a consensus among deposit insurance practitioners on what features they consider constitute good practice and what practices should be eschewed. The FSF good practices represent consensus formed from the combined experience of the 12 working group member deposit insurers (mentioned in note 3) plus deposit insurance experts from the IMF and World Bank. They also had the benefit of input from individuals and representatives of non-member organizations who have participated in the working group's outreach events.

Garcia adopted a second approach by attempting to identify the features of an incentive-compatible deposit insurance system partly from the principles of finance theory. These principles recommend incentive-compatible practices that are intended to encourage all parties affected by deposit insurance to keep banks safe and sound. These different parties include bankers, shareholders, creditors, depositors, borrowers, supervisors, regulators and politicians.

The IMF and Garcia also appealed to country experiences, as documented by the IMF, as a third method of identifying which practices have been successful and why they have proved efficacious and which have failed to protect consumers and/or to produce financial stability. Thus the IMF's and Garcia's good practice recommendations derive partly from a judgemental evaluation of the collected experience of IMF missions in different countries, in different parts of the world, at different stages of development and with different legal and cultural traditions.

Fourth, good practice has been approached from a different, innovative direction in empirical work by, for example, Demirguc-Kunt and Detragiache (1998; 2000). Demirguc-Kunt and Detragiache and others subsequently, have used statistical analysis to examine the relationship between the occurrence of a systemic crisis and features of the financial system including its system of deposit protection. The existence of an explicit system of deposit protection and some of its individual features appear as explanatory variables in logit regression equations that explain the occurrence of a financial crisis. Those features that are positively associated with the occurrence of crises are judged to constitute bad practice.

A Comparison of Good Practices as Derived from the Different Approaches

Table 9.1 summarizes good practices as seen by the IMF, Garcia, the FSF and Demirguc-Kunt and Detragiache. It suggests that, despite perceived disagreements, the sets of recommendations are remarkably similar once the one major divergence of opinion that exists is overcome. The first three analysts in Table 9.1 (IMF, FSF and Garcia) all favour a well-designed system of explicit insurance over an implicit system. Demirguc-Kunt and Detragiache, on the other hand, find an association between the existence of explicit deposit insurance coverage and the incidence of financial crises among a sample of 61 countries over the period 1980–97. They also, however, find that many of the characteristics of a well-designed system as recommended by the IMF, FSF and Garcia ameliorate the adverse impact they find for an explicit system of protection.

Where Agreement Has Been Reached

It is reassuring that there is, in fact, a convergence of opinion in favour of many elements of deposit insurance design. As Table 9.1 illustrates, there is a preference for (1) compulsory systems over voluntary ones; (2) limitations on coverage; (3) a strong legal, judicial and political infrastructure; and (4) an effective system of bank supervision and regulation. Such agreement is interesting and perhaps surprising because it is derived from such different sources and relies of different methodologies.

Demirguc-Kunt and Detragiache offer advice on a more limited set of characteristics than the other three analysts do. The other three show remarkable agreement on six additional factors that Demirguc-Kunt and Detragiache do not address. These factors are the need for: (1) supervisors to have a system of prompt corrective actions to reduce the number of failures; (2) the authorities to resolve failed banks promptly; (3) close co-ordination between depositors insurers and other safety-net providers (lenders of last resort and supervisors); (4) prompt reimbursement for depositors; (5) accurate sources of information for supervisors and deposit insurers; and (6) adequate disclosure of banks' financial condition.

Where Disagreement Remains

There is less agreement on some other characteristics of deposit insurance. The first three analysts listed in Table 9.1 are agnostic on the issue of whether deposit insurance systems should be publicly or privately run, whereas Demirguc-Kunt and Detragiache favour privately run systems. There is some difference of opinion on the issue of coinsurance. The IMF and Demirguc-Kunt and Detragiache favour it, while Garcia and the FSF see both advantages and disadvantages but argue the small depositor should be protected in full up to the coverage limit, while coinsurance may be an option to apply to higher deposit tranches. The IMF, Garcia, and FSF argue in favour of adequately

Table 9.1 Convergence to good practices

IMF good practices	Garcia's recommendations	Guidance from the FSF	Demirguc-Kunt and Detragiache's findings
Infrastructure The primary objective is to provide a safe asset to small savers	Have realistic objectives	Contribute to system stability and protect unsophisticated depositors (p. 42)	
	Choose carefully between a public or private deposit insurance system	Either a public or private system is acceptable	Government-run systems are more prone to systemic crises
	Define the deposit insurer's mandate accordingly	The deposit insurers' mandate may be broad or narrow (p. 17)	
Strong institutions are needed	Have a good legal, judicial, accounting, financial, and political infrastructure	Need robust legal, prudential regulatory, supervisory, accounting and disclosure regimes (p. 13)	A good infrastructure curbs the insurance's negative effects
To contain moral hazard Explicitly define in law/ regulation	Explicitly define in law and regulation	Define clearly in law, regulation, or private contract (p. 23)	Explicit systems reduce market discipline and cause instability
	Conduct a public awareness campaign	Public awareness programme necessary (p. 29)	
Take prompt remedial actions	Give the supervisor a system of prompt remedial actions	Members should be subject to strong prudential supervision and regulation with early intervention and PCA (p. 13)	
Resolve failed depository institutions promptly	Resolve failed depository institutions promptly	Need timely and effective exit strategies for failed banks (p. 31)	

Impose limitations on coverage	Provide low coverage	Determine scope, then set an appropriate limit based on deposit-distribution data – on a per depositor per bank basis (pp. 24, 47)	Bank instability increases with wider coverage – encompassing forex and inter-bank deposits
Coinsurance is advisable	Coinsurance should be imposed only above the coverage threshold	Coinsurance has both negative and positive effects, but imposing it only above the threshold helps (p. 24)	Coinsurance reduces the probability of a crisis
	Net (offset) loans in default against deposits	Is a country-specific choice	
To avoid adverse selection			
All banks should be members	Make membership compulsory	In general, it should be compulsory (p. 21)	Compulsory schemes are less destabilizing
Charge risk-adjusted premiums (if risks can be accurately measured)	Risk-adjust premiums, once the DIS has sufficient experience	When necessary information is available, risk-basing assessment is preferable (p. 28)	
To reduce agency problems	Create an independent but accountable DIS agency	Governance should reflect the mandate but be transparent and accountable (p. 44)	
Grant *no* decision-making authority to bankers within the deposit insurance scheme	Have bankers on an advisory board, not the main board of a publicly run DIS with access to financial support from the government	Board members should be subject to a fit-and-proper test and be free from conflicts of interest (p. 18)	Government-run schemes are more prone to crises
Have close relations with the lender of last resort and the supervisor	Ensure close relations with the LOLR and the supervisor	Close co-ordination necessary (p. 19), formalize information-sharing agreements (p. 46)	

Table 9.1 (continued)

IMF good practices	Garcia's recommendations	Guidance from the FSF	Demirguc-Kunt and Detragiache's findings
To ensure credibility			
Have adequate sources of funding to avoid insolvency (*ex ante* or *ex post*)	Start when banks are sound	Need to consider the capacity of the banking system to fund a new system (p. 14)	Funded schemes increase moral hazard
	Ensure adequate sources of funding (*ex ante* or *ex post*) to avoid insolvency	Sound funding critical for confidence (p. 26). Can be *ex ante* or *ex post* or hybrid	
	Enact depositor priority	Be aware of the implications of granting priority (p. 38)	
	Invest fund resources wisely	Funds should be well managed, with appropriate policies and procedures (p. 48)	
Pay deposits quickly	Pay out or transfer deposits quickly	Ensure prompt reimbursement (p. 47)	
Have accurate information on an insured bank's financial condition	Organize good information on the condition of individual institutions and the distribution of deposits by size	Information needs vary with breadth of the mandate, but all need data on individual banks' deposit bases (p. 45)	
Make accurate disclosure on an insured bank's financial condition	Make appropriate disclosure to maintain confidence while enabling depositors to protect their interest	Accurate, reliable, timely information helps management, depositors, markets and authorities make decisions and increases market, regulatory, and supervisory discipline (p. 13)	

Sources: Folkerts-Landau and Lindgren (1998), Garcia (1999; 2000), FSF (2001), and Demirguc-Kunt and Detragiache (2000).

120

Table 9.2 Areas of agreement and disagreement

Status characteristic		Positions	Revealed preferences
Major disagreement			
3:1	Explicit or implicitly defined system	IMF, FSF, Garcia favour explicit, but not Demirguc-Kunt and Detragiache	Explicit systems have increased from 47 to 74 since 1995
Unanimity			
All 4	Good infrastructure	All agree it is needed	Many donors are working toward it
	Coverage should be limited	All agree limits needed	92.5% systems offer limited cover
	Compulsory membership	All agree membership should be compulsory	92% of systems are compulsory
Other disagreements			
3:1	Government in charge	Demirguc-Kunt and Detragiache favour private system; IMF, FSF, Garcia allow private or public	60% of systems are run by the government, the rest are privately or jointly run
2:2	Coinsurance	Demirguc-Kunt and Detragiache and IMF favour, FSF and Garcia would confine to excess coverage	Only 26% have adopted coinsurance and 1/4 of these apply it only above the basic minimum coverage
3:1	Funding: *Ex post or ex ante*	IMF, Garcia, FSF have no preference, Demirguc-Kunt and Detragiache prefer *ex post*	82% of explicit systems maintain a fund as their principal financing vehicle
3:1	Adequate funding	IMF, FSF, Garcia call for adequate funding, Demirguc-Kunt and Detragiache disagree	Many schemes appear to be under-funded
Unanimity of 3			
3:0	Risk-base premiums	IMF, FSF, Garcia favour when accurate	35% of systems charge risk-adjusted premiums, up from 8.5% in 1995
3:0	Adequate information	IMF, FSF, Garcia	68% of supervisors share data with the insurer, but problems are widespread
3:0	Reimburse depositors quickly	IMF, FSF, Garcia	Honoured in the breach

funded schemes, regardless of whether they are financed *ex ante* or *ex post*, while Demirguc-Kunt and Detragiache demur by demonstrating that pre-funded schemes have been more prone to crises.

In summary, as demonstrated in Table 9.2, remarkable progress has been made in the past six years towards reaching consensus on many factors that are considered to be important components of a well-structured system of deposit protection. The next section of the chapter will show the extent to which different countries conform to, or diverge from, these good practices. The convergence is strong and reassuring, especially as the revealed preferences of countries around the world, and in Western Europe, conform in many, but not all, instances to the good practices that the different analysts recommend.

Countries' Revealed Preferences

This section shows where countries world-wide and in Western Europe have agreed to adopt good practice, where they retain differences in system characteristics and where more work needs to be done to emulate good practice.

CONVERGENCE

In 1995, Kyei conducted a survey to identify deposit protection arrangements in operation in the early 1990s. Garcia (1999; 2000) has subsequently recorded country practices. Kyei's findings are used as a basis of comparison with Garcia's 2000 results, updated through 2001, in order to identify convergence toward good practice.

There are a number of important instances where deposit insurance systems in Western Europe and around the world have already converged toward uniformity – and, fortunately, have converged on good practice. As shown in Figure 9.1, 92 per cent of explicit deposit insurance systems worldwide were compulsory in 2001. This represents a substantial increase from the 55 per cent of systems that Kyei found to be mandatory in 1995. Further, 97.3 per cent of systems in 2001 had at least some private funding from the system's membership – up from 87 per cent in 1995. In 2001, more systems were concerned about limiting cover to contain moral hazard so that the percentage of countries that excluded certain types of deposits from coverage had risen from 45 to 81, and those that applied the coverage limit per depositor rather than per deposit, had risen from 91 per cent in 1995 to 99 per cent in 2001.

Figure 9.1 shows that, although not noted as necessarily good practice, more systems (82 per cent in 2001 compared with 72 per cent in 1995) maintained a fund, as opposed to collecting monies *ex post*. In fact, new and

System features

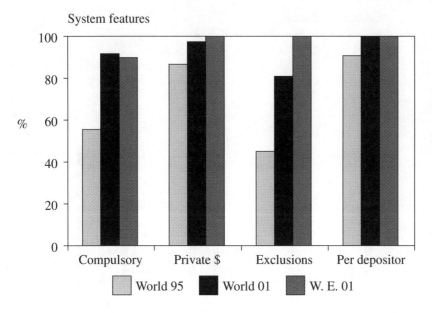

Figure 9.1   Convergence to good practice

reformed systems are moving towards a balance between *ex ante* and *ex post* funding that maintains a smaller fund and supplements it with *ex post* levies when necessary. The system being currently designed in Hong Kong has explicitly modelled this balance.

In other instances there are movements in one-direction movements that have not yet reached uniformity. Sometimes these movements are towards good practice as identified in Table 9.1. Perhaps the most notable change is in the adoption of explicit systems of deposit protection. This movement accords with the advice of the FSF, the IMF and Garcia, but disregards Demirguc-Kunt and Detragiache's finding that explicit systems are more prone to crises. Figure 9.2 shows the number of systems adopted by decade. Only one of the currently operating systems (that of the USA) was in existence before the 1960s. Twelve systems were initiated in the 1960s, seven in the 1970s, 23 in the 80s and 31 in the 1990s. The proliferation continues: five new systems were initiated in the first two years of the new millennium. Should we regard this trend as a 'fad' as Demirguc-Kunt and Detragiache suggest, or as a wisely considered move to increase stability in the domestic and international financial system and protect consumers? Time and experience in the next few years must provide the answer to this question. This makes a total of 79 explicit deposit insurance systems, of which 77 provide limited coverage in normal (no crisis) times.

Number of systems

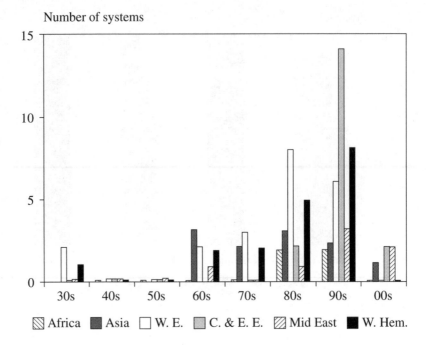

Figure 9.2   Decade of system initiation

Explicit Systems

The countries hosting the 77 limited explicit systems are listed in Table 9.3. It shows a large variation from continent to continent. European countries almost universally offer their citizens a system of deposit protection, while only four countries in Africa do so. But further pursuit of regional differences in deposit insurance practices – differences that can be quite marked – are a topic for another day.

Progress on Funding, Coinsurance and Management

Figure 9.3 shows that the percentage has risen of systems that adjust premiums in an attempt to reflect the risk that the member institution imposes on the insurance system. That percentage was only 8.5 in 1995, but 35 in 2001, showing that an increasing number of countries are attempting to emulate this good practice. As Figure 9.3 illustrates, there have also been increasing percentages of countries worldwide that run their deposit insurance systems officially, impose coinsurance, and are funded.[4] Although not shown in the

Table 9.3 Countries with explicit, limited deposit insurance systems

Africa	Asia	Europe	Middle East	Western hemisphere
Kenya	Bangladesh	Austria	Bahrain	Argentina
Nigeria	India	Belgium	Jordan	Bahamas
Tanzania	Japan	Bosnia & Herzegovina	Kuwait	Brazil
Uganda	Kazakhstan	Bulgaria	Lebanon	Canada
	Korea	Croatia	Morocco	Chile
	Marshall Islands	Cyprus	Oman	Colombia
	Micronesia	Czech Rep.		Dominican Republic
	Philippines	Denmark		Ecuador
	Sri Lanka	Estonia		El Salvador
	Taiwan Province of China	Finland		Guatemala
	Vietnam	France		Honduras
		Germany		Jamaica
		Gibraltar		Mexico
		Greece		Paraguay
		Hungary		Peru
		Iceland		Trinidad & Tobago
		Ireland		United States
		Isle of Man		Venezuela
		Italy		
		Latvia		
		Liechtenstein		
		Lithuania		
		Luxembourg		
		Macedonia		
		Netherlands		
		Norway		
		Poland		
		Portugal		
		Romania		
		Slovak Rep.		
		Slovenia		
		Spain		
		Sweden		
		Switzerland		
		Turkey		
		Ukraine		
		United Kingdom		
		Yugoslavia		
4	11	38	6	18
				Total: 77 countries

Source: Garcia (2000), updated.

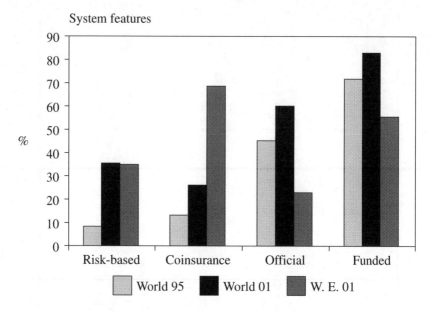

Figure 9.3   Moving toward agreement

figure, in 2001 more countries assessed premiums only on insured deposits as opposed to total deposits.

Progress on Coverage

In addition, an increasing number of countries are placing limitations of the level of coverage they provide. The USA does this by covering all domestic deposits up to a limit fixed by statute. Other countries set a maximum level for coverage but in addition exclude certain classes of depositors from coverage. Figure 9.4 shows that the percentage numbers of countries worldwide and in Western Europe that exclude one or other type of deposit. The number of countries excluding deposits denominated in foreign currencies, and/or inter-bank deposits, have all increased since 1995. The percentage of countries confining coverage to household deposits has also increased. Figure 9.5 shows that a substantial percentage of countries also excluded government, illegal, insider or high-rate deposits in 2001. Exlusions from coverage are particularly popular in Western Europe.

Exclusions

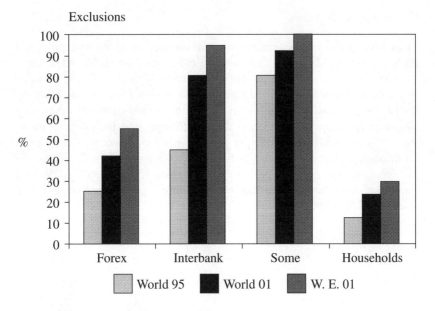

Figure 9.4   Convergence on exclusions

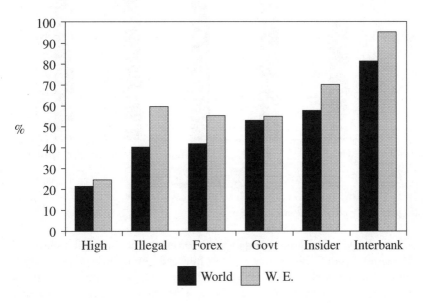

Figure 9.5   Exclusions in 2001

Continuing Differences

Many divergences in practices remain and some reflect departures from good practice. Figure 9.6 shows that only 46 per cent of countries set a target amount or ratio to insured deposits for their fund. Setting a target in a funded system would appear to aid fund management and make it more likely for the fund to be adequately funded. Only half of the countries worldwide, and a significantly smaller proportion in Western Europe, give their deposit insurance systems wide responsibility, only two-thirds have access to good information, only three-quarters of countries offset a depositor's loans against his deposits, and only 53 per cent of countries (30 per cent in Western Europe) contain the fund's obligations by giving depositors priority over the assets of a failed bank.

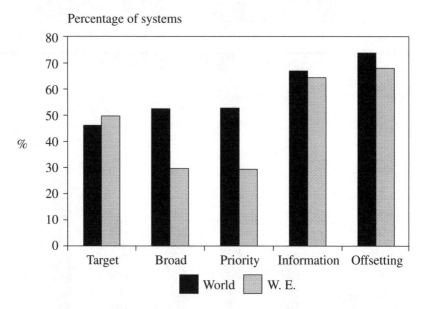

Figure 9.6   Divergences in 2001

Two things are of primary importance for effectively protecting the small depositor – getting his money back to him and getting it back promptly. I know of no research that has investigated whether deposit insurance systems have fulfilled their promises to reimburse depositors. The fact that a number of systems in Garcia (2000) appear to be under-funded suggests that a problem may exist in this regard. It is possible that some depositors have not been paid when their bank is closed. Observation of country practices suggests, however, that it is more likely that government money has footed the bill, or that insolvent banks have been allowed to continue operating and/or that failed institutions have been merged into (willing or unwilling) sounder banks.

But countries' promises as to when they will repay depositors have been surveyed. The results have been disappointing. Only the USA pays promptly, usually over the weekend of the failure. Generally elsewhere the speed of reimbursement is not good, ranging from two weeks at best to well over a year at worst.

CONCLUSIONS

The results of the latest survey of country practices suggest that notable strides have been taken towards identifying and implementing good practices for an effective system of deposit protection. Uniformity is being approached on making membership compulsory, providing per-depositor coverage at a failed bank (by aggregating depositors several accounts at the same bank), and requiring member institutions to provide at least some of the funding for the coverage their depositors receive.

Convergence has begun on risk-basing insurance assessments but further efforts are needed. The major lacunae in achieving effective systems of deposit protection appear to concern sources of information, adequacy of funding and speed of reimbursement.

NOTES

1. Garcia (1996) discusses the relevance of a list of different objectives.
2. For example, the Policy Research arm of the World Bank argues that explicit systems of deposit protection increase the probability of a banking crisis, whereas it operational/ country departments frequently help to design explicit deposit insurance systems.
3. The working group was led by the Canada Deposit Insurance Corporation and included representatives from the explicit protection systems in Argentina, Canada, Chile, France, Germany, Hungary, Italy, Jamaica, Japan, Mexico, the Philippines and the USA. The IMF and the World Bank were also members.
4. Figure 9.3 shows that, although not noted as necessarily good practice, more systems (82 per cent in 2001 compared with 72 per cent in 1995) maintained a fund, as opposed to collecting monies *ex post*. In fact, new and reformed systems are moving towards a balance between *ex ante* and *ex post* funding that maintains a smaller fund and supplements it with *ex post* levies when necessary. The system currently being designed in Hong Kong has explicitly modelled this balance.

REFERENCES

Demirguc-Kunt, A. and E. Detragiache (1998), 'The determinants of banking crises in developing and developed countries', *IMF Staff Papers*, **45** (1), March, 81–109.

Demirguc-Kunt, A. and E. Detragiache (2000), 'Does deposit insurance increase banking system stability?', IMF Working Paper, No. 00/3, January.

European Parliament (1994), 'Directive 94/19/EC of the European Parliament and Council of 30 May 1994 on Deposit Guarantee Schemes', No. L 135/5, *Official Journal of the European Communities*.

Financial Stability Forum (FSF) (2001), *Guidance for Developing Effective Deposit Insurance Systems*, Basle: Financial Stability Forum.

Folkerts-Landau, D. and C.-J. Lindgren (1998), *Toward a Framework for Financial Stability*, Washington, DC: International Monetary Fund.

Garcia, G.G.H. (1996), 'Deposit insurance: obtaining the benefits and avoiding the pitfalls', IMF Working Paper No. 96/83, August.

Garcia, G.G.H. (1999), 'Deposit insurance: a survey of actual and best practices', IMF Working Paper No. 99/54, April.

Garcia, G.G.H. (2000), *Deposit Insurance: Actual and Good Practices*, Washington, DC: International Monetary Fund.

Hall, M.J.B. (2001), 'How good are EU deposit insurance schemes?', *The Financial Safety Net: Costs, Benefits, and Implications for Regulation*, Proceedings of the 37th Annual Conference on Bank Structure and Competition, Chicago: Federal Reserve Bank of Chicago.

Hawke, J.D. (2001), 'Deposit insurance and bank supervision', address to the Exchequer Club, 20 December 2001.

Kyei, A. (1995), 'Deposit protection arrangements: a survey', IMF Working Paper No. 95/134, December.

Monetary and Exchange Affairs Department (MAE) (1996), 'Deposit insurance and crisis management', MAE Operational Paper No. 3, December.

COMMENT ON 'THE EFFECTIVENESS OF DEPOSIT INSURANCE'

Wilko Bolt

The paper by Garcia on the effectiveness of deposit insurance focuses on three themes that are also at the core of the conference 'Banking supervision at the crossroads'. First, in her paper Garcia analyses the interplay between prudential supervision and deposit insurance. Second, she examines the effectiveness of deposit insurance schemes. Third, she addresses the issue of convergence of various deposit insurance configurations, a topic that runs parallel to the issue of convergence of supervisory practices. Garcia's paper is elegantly written and provides interesting insights in the workings of different insurance schemes. Still, a few questions and remarks remain that give further food for thought.

As Garcia claims, and I support this view, it has been recognized that there are two principal rationales for deposit insurance. The foremost reason to insure deposits is to protect consumers and to safeguard their interests. A second important reason is to foster financial stability by avoiding bank panics and widespread contagion effects. It is obvious that those two objectives are complementary. By convincing small depositors that there is no need to run to a troubled bank since their deposits are insured, the financial system will be correspondingly more stable from a systemic viewpoint. However, although many deposit insurers may regard themselves as independent institutions, deposit insurance can only be effective if there is adequate prudential supervision. Deposit insurance and supervision being inextricably intertwined, delicate fine-tuning is required to find the right balance. This fine-tuning is very well put in Garcia's paper: 'We need a Goldilock's world where the insurance/supervisory porridge is not too hot, nor too cold, not too sweet nor too tart, and the insurance/supervisory bed is not too large nor too small, not too soft nor too hard.' But does a recipe for this porridge actually exist? Essentially, this fine-tuning problem points to the basic problem of any type of insurance: moral hazard and adverse selection.

Although deposit insurance solves one informational problem, namely that of the small depositor in assessing the state of the world, it creates another at the same time. The basic problem of moral hazard and adverse selection comes into play. Adverse selection may be regarded as a problem *ex ante*, before the contract between the insurer and the insured is written, in the sense that the 'type' of the insured agent, here the bank, is unknown. Adequate but costly screening may in general mitigate this problem. Moral hazard points to a problem *ex post*, after the contract has been signed, and involves the unobservable effort of the insured agent to do its best. Adequate monitoring may discipline the insured agent, but again effective monitoring comes at a cost. That is why Garcia calls for 'good' or 'best' practices for deposit insurance: to which extent can adverse selection be avoided and can moral hazard be curbed?

This brings me to my more specific discussion. Below, I will briefly discuss four points, which in my opinion are important for prudential supervision and deposit insurance, and deserve further attention.

My first remark concerns fair pricing of the deposit insurance scheme. From a theoretic perspective, it is easy to show that a 'flat' insurance premium produces moral hazard. But the deeper question arises whether fair pricing is actually possible. Following Freixas and Rochet (1998), using a simple model of banking behaviour with stochastic returns on investment projects, it can be shown that, in an attempt to price deposits fairly, the optimal level of deposits is zero! Further, it is well known that in an adverse selection environment the possibility of side payments between banks may actually be welfare improving. More generally, in a world with imperfect information, fair pricing is never completely desirable, since it generates a trade-off between static and dynamic efficiency. So, what guidelines does Garcia's paper offer to solve this informational dilemma?

Second, over the last decades, financial crises have been witnessed in countries with and without formal deposit insurance systems, suggesting – and Garcia admits to that herself – that deposit insurance does not solve all problems. Moreover, in the event of a financial crisis it is highly likely that there will be bailout, so that at the end of the day it is the taxpayer who pays, insured or not. In a recent article Hellman, Murdock and Stiglitz (2000) state: 'there are two kinds of countries: those that have deposit insurance, and those that don't know yet that they have it'. Hence, in this view one need not only question the use and merits of deposit insurance but, perhaps more importantly, one needs to assess and investigate the credibility of a no-bailout clause.

A third comment focuses on possible regulatory burden in supervision. Deposit insurance is not the only regulatory instrument; several other types of instruments may be distinguished. Indeed, one may think of capital requirements, deposit rate controls, entry and exit regulation, disclosure requirements, and so on. More often than not, the financial system is faced with not one supervisory authority, but with two or even three different authorities. This interplay between instruments and authorities requires adequate and balanced banking supervision. This is costly and these costs show up in different formats. Direct costs are involved simply because of allocated resources. Indirect costs may arise, because supervision in itself may create economic distortions. The obvious example is that too much insurance leads to moral hazard incentives and possibly to too much risk-taking. Additional costs may come from regulatory capture: self-interested regulators may not be trying to achieve socially desired goals but pursue their own objectives. All this may lead to many regulatory burdens on the financial sector, which could strangle the necessary entrepreneurial spirit. One modern response might be to move to a more incentive-based, market-orientated banking system where market discipline induces prudent behaviour. How do Garcia's best practices fit into this new perspective?

My last point concerns competition policy. The first aspect has to do with private versus public insurance schemes. In general, market competition provides the right incentives for information extraction and accurate pricing. However, in the event of a severe adverse macroeconomic shock it is most likely, as discussed earlier, that the government must ultimately jump in. Anticipating this government behaviour, perverse moral hazard incentives may again pop up. Secondly, introducing more banking competition may have negative side effects. As shown in Bolt and Tieman (2001) for example, in an attempt to sustain current profits and market power, banking competition could effectively aggravate risk-taking behaviour by banks. Fierce competition may reinforce so-called 'gambles for resurrection'. Is there an explicit role for deposit insurance in this context and, more importantly, how should regulators in general react to increased competition in the banking sector?

All in all, Garcia's paper opens up new insights into the workings of different insurance schemes and provides a better understanding of the effectivity of deposit insurance in general. Still, as I tried to indicate, some questions remain, which hopefully will trigger more debate and analysis in the important area of banking supervision.

REFERENCES

Bolt, W. and A. Tieman (2001), 'Banking competition, risk and regulation', DNB Staff Reports, 70.
Freixas, X. and J.C. Rochet (1997), *The Microeconomics of Banking*, Cambridge, MA: MIT Press.
Hellman, T., K. Murdock and J. Stiglitz (2000), 'Liberalisation, moral hazard in banking and prudential regulation: are capital requirements enough?', *American Economic Review*, **90**, 147–65.

REPLY

Gillian G.H. Garcia

Starting from a state of underdevelopment, economic theory has made substantial strides in the past two decades towards understanding how to design incentive-compatible systems of regulation and supervision in a liberalized, competitive and, as is now recognized, more risky, financial system. Mr Bolt's citations in his gracious comments illustrate these advances. In some areas – providing a credible no-bailout commitment, balancing power between multiple regulators with different objective functions, avoiding regulatory capture, designing risk-based capital requirements and utilizing interest rate ceilings – prudential supervisors have progressed in tandem with economic theorists. In setting deposit insurance premiums that are effectively and fairly risk based, however, much work remains to be done.

With regard to the no-bailout commitment, for example, the 1991 FDIC Improvement Act (FDICIA) in the USA dealt with a previous lack of credibility in the threat of closure arising from supervisors' practice of forbearance. Freixas and Rochet (1997) show that forbearance may be rational for the regulators, but the US Congress believed that it was typically contrary to the public interest and contained it by requiring supervisors to take prompt corrective actions to remedy deficiencies in bank soundness and to close a bank early – when its equity capital fell to 2 per cent of its assets. Congress also appreciated that, as Freixas and Rochet later observed, the Federal Deposit Insurance Corporation (FDIC) was likely to be more risk averse than a supervisor. So, wishing to protect taxpayers from additional losses, Congress gave the FDIC new authority to close failing banks in cases where the supervisor delayed action. This does not, of course, resolve all the problem of multiple supervisors – a problem that the USA has in spades. The UK and Australia have installed a monolithic regulator, while other countries are considering this remedy. Experience will tell if this proves to be a practical solution.

A number of other countries around the world now recognize that weak banks may offer high rates in order to garner deposits to use to 'gamble for redemption'. Consequently, an increasing number of countries (15 of the 75 last studied), both industrial and developing, now impose restrictions on what they regard as excessively high deposit interest rates. They are, in effect, implementing the recommendation of Hellman, Murdock, and Stiglitz (2000) that a combination of (Basle Committee) capital requirements and deposit interest-rate ceilings provides a more effective restraint on bank risk-taking than either alone.

Theoreticians and policy-makers alike now recognize that financial liberalization must be attended by the regulatory and supervisory advances needed to counter the increased risk-taking and propensity to fail that result from greater competition. This has been a repeated theme of studies and advice of the International Monetary Fund and the World Bank. Bolt and Tieman (2001) favour constraint by risk-adjusted capital requirements – the objective of the new Basle Capital Accord. A well-designed system of deposit protection can also play a part by making it politically and administratively easier to firmly resolve failed banks and set incentives for banks to innovate, but to do so wisely. More generally, one wonders whether the current US experience with fraud and conflicts of interest may come to be attributed to the liberalized structure of the financial sector and the increase in banks' asset powers enacted under the Gramm-Leach-Blilely Act of 1999 that repealed the Glass-Steagall Act. In other respects, it is clear that both policy and theory need more work to reach a satisfactory understanding of how to set appropriate risk-adjusted interest rates. Here, recommendations, including those offered by the author, may be seen as groping their way toward setting the right incentives to convince private agents to behave in a public-spirited manner.

10. Credit risk measurement and procyclicality

Philip Lowe

INTRODUCTION

The idea that a bank's capital should be related to the 'riskiness' of its assets enjoys widespread support. This idea underlies many banks' internal decisions about capital and is central to the current proposals for reform of the Basle Capital Accord. Yet, despite the appeal of the idea, its application is far from straightforward. In particular, it requires that the 'riskiness' of a bank's assets be measured. This is a difficult task and, while much progress has been made on this front over recent years, much remains to be done. Amongst the challenges is to measure not only the relative riskiness of different assets at a point in time, but also to measure how the overall level of risk changes through time and, in particular, how the level of risk is related to the macroeconomy.

This latter issue is critically important, not only to banks and their supervisors, but also to central banks and other policy-makers concerned with macroeconomic and financial stability. If banks misassess risk over the course of the business cycle – underestimating it in booms and overestimating it in downturns – the potential for credit booms and busts is increased. In turn, this can lead to greater financial amplification of the business cycle and a heightened risk of financial instability.

At a practical level, the difficulty facing banks and their supervisors is determining exactly how the level of credit risk changes with the evolving state of the macroeconomy and, by implication, how the level of required capital (either from application of a credit risk model or to meet regulatory standards) should change through time. On the one hand, there are strong arguments that capital should be built up in good times, so that when the bad times come a sufficient buffer exists so that losses can be absorbed without the solvency of the bank, or more generally the stability of the financial system, being threatened. On the other hand, credit risk models and the proposed regulatory approach to measuring risk for purposes of minimum capital requirements may well deliver measures of credit risk that fall in good times and increase in bad times. To the extent that actual capital levels follow this same pattern, the capacity for the financial system to weather business cycle fluctuations may be affected.

The apparent tension in the ideas that risk is low in good times but that capital should be built up in good times raises three interrelated questions that are the focus of this chapter. First, how is credit risk related to the state of the macroeconomy? Second, how do credit risk measurement techniques, including those proposed under Basle 2, deal with macroeconomic effects? And third, are risk-based capital arrangements likely to increase financial procyclicality or, in other words, are they likely to unnecessarily increase the financial amplification of economic cycles?

These questions are difficult to answer. The issue of how credit risk evolves with the macroeconomy is inextricably linked to how one views the basic forces driving the business cycle. And on this important issue there is little consensus within the economics profession. Furthermore, the use of formal credit risk models for purposes of determining a bank's overall level of capital is still in its infancy and the implementation of risk-based capital requirements is still some way off. This means that there is limited evidence upon which to draw. Moreover, the evidence that does exist is subject to the 'Lucas critique'; namely, that structural changes that are likely to occur after the implementation of risk-based capital requirements mean that evidence from the current regime says little about the future.

Notwithstanding these difficulties, the chapter attempts to shed some light on these three questions. Its main observations can be summarized as follows.

First, while some business cycle expansions might reasonably be characterized by a relatively low level of credit risk, others might be better characterized by a relatively high level of risk. This latter characterization is arguably more relevant where the expansion is associated with rapid credit growth, large increases in asset prices and high levels of investment. These developments are often symptomatic of the emergence of financial imbalances, and the unwinding of these imbalances can cause significant losses for financial institutions.

Second, most approaches to measuring credit risk pay little attention, at least explicitly, to the business cycle. Key parameters in credit risk models are generally assumed fixed, or at least do not move with the macroeconomic environment. The main cyclical element comes from ratings migration. Typically, both internal and external credit ratings improve during economic expansions and deteriorate during contractions, so that measured risk falls in good times and increases in bad times. Allowing the parameters of credit risk models to move with the macroeconomy risks increasing this cyclical pattern in measured credit risk.

Third, given the way that risk is measured, the level of capital suggested by credit risk models and required under the proposed reforms to the Basle Capital Accord is likely to fall in economic booms and increase in downturns. Even for moderate business cycle fluctuations, the changes in required capital are likely to be significant, the more so for measurement systems that rely on market prices for risk measurement.

Fourth, to the extent that under the new Capital Accord minimum capital requirements increase in downturns, it will be important that banks build up buffers over the regulatory minimum before the downturn. Both supervisors and the markets have an important role to play here. If these buffers over regulatory minimum are not built up there is the potential for adverse macro-economic effects.

The remainder of the chapter is structured as follows. The following section briefly discusses the various views concerning the relationship between the macroeconomy and credit risk. The third section identifies the building blocks of credit risk measurement and discusses how these building blocks are treated in credit risk models and in the proposed approach for measuring the minimum level of regulatory capital, paying particular attention to if, and how, macroeconomic considerations are incorporated. The fourth section then examines the limited evidence regarding how minimum capital requirements might move through time under a system of risk-based capital, and the penultimate section discusses the possible macroeconomic effects of such a system. The final section summarizes the chapter.

CREDIT RISK AND THE MACROECONOMY

A key element in many approaches to credit risk measurement is a credit ratings system. Although these systems vary considerably in detail, they are generally recognized as being reasonably successful at distinguishing the relative riskiness of different borrowers at a given point in time. In contrast, their performance in assessing how risk changes through time is subject to less agreement.[1]

At a general level, a lack of consensus on this issue reflects different views regarding the relationship between the macroeconomy and credit risk. These different views can perhaps be best illustrated by considering two highly stylized economies. In the first economy, the evolution of economic activity is roughly described by a sine wave. Thus, a boom will almost surely be followed by a recession and a recession by a recovery. In this economy, a forward-looking ratings system would be likely to show an increase in average credit risk around the peak of the business cycle, given the imminent recession, and perhaps a reduction in credit risk around the trough of the cycle, given the imminent recovery.

In the second economy, while business cycles may be discernible *ex post* they are so irregular that the economy's current performance is the best indicator of the future. Thus a boom does not mean that a recession is imminent and a recession does not mean that a recovery is likely. In this economy a forward-looking ratings system would be likely to show a decline in credit risk when macroeconomic conditions are strong – on the basis that the strong conditions are likely to continue and an increase in credit risk when economic conditions were depressed.

Clearly, the economies in which real banks and supervisors operate do not fit neatly into either of these polar cases. A common view, however, is that economic forecasters have such a poor record that, at least to a first approximation, the current performance of the economy can be taken as the best guess of its future performance. This view leads to ratings systems that eschew economic forecasting and that rely heavily on the current state of the economy and firms' current financial condition. As a general characterization this view underlies many, although certainly not all, ratings systems currently employed by banks. It leads to risk being measured as low in an expansion and high in a recession.

An alternative view is that the forces that drive economic expansions often (although not always) sow the seeds of future contractions by generating imbalances in either the financial system or the real economy. This means that while the economy does not follow a sine wave, a strong economic expansion, particularly if it is associated with the development of imbalances in the financial system, can increase the likelihood of an economic downturn. Such financial imbalances can arise from rapid and sustained growth in credit and asset prices and excessive capital accumulation, and when they are unwound they can pose considerable costs to the macroeconomy. According to this view, while these imbalances cannot be measured perfectly, they can be measured *ex ante* at least to some degree. Accordingly, periods of strong economic growth might, under some circumstances, be characterized by an above average level of credit risk. This view is consistent with the proposition that risk is built up in the boom but materializes in the downturn.

The distinction between these two worlds underlies much of the rest of the chapter. It is more than academic. Over the past two decades, a large number of countries have experienced a banking system crisis after a period of strong economic growth, rapidly increasing asset prices and significant increases in credit.[2] During the period of strong growth, risk often appeared to be low, but in reality, serious imbalances were building up. The unwinding of these imbalances later caused severe financial and macroeconomic stress. From a risk measurement perspective, a central issue is whether these imbalances can be measured *ex ante* in any meaningful way, and if they can, how they can be incorporated into measures of credit risk.

The existing empirical literature provides mixed guidance. On the one hand, there is considerable statistical evidence that gross domestic product (GDP) is a 'unit root' process. In other words, most movements in GDP can be viewed as permanent, rather than as temporary fluctuations around a trend. This means that a period of strong growth need not automatically be followed by a period of weak growth. Broadly consistent with this, there appears to be little empirical support for the proposition that the longer an economic expansion runs, the greater is the likelihood of an economic downturn.[3] This suggests that economic expansions do not simply die of old age, and thus there should be no presumption that simply because an expansion has gone on for a number of years, credit risk has increased. In contrast to these findings, a number of authors have recently suggested that useful indicators of banking system stress can be developed using only *ex ante* information.[4] This later research does not suggest that the business cycle can be forecast with any degree of accuracy but, rather, makes the more modest claim that the combination of particularly fast credit growth and rapidly increasing asset prices makes an episode of financial stress more likely. An implication of this is that when such developments occur, the level of credit risk should be judged to have increased.

Unfortunately, none of this evidence is conclusive and there is plenty of room for disagreement about the use of techniques and interpretation. This is what makes the issue so difficult. Nevertheless, a reasonable interpretation of the evidence is that during a period of strong growth there need be no presumption that a period of weak growth will follow. At the same time, during some episodes of strong growth uncertainty about the future can be said to be higher than average due to the emergence of identifiable imbalances in either the financial system or the real economy. This then opens the possibility of measured credit risk being relatively high in a booming economy.

We now turn to a more practical discussion of how macroeconomic factors are dealt with in credit risk models and in the risk measurement approach that underlies the internal ratings based (IRB) approach to determining regulatory capital proposed by the Basle Committee on Banking Supervision (hereafter the Basle Committee or BCBS).[5]

MEASUREMENT OF CREDIT RISK: THE BUILDING BLOCKS AND THE MACROECONOMY

Loosely speaking, when measuring risk what we are trying to do is to obtain some measure of the dispersion of possible future outcomes. For an individual bank, it is the dispersion of future returns on its own portfolio that is of concern, while for a policy-maker charged with financial stability, it is the dispersion of possible future outcomes for the system as a whole. In practice, the focus of risk measurement is on downside outcomes, rather than upside outcomes, so that measures of risk tend to focus on the likelihood of losses, rather than characterizing the entire distribution of possible future outcomes.

This focus is clearly evident in the increasing use of value-at-risk (VaR) based models to measure credit risk. These models include amongst others JP Morgan's Credit Metrics, McKinsey's Credit Portfolio View, Credit Risk Financial Products' CreditRisk+ and KMV's Credit Portfolio Manager. Although the various approaches have different structures, all are trying to measure the potential loss that a portfolio of credit exposures could suffer, with a predetermined confidence level, within a specified time horizon. Most often, this horizon is one year.

In measuring the range of possible future outcomes all such models can be thought of as having a number of common building blocks. These include:

- a system for rating loans (generally based on some concept of the probability of the borrower defaulting);
- assumptions about the correlation of default probabilities (PDs) across borrowers;
- assumptions about the loss incurred in the case of default (commonly referred to as the LGD); and
- assumptions regarding the correlation between the PD and the LGD.

Each of these elements can also be found in the IRB approach to calculating regulatory capital. In the remainder of this section we consider if, and how, these various building blocks deal with cyclical or macroeconomic considerations. We do not review the various credit risk models in any detail, but instead our focus is on how these various elements of credit risk measurement affect the way in which credit risk is assessed through time.[6]

Probability of Borrowers Defaulting

For the purposes of this chapter it is useful to think of the first building block of most credit risk models as having two elements. The first is a system for rating individual borrowers according to their creditworthiness, and the second is a transition matrix which provides details of how borrowers are expected to migrate, on average, to different ratings classes (including to default) over a given horizon. With these two elements it is possible to calculate the VaR for each borrower over the relevant horizon. Given the nature of transition matrices, the lower the credit rating of the borrower the greater is the VaR on loans to that borrower.

For a portfolio of loans the VaR will change through time if the distribution of borrowers across ratings classes changes or if the transition matrix itself changes. For instance, a general downgrading of borrowers or an increase in probability of a downgrade (for a given grade) would both lead to an increase in measured credit risk. In practice, transition matrices are often treated as fixed, so it is the movement of borrowers across ratings classes that drives changes in measured credit risk. This means that in the context of the procyclicality debate the nature of the ratings system is especially important.

Ratings Systems

While a variety of ratings systems are currently used in practice, it is useful to distinguish between two broad classes: those that rely on market-based information, and those that rely on a much broader set of information. The two classes can have quite different implications for the cyclical properties of measured credit risk.

Market-based ratings systems typically rely on a version of the Merton model to derive probabilities of default from equity prices. KMV is perhaps the best-known example of this approach. For a given firm the PD (and thus implicitly the rating) is a decreasing function of the firm's equity price, and an increasing function of the volatility of the equity price and the firm's leverage. In principle, this type of ratings system is quite forward looking. If the market generally expects deterioration in the macroeconomy, and as a result stock prices decline, implied PDs would rise even if current economic conditions remained robust. Similarly, if the level of uncertainty about the future increases due to the emergence of imbalances in the financial system and this leads to an increase in volatility of the equity market PDs would again rise.

Despite the appeal of this type of system there are a couple of potential difficulties. The first is that, occasionally, equity values appear to move away from those suggested by fundamentals, distorting measures of risk. If, for example, the market is 'overvalued', calculated PDs are likely to underestimate true probabilities, and perhaps suggest a relatively low level of risk. This is despite the fact that the very existence of an overvalued equity market might be symptomatic of more widespread financial imbalances and thus a relatively high level of risk.

The second potential difficulty arises from the fact that the volatility of the equity market means that changes in PDs can be reversed quite quickly and that PDs can move by a significant amount in a relatively short period of time. Figure 10.1 shows KMV's median EDF calculated for BBB rated firms

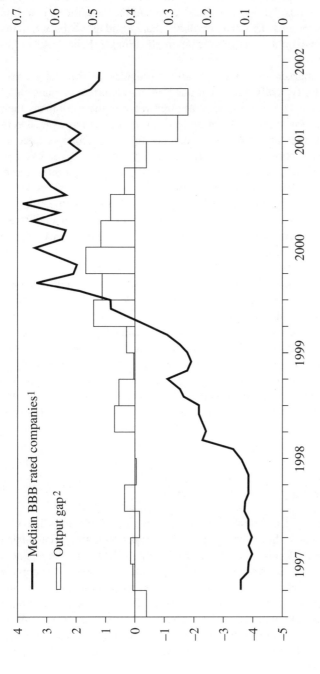

Notes: [1]Right-hand scale. [2]Left-hand scale; HP filter applied (BIS).

Source: KMV.

Figure 10.1 Expected probability of default of US companies currently rated BBB

since the beginning of 1997. It indicates that in 1997, the EDF averaged around 10 basis points, but by 2000 this figure had increased around sixfold to around 60 basis points. This is a very large change and as we discuss in the following section would have significant implications for the level of required capital.

In contrast to market-based ratings, ratings provided by the major credit rating agencies are typically not conditioned on market prices or the state of the economy. Moody's, for example, states that when rating a company their aim is to measure the company's ability to meet its obligations against economic scenarios that are reasonably adverse to the company's specific circumstances. The ratings do not incorporate a single economic forecast but, rather, are based on examination of a variety of scenarios. Furthermore, rating agencies are averse to reversing ratings changes within a short period of time. As a result, ratings tend to be quite 'sticky'. In principle, such an approach should not lead to a significant pick-up in measured credit risk simply because the economy is experiencing a period of slow growth, or the stock market has declined.

The ratings systems employed by banks vary considerably, with some systems closely aligned with the approach used by credit rating agencies, while other (but fewer) systems rely on KMV-style default probabilities.[7] Furthermore, many banks use ratings systems that rate borrowers on the PD over the next year (as with KMV), but derive the probability not from market prices, but from internal models and/or the judgement of expert internal credit offices. The volatility in ratings produced by such systems is likely to lie somewhere between the volatility of the agencies' ratings and KMV's implicit ratings. However, the measures of risk produced by such systems may be quite sensitive to current state of the business cycle, particularly if those responsible for rating borrowers are unwilling to make assessments of the implications of current macroeconomic and financial imbalances for the future.

Transition Matrices

As indicated above, it is common practice to treat the transition matrix as fixed. Recent research, however, suggests that transition matrices calculated using ratings from Moody's and Standard & Poor's vary with the business cycle.[8] In particular, the probabilities of downgrade and default (for a given grade) appear to increase significantly in economic contractions, and the probability of upgrades increases in expansions. Two approaches have been advocated for dealing with this issue. The first is to calculate transition matrices for different points of the cycle: say, for a boom, for a recession, and for normal times. The second is to explicitly model the elements of the transition matrix as a function of macroeconomic and financial variables. The latter approach is adopted by Credit Portfolio View.

The effect of using transition matrices that are conditional on the state of the economy on VaR calculations can be substantial. For instance, simulations conducted by Bangia, Diebold and Schuermann (2000) suggest that for a given loan portfolio the use of a 'recession transition matrix' delivers a VaR estimate that is 25 to 30 per cent higher than that delivered by an 'expansion transition matrix'.

Introducing transition matrices that are conditional on the state of the economy could both increase measured risk in downturns and reduces it in booms, or vice versa. Much depends upon how the conditioning is implemented. In principle, one could imagine that, during a period of strong growth characterized by the emergence of financial and real sector imbalances, the distribution of borrowers across ratings classes would be unaffected, but that the weight on the diagonal elements of the transition matrix would be reduced. Such a move could reflect a view that the strong growth increased the possibility of both upgrades (if the higher growth is sustained) and downgrades (if the unwinding of the imbalances causes macroeconomic effects). In such a situation measured credit risk could increase without any change in the distribution of borrower ratings. Such an approach would tend to push up measured credit risk in the good times.

Much more likely, though, is that in a boom the conditional transition matrix would assign a lower than average probability to ratings downgrades. In effect, this is the outcome of the Credit Portfolio View approach which models default probabilities for a given rating grade as a function of the expected value of macroeconomic variables at the relevant horizon. To obtain the expected value of these variables, simple econometric time-series models are used. This means that if times are good today, they are likely to be forecast as good tomorrow and thus there will be few downgrades or defaults. Once again, whether or not this is desirable depends upon one's view of the forces driving the business cycle.

Regulatory Treatment

The calculation of regulatory capital using the IRB approach also commences with borrowers being assigned to ratings classes. In particular, the January 2001 Consultative Paper requires that banks have a minimum of six to nine grades for performing loans and a minimum of two grades for non-performing loans. It also requires that no more than 30 per cent of the gross exposures should fall into any one grade.

The Basle Committee has not been prescriptive as to how ratings are assigned. Nevertheless, it has set out minimum requirements with a number of these requirements being particularly relevant for the issues discussed in this chapter. The first is that borrowers should be rated or reviewed at least annually, or whenever new information about the borrower comes to light. The second is that in assigning borrowers to grades, banks must assess 'risk factors for the future horizon based on current information' (BCBS, 2001a, p. 50). And the third is that for risk quantification purposes the bank must assign to each grade a probability of default over the next year.

Importantly, the assignment of one-year PDs to each risk grade does not mean that loans must be rated according to these PDs. In principle, a bank could employ a qualitative ratings system whereby borrowers are rated on the basis of their long-term prospects but assign a one-year PD to each of the ratings grades for purposes of quantification for the purposes of calculating regulatory capital. Under such a system the PD over the next year might increase due to an increased probability of an economic downturn, but the rating, and thus the measurement of risk, could remain unchanged if the borrower's long-term prospects were unaffected. Such a system would be similar in spirit to that used by the credit rating agencies. In contrast, under an alternative system in which borrowers are rated exclusively according to the their one-year PDs, borrowers would be downgraded as the one-year PDs rose. From a validation perspective this latter approach may have some advantages, although it may lead to very cyclical minimum capital requirements.

The Basle Committee does not address the issue of the calculation of transition matrices. The model underlying the calculation of regulatory capital charges only requires an estimate of the probability of default for each rating grade, and not the probability of downgrade.[9]

Correlation of PDs across Borrowers

The second building block in the measurement of credit risk is the correlation in asset returns across borrowers. If asset returns were uncorrelated, then for sufficiently large portfolios, the potential for unexpected losses would be essentially zero, for while some borrowers would inevitably default, there would be no uncertainty regarding the average rate of default.

All credit risk models include estimates of correlation amongst borrowers. While there are numerous ways of obtaining these correlations, they are typically derived from multifactor models of equity returns, with the factors related to industry, sectoral and country characteristics. These various factors are reestimated periodically, although they tend to change slowly through time. The state of the macroeconomy and the existence of imbalances in the financial system are generally not explicitly considered. Despite this there is some evidence that during periods of financial stress asset correlations tend to increase. Finger (1999) suggests that this is one reason why the distribution of credit losses through time appears to be bi-modal. Either default probabilities and asset correlations are both low, or they are both high, so that actual default rates are either much lower than average, or much higher than average. Typically, credit risk models do not take this into account.

In measuring risk for regulatory purposes, the Basle Committee has also recognized the importance of correlations. Its approach, however, is somewhat simpler. In particular, it assumes that there is only a single systematic risk factor that drives correlations. While the Committee has contemplated allowing more complex correlation structures, it has argued that the difficulties of measuring and validating correlations make it premature to do so for purposes of calculating regulatory capital.

A major advantage of the single factor model is that the capital requirement assigned to a given borrower is determined solely by the characteristics of that borrower. In multi-factor models, by contrast, the marginal capital requirement depends not only on the borrower's own characteristics, but also on the characteristics of other borrowers in the portfolio.[10] For this reason, most banks still use a risk-bucketing approach for internal capital allocation on individual loans, rather than a credit risk model with full correlation structure. The use of credit risk models is often restricted to assessing the overall level of capital for a portfolio or sub-portfolio of loans.

In its January 2001 proposals, the Basle Committee made the further simplifying assumption that all borrowers share the same sensitivity to the single risk factor. This assumption is reflected in the assignment of an asset correlation of 0.2 to all borrowers. In contrast, in its November 2001 proposals the Basle Committee raised the possibility of allowing the sensitivity to the common risk factor to be a decreasing function of the probability of default.[11] One justification for this is that, at least in a cross-section of borrowers, as PDs rise, the importance of idiosyncratic risk, relative to systematic risk, also appears to rise (that is, the asset correlation falls). In operationalizing this approach, the Committee has proposed that an asset correlation of 0.2 be retained for the highest quality borrowers, but that the correlation be allowed to fall to a minimum of 0.1 for high-risk borrowers. This change has the effect of reducing the measured risk associated with high PD loans. This can be seen in Figure 10.2.

An important consequence of this proposed change is that during periods in which borrowers are, on average, being rated downwards (to grades with higher PDs), the implicit average asset correlation across the portfolio will decline. To the extent that loans are downgraded in downturns, average asset correlations will implicitly be lower in a downturn than in an expansion. In turn, the increase in measured credit risk in downturns will be lower than it

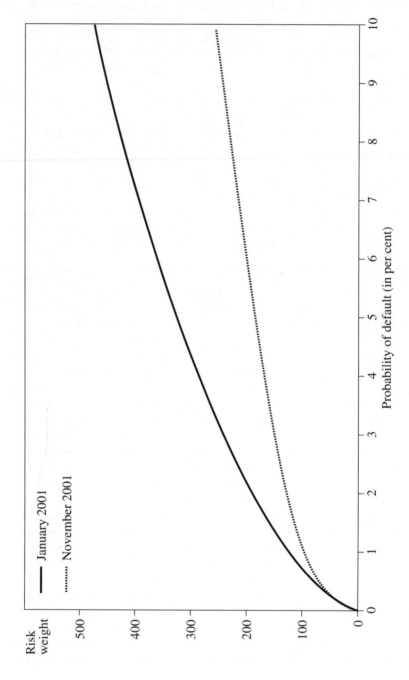

Figure 10.2 Proposed risk weights for corporate loans

would have been with the assumption of a constant asset correlation. Simulations suggest that this effect is potentially substantial, with the increase in measured credit risk in a typical downturn being reduced by perhaps 30 per cent.

The Loss Experienced in the Event of Default

The third building block in credit risk measurement is the loss incurred in the event of default (the LGD). If a bank were guaranteed to receive all monies owed even in the event of a borrower defaulting, credit risk would be zero regardless of the probability of default and the asset correlation. Another potentially important factor in the measurement of credit risk is the uncertainty about LGDs, with the greater the uncertainty the greater the risk.

Most credit risk models treat the LGD as either a stochastic variable independent of the PD, or as a parameter that must be specified for each exposure. LGDs are generally not treated as being a function of the state of the macroeconomy. Further, where LGDs are modelled as stochastic variables, the degree of variability is not modelled as a function of the macroeconomy.

The approach adopted by the Basle Committee is broadly similar. In the Foundation IRB approach the LGD is set at 50 per cent for unsecured loans, while for loans secured with real estate the figure is between 40 and 50 per cent depending upon the value of the collateral relative to the loan. For loans secured by some other types of physical collateral, the Committee is considering the use of an LGD of 45 per cent. These various LGD values do not move with the state of the economy. They are also treated as known variables, so that any uncertainty about the future losses in the event of default is ignored when quantifying credit risk.

In the advanced IRB approach banks are able to use their own estimates of LGD, subject to the estimation process meeting minimum standards. Whether or not banks will adjust their estimates based on cyclical factors remains to be seen. When asset prices are very strong, one approach would be to recognize that higher collateral values mean lower LGDs. A contrasting approach would be to recognize that (at least in some cases) if prices have increased substantially, a correction is likely, and that the correction is likely to occur during a period of weak economic activity. The result might be an increase in LGD estimates, particularly on newly issued loans. Again, it all depends on how the bank views the business cycle and the sustainability of movements in asset prices.

Correlation between PD and LGD

The fourth building block is the correlation between PDs and LGDs. As the correlation between these two variables increases, so does the level of credit risk.

Generally, credit risk models treat the PD and the LGD as independent variables. The Basle Committee makes the same assumption.

In contrast, there is considerable empirical research showing a reasonably strong positive correlation between these two variables.[12] The basic intuition for this result is not hard to understand. Aggregate default rates are usually higher than average in economic downturns. Such periods also tend to be associated with depressed asset values and thus higher than average losses when loans default. While the empirical results are broadly consistent with this intuition, Altman, Resti and Sironi (2002) argue that the story is a little more complicated. Although they find a strong positive correlation between PDs and LGDs they question whether the economic cycle is the sole reason for this. They suggest that LGDs are influenced independently by supply and demand considerations for defaulted securities. In particular, they argue that an increase in defaults leads to an increase in the supply of defaulted securities, and correspondingly to a reduction in their price and to larger losses for investors.

Altman, Resti and Sironi (2002) also explore through simulation analysis what effect incorporating the positive correlation between PDs and LGDs has on the VaR for a broadly representative loan portfolio. For their particular simulations they find that setting the correlation between the PD and LGD to zero (as is usual practice), rather than to its estimated value, leads to a reduction in the VaR of at least one-quarter.

As above, the implication of the zero correlation assumption for how measured risk evolves with the business cycle depends upon the stage of the cycle at which ratings deteriorate. If ratings decline when economic conditions are depressed, the increase in measured risk in the downturn will be larger if a positive correlation is assumed. On the other hand, if ratings deteriorate as financial imbalances emerge in the good times, recognizing the positive correlation will contribute to the increase in measured risk when the economy is strong.

Finally, the Basle Committee has indirectly attempted to address the correlation issue by requiring that when banks calculate LGDs from historical data they use a default-weighted average, rather than simply taking the LGD for each year and then averaging the yearly LGDs. Since most defaults occur when economic conditions are weak, the default-weighted estimate is likely to be close to the estimate that applies when PDs are high. Thus it could be viewed as a conservative approach, in that it does not recognize a fall in the LGD when the PD declines.

Summary

Significant advances have been made in the measurement of credit risk over recent years. Despite this, macroeconomic considerations still play only a small role in most measurement approaches. This is despite the fact that, in the past, the development of macroeconomic imbalances has often been at the root of major credit quality problems.

Whether or not a more thorough treatment of macroeconomic factors would improve the measurement of credit risk depends, in part, upon how one views the business cycle and the forces that drive the evolution of economies.

If one takes the view that major system-wide credit quality problems arise from the unwinding of imbalances, there is a case for incorporating measures of these imbalances, however imperfect, into the risk measurement framework. This is particularly the case if this framework is used for decisions about bank capital. On the other hand, if one takes either the view that these imbalances cannot be measured *ex ante*, or that they have little effect on credit quality, there is little point in moving in this direction.

Within the context of the current measurement approaches, business cycle considerations have the potential to enter in a number of ways. For example, ratings transition matrices, asset correlations and LGDs can all be made a function of macroeconomic variables, and there is reasonable evidence to support doing so. But there are risks in proceeding in this direction. In particular, there is the potential for larger increases in measured risk in downturns, and declines in booms. For example, if, when the economy enters into a recession, a recession transition matrix is substituted for an expansion matrix, higher asset correlations are used and assumed LGDs are increased, measured credit risk is likely to increase by considerably more than if these changes were not made. To repeat a theme, whether or not this is desirable depends upon how one views the forces the drive the macroeconomy. If one has the 'imbalances' perspective, then such changes are probably undesirable. Rather, they should be made during the boom if it is judged that risk is increasing, rather than being made when bad loans begin to materialize in the downturn. If one has the alternative view, such shifts in the key parameters of credit risk measurement during economic downturns are probably desirable.

MOVEMENTS IN CAPITAL REQUIREMENTS THROUGH TIME: SOME LIMITED EVIDENCE

We now turn to a review of the existing evidence on how minimum regulatory capital requirements are likely to change through time under a system of risk-based capital. Our interest is in two questions. The first is how large are the changes in minimum requirements likely to be? The second is at what point of the cycle the changes are likely to take place?

The above two questions are difficult to answer with any degree of precision. They are particularly difficult for risk measurement systems that rely on internal ratings. This largely reflects the relative lack of publicly available data about the migration properties of these systems. Many banks are only now developing ratings systems and in the relatively few cases, which they have been in place for some time, the data are normally proprietary and often do not cover a full business cycle. It is also unclear as to whether the introduction of capital requirements linked to these ratings will change the nature of the ratings process and the migration properties of the ratings.

Despite these difficulties a number of studies have recently been conducted which throw some light on these questions. One of the most comprehensive is that undertaken by Jordan, Peek and Rosengren (2002). They examine how hypothetical capital requirements would have moved between 1996 and 2001 on a portfolio of 339 loans in the shared national credit programme in the USA. The loans in the portfolio are, on average, relatively high quality, they are all large (exceeding US$20 million) and they all have at least three participating banks. The capital requirements are calculated using the formulae set out in the Basle Committee's January 2001 Consultative Paper, and the relevant PDs are calculated in two separate ways: the first uses KMV's expected default frequency for each borrower, and the second uses the PD associated with the borrower's Standard & Poor's (S&P) rating.

The main findings are reproduced in Figure 10.3, which also shows a measure of the output gap in the USA. Perhaps the most striking aspect of the results is the large increase in hypothetical capital requirements over recent years generated by using KMVs EDFs. In 1996–98, the capital requirement was around 2½ to 3 per cent of the loan portfolio, but by mid-2000 this had risen to around 7 per cent! Using S&P's default probabilities, capital requirements also increase, but the change is much smaller; in 1996 the requirement was around 2½ per cent and this increased to just over 3 per cent by 2001. This marked difference reflects the much greater stability of external ratings discussed in the previous section.

Another interesting aspect of the results is the timing of the increase in capital requirements. Using KMV's EDFs the big increase took place between mid-1998 and early 2000. This was a period of strong expansion in the USA as evidenced by the positive output gap. While Jordan, Peek and Rosengren only report the hypothetical capital requirements up to mid-2001, an examination of average EDFs over the rest of the year does not suggest that requirements would have increased further, despite the recession in the USA. This highlights another of the points made in the previous section. Ratings systems based on market information will lead to capital require-

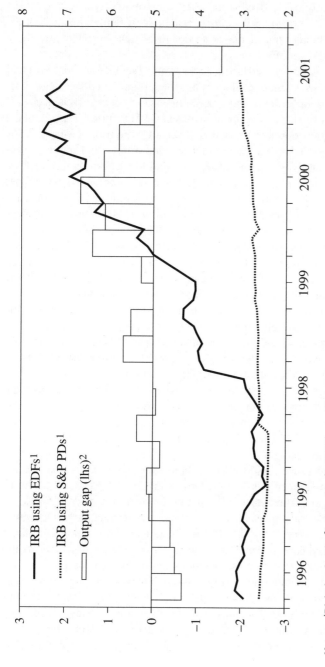

Notes: [1]Right-hand scale. [2]Left-had scale. HP filter applied (BIS).

Source: Jordan, Peek and Rosengren (2002), Figure 1.

Figure 10.3 Capital ratio using EDF and S&P rating PDs for the probability of default

- IRB using EDFs[1]
.... IRB using S&P PDs[1]
▢ Output gap (lhs)[2]

ments increasing in good economic times if the equity market becomes more volatile, or if equity prices decline in anticipation of a downturn. The capital requirements derived from S&P's ratings also increase before the onset of the US recession, although the increases appear to be delayed relative to those generated by KMV's EDFs.

In another study, Catarineu-Rabell, Jackson and Tsomocos (2002) also find large, albeit somewhat smaller, changes in capital requirements through time. The authors use data on the actual distribution of loans across ratings classes (at one point in time) for a selection of banks in G10 countries. They combine these data with transition matrices calculated using data from the early 1990s recession. Using the January 2001 proposals and a transition matrix calculated based on KMV-style ratings, they find that the capital requirement on non-defaulted loans for high-quality portfolios might increase by up to 80 per cent in an early 1990s-style recession. Under the November 2001 proposals, the figure is around 50 per cent. Once again, using transition matrices calculated from Moody's data the increases are considerably smaller.

Neither of these two studies has access to data on the evolution of banks' internal ratings through time. In contrast, Carling et al. (2001) uses data on the internal ratings of a large Swedish bank over the period since 1994. Their results are striking. They find that the capital charge for this bank would have fallen from around 20 per cent in 1994 to around 1 per cent by the end of the decade. This decline largely reflects the gradual improvement in the Swedish economy after the financial problems of the early 1990s. However, the decline is significantly overstated, as the authors use a four-quarter moving average to determine the default probabilities for each grade. This means that unexpectedly low actual defaults for a given ratings grade (because the economy has performed better than expected) lead to low expected defaults for that grade and thus low capital requirements. In contrast, the Basle Committee requires that the PDs associated with each grade be determined on the basis of long-term averages.

Segoviano and Lowe (2002) also use time-series data on internal ratings, having access to the ratings assigned by a number of Mexican banks to business borrowers. Their data cover the period from the mid-1990s to the late 1990s, and so encompass the crisis-driven peso devaluation of December 1994 and the recovery of the late 1990s. Once again, the authors find large swings in required capital. This can be seen in Figure 10.4, which shows the hypothetical capital requirements, together with the Mexican output gap.

The aggregate capital requirement (including the provisioning requirement on defaulted loans) almost doubles after the devaluation, before returning close to the original level. The authors find similar results using a credit risk model similar in spirit to the Credit Metrics model. In terms of timing, loans migrate downwards relatively slowly after the devaluation, so that it takes

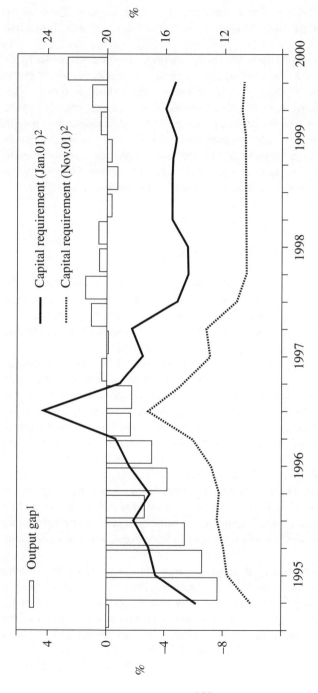

Notes: [1]Left-hand scale; HP filter applied (BIS). [2]Right-hand scale.

Source: Segoviano and Lowe (2002).

Figure 10.4 Mexican output gap and hypothetical IRB capital requirements

around two years for the capital requirement to reach its peak. Then, as the economy recovers, the capital requirements fall as loans migrate to lower-risk classes.

Overall, while each of these studies has its own shortcomings, collectively they suggest that risk-sensitive regulatory capital requirements are likely to lead to quite large changes in capital requirements through time.[13] Risk measurement systems that rely on market prices will almost certainly deliver the largest changes. These systems, however, may lead to earlier increases in required capital than would systems based on external ratings or ratings methodologies similar to that used by the rating agencies. Clearly though, more work is needed before robust conclusions can be drawn. We now turn to a discussion of the potential macroeconomic consequences of large changes in minimum capital requirements.

POSSIBLE MACRO CONSEQUENCES?

The banking industry is inherently procyclical. Economic expansions are supported by an increased willingness of banks to take on risks, by increased competition in credit markets, by lower credit spreads and by easier access to credit as collateral values rise. In downturns the process can work in reverse, with the banking industry acting as a drag on recovery.[14]

Whether or not a system of risk-based capital will add to, or attenuate, these procyclical forces is subject to many debates. A number of submissions to the Basle Committee, for example, have expressed a concern that the proposed changes to the Capital Accord could unintentionally increase the amplitude of the business cycle.[15] The fear is that a decline in capital requirements in a boom will fuel the boom, and that an increase in capital requirements in a downturn will lead to credit supply constraints as banks suffer capital shortages and perhaps even fail as a consequence of having earlier run down the level of capital. On the other hand, others have argued that a system of risk-based capital will contribute to a more stable financial system, and while it may not attenuate normal swings in the business cycle, it will help avoid the type of financial crises that occasionally have very large macroeconomic effects.

The existing literature is of relatively little help in resolving the debate. While it is suggestive of the fact that binding capital requirements can have macroeconomic effects, the evidence is largely inconclusive. In surveying this evidence, Jackson et al. (1999) conclude that reductions in bank lending in some countries following financial stresses do not appear to have been fully offset by increases in lending from other intermediaries or markets. The impact on the macroeconomy is, however, more difficult to establish. In particular, the existing research suggests that binding capital requirements have adversely affected output in some sectors – most notably real estate and small business – but it has not established a robust link between binding capital requirements and macroeconomic outcomes.[16]

The existing studies, however, probably provide little guide to the future. Under the current Basle Accord minimum capital requirements, on a given portfolio, are fixed through time. Thus capital requirements typically become binding through a fall in a bank's capital following the recognition of credit losses. In contrast, under a system of risk-based capital, requirements could become binding not only through a decline in capital due to credit losses, but also through an increase in minimum requirements as loans migrate to higher risk classes. Indeed, the above discussion suggests that just at the time that banks are most likely to be recording losses, the minimum capital requirements could themselves be increasing, perhaps substantially so. Indeed, the increase in the minimum requirements may pose more of a difficulty than the reduction in capital.

This line of argument, by itself, suggests that risk-based capital requirements may lead to greater financial amplification of the business cycle. Such an outcome would, at the least, be ironic, particularly given that a central underlying motivation for reform of the Capital Accord and the improvement of credit risk measurement is to increase the resilience of both individual banks and the financial system as a whole. The likelihood of such an outcome, though, depends in large part on what else changes with the implementation of risk-based capital requirements. At least three such changes are possible.

Improvements in Credit Risk Management

The first, and arguably most important change is that the increasing use of credit risk models and ratings systems is contributing to a revolution in the measurement and management of credit risk in financial institutions. Until recently, many banks did not have formal ratings systems or a metric for measuring changes in credit quality, short of default. This is now clearly changing. And when risk is formally measured, arguably this leads to better management reporting and a more structured decision-making process. One significant benefit of this is that credit-quality problems should be recognized earlier in the business cycle, and with earlier recognition should come earlier corrective action by management, supervisors and the market. In turn, earlier corrective action is likely to increase the probability that difficulties are contained before they reach the point where they threaten either the health of the bank, or the banking system more generally.

Buffers over the Regulatory Minimum

The second change is that the capital buffers over the regulatory minimum are likely to become much more cyclical than is currently the case. In particular, buffers are likely to increase when economic conditions are strong and fall when they are weak.

Under the current Capital Accord banks typically hold more capital than required, although the relative size of the buffer does not appear to co-vary in a consistent way with the business cycle.[17] Over the second half of the 1990s, for example, when most countries experienced reasonably strong economic growth, capital ratios fell in some countries, while they rose in others. Looking forward, we are likely to see a much more consistent pattern.

The reason is as follows. As a bank re-rates its loans upwards in good times, its risk-weighted assets will fall and its capital ratio calculated for regulatory purposes will increase (all else staying constant). In response, the bank could undertake additional lending (or a share buyback), and in so doing increase its leverage and reverse the rise in its regulatory capital ratio. If this were to occur, it would contribute to the procyclicality of the financial system. However, if the bank were to behave in this way, it would likely suffer adverse consequences either in the capital markets or from the rating agencies. Its counter-parties would be rightly concerned that if the cycle turned, and the favourable migration had to be reversed, the bank could find itself with a capital shortage, given that it might be unable quickly to undo the increase in lending. As a result, during good times the rating agencies and the markets may well be intolerant of banks that use favourable ratings migration to support additional lending. Consequently, when times are good banks may be required by the market, and/or by their own management, to hold larger buffers over the regulatory minimum. Over time, markets may also impose some form of penalty (in terms of higher funding costs, a discount in equity valuations or lower ratings) on banks that exhibit 'excessive' loan migration. This may encourage banks to use ratings systems that more closely resemble those used by rating agencies than market-based systems.

For this type of market discipline to work effectively, at least two conditions need to be satisfied. The first is that disclosure is comprehensive, for without adequate disclosure analysts will have difficulty in judging the source of any change in a bank's reported capital ratio. The second is that the market as a whole does not treat favourable loan migration due to business cycle considerations as likely to persist. If it were to do so there might be no penalty for banks that used favourable loan migration to increase their leverage.

Changes in Supervisory Practices

The third change is to supervisory practices. Here there are two important elements.

The first is the recognition that supervisors must assess whether a bank is adequately capitalized even if it is meeting the minimum requirements as set out under Pillar I of the Accord. In making this assessment, the Basle Committee states that supervisors should take into account 'external factors', and this could include business cycle effects. Furthermore, the Basle Committee requires that when banks and their supervisors are assessing the adequacy of capital they are 'mindful of the particular stage of the business cycle in which the bank is operating' (BCBS, 2001c, p. 3). Presumably, if the supervisory authority thought that the bank was inadequately capitalized for the particular point in the cycle, it would suggest, or even require, that the bank raise more capital.

While the possibility of such action might help limit downward pressure on capital in good times, it remains an open question as to whether supervisors will be prepared to act in this way. The difficulty is that for them to do so they need to take a view about future macroeconomic developments, and this can be difficult to do. One way of strengthening their hand is to require banks to undertake and then publish some form of macroeconomic stress test. This could at least form the basis of a dialogue between the bank and its supervisors and strengthen the market discipline discussed above.

The second element is that a system of risk-based capital requirements limits the ability of the supervisory authority to engage in undisclosed forbearance. As noted above, credit quality problems should become evident much earlier, not only because of better measurement but also because of more comprehensive disclosure. This will make it difficult for supervisors to ignore deteriorations in the quality of banks' portfolios, and help overcome the problems that arise from distorted incentives when banks in very poor condition are allowed to continue operating.

Evaluating the impact of these various potential changes in the behaviour of banks and their supervisors is difficult. Yet, these changes are probably the most important consequences of the new Basle Capital Accord. If they were not to take place and the actual level of capital that banks hold was to move in line with changes in the minimum level of required capital under Pillar I, then the potential for adverse macroeconomic effects would be increased. In ensuring that these changes take place, the use of macroeconomic stress tests and the increased disclosure of information are both of considerable importance.

CONCLUSION

Measuring the cyclical dimension of credit risk is fundamentally difficult. Yet, as the recurrence of banking crises suggests, it is fundamentally important.

One reason for the difficulty is that the economics profession is divided over the forces that drive business cycles and whether financial imbalances can be identified *ex ante* in any meaningful way. Without agreement on these important issues, it is difficult for banks and for their supervisors to incorporate business cycle considerations in a mechanical fashion into their risk measurement approaches. Attempts to do so could even be counterproductive, particularly if during a period of weak economic growth they led to changes in key parameters that amplified the increase in measured risk, and in turn accentuated the increase in required capital.

This difficulty, however, does not mean that progress is impossible. Good credit risk measurement cannot be blind to developments in the macroeconomy and to the evolving nature of the balance of macroeconomic risks. Even if the balance of risks cannot be easily quantified and incorporated into formal risk measurement approaches, an assessment of the full range of possible macroeconomic outcomes needs to be made when judging the appropriateness of a bank's capital. When imbalances appear to be developing in the economy, it would seem undesirable for the level of capital in the banking system to decline, irrespective of the outcome of formal risk measurement approaches. Both markets and supervisors have an important role to play in ensuring that the difficulties in formally measuring the evolution of risk through time do not, under a system of risk-based capital, translate into larger macroeconomic fluctuations.

NOTES

1. See Borio, Furfine and Lowe (2001) for further discussion of the distinctions between relative risk and changes in risk through time. See also Goodhart (2001).
2. See Bank for International Settlements (2001).
3. Diebold, Rudebusch and Sichel (1999), for example, find that for the post-war period there is no evidence that expansions in the USA become more likely to end as they grow older. In contrast, they find that contractions are more likely to end the longer that they go on. Interestingly, in the period from 1850 to 1939 the reverse appears to be the case: expansions exhibit duration dependence, but contractions do not.
4. See for example Borio and Lowe (2002) and Gourinchas, Valdes and Landerretche (2001).
5. For details see BCBS (2001a; 2001b; 2001c; 2001d).
6. For reviews of the various models see Saunders and Allen (2002), Crouhy, Galai and Mark (2000) and Gordy (2000).
7. For a comprehensive review of banks' internal ratings systems see BCBS (2000).
8. See for example Nickell, Perraudin and Varotto (2000) and Bangia, Diebold and Schuermann (2000).
9. The only exception is in the calculation of the mark-to-market maturity adjustments.

10. See Gordy (2001) for an extensive discussion of this point.
11. See Lopez (2002) for empirical evidence in support of this assumption. Lopez also presents evidence that the sensitivity to the common factor is an increasing function of firm size.
12. See for example Altman, Resti and Sironi (2002), Frye (2000) and Hamilton, Gupton and Berthault (2001).
13. For other studies see Carpenter, Whitesell and Zakrajšek (2001) and Ervin and Wilde (2001).
14. For a fuller discussion of this issue see BIS (2001) and Borio, Furfine and Lowe (2001).
15. See for example, Danielsson et al. (2001), European Central Bank (2001), Federal Banking Supervisory Office of Germany (2001), International Monetary Fund (2001) and Spanish Banking Association (2001).
16. See for example Hancock and Wilcox (1997; 1998), Peek and Rosengren (1997) and the references in Jackson et al. (1999).
17. For a cross-country comparison see BIS (2001). See also Ayuso, Pérez and Saurina (2002), who present evidence that in Spain under the current Capital Accord capital buffers over the regulatory minimum are substantially eroded during upturns.

REFERENCES

Altman, E., A. Resti and A. Sironi (2002), 'The link between default and recovery rates: effects on the procyclicality of regulatory capital ratios', paper prepared by a conference on Changes in Risk through Time: Measurement and Policy Options, BIS, Basle, 6 March.

Ayuso, J., D. Pérez and J. Saurina (2002), 'Are capital buffers pro-cyclical?', paper prepared for a conference Basle II: An Economic Assessment, Bank for International Settlements, May.

Bangia, A., F. Diebold and T. Schuermann (2000), 'Ratings migration and the business vycle, with applications to credit portfolio stress testing', Wharton Financial Institutions Center, Working Paper 26, April.

Bank for International Settlements (BIS) (2001), *71st Annual Report*, June.

Basle Committee on Banking Supervision (BCBS) (2001a), The new Basle Capital Accord, consultative document, January.

Basle Committee on Banking Supervision (BCBS) (2001b), The internal ratings-based approach, consultative document, January.

Basle Committee on Banking Supervision (BCBS) (2001c), Pillar two (Supervisory Review Process), consultative document, January.

Basle Committee on Banking Supervision (BCBS) (2001d), Potential modifications to the committee's proposals, 5 November.

Basle Committee on Banking Supervision (BCBS) (2000), Range of practice in banks' internal ratings systems, Discussion Paper No. 66.

Borio, C. and P. Lowe (2002), 'Asset prices, financial and monetary stability: exploring the nexus', paper prepared for the conference on Asset Price Bubbles: Implications for Monetary, Regulatory and International Policies, co-sponsored by the Federal Reserve Bank of Chicago and the World Bank Group, 22–24 April.

Borio, C., C. Furfine and P. Lowe (2001), 'Procyclicality of the financial system and financial stability: issues and policy options', in *Marrying the Macro- and Micro-prudential Dimensions of Financial Stability*, BIS Papers, No. 1, 1–57.

Carling, K., T. Jacobson, J. Linde and K. Roszbach (2001), 'The internal ratings based approach for capital adequacy determination: empirical evidence from Sweden', paper prepared for the Workshop on Applied Banking Research, Oslo, 12–13 June.

Carpenter, S., W. Whitesell and E. Zakrajšek (2001), 'Capital requirements, business loans, and business cycles: an empirical analysis of the standardised approach in the New Basle Capital Accord', Board of Governors of the Federal Reserve System, Finance and Economic Discussion Series No. 2001-48, Federal Reserve Board.

Catarineu-Rabell, E., P. Jackson and D. Tsomocos (2002), 'Procyclicality and the new Basle accord – banks' choice of loan rating system', paper presented at conference on The Impact of Economic Slowdowns on Financial Institutions and their Regulators, Federal Reserve Bank of Boston, 17–19 April.

Crouhy, M., D. Galai and R. Mark (2000), 'A comparative analysis of current credit risk models', *Journal of Banking and Finance*, January, 57–117.

Danielsson, J., P. Embrechts, C. Goodhart, C. Keating, F. Muennich, O. Renault and H.S. Shin (2001), 'An academic response to Basle II', Special Paper No 130, London School of Economics Financial Markets Group.

Diebold, F., G. Rudebusch and D. Sichel (1999), 'Further evidence on business cycle duration dependence', in F. Diebold and G. Rudebusch (eds), *Business Cycles: Durations, Dynamics and Forecasting*, Princeton, NJ: Princeton University Press, pp. 86–116.

European Central Bank (2001), 'The new Basle capital accord: comments of the European Central Bank', comments to the Basle Committee.

Ervin, W. and T. Wilde (2001), 'Capital volatility and pro-cyclicality in the New Accord', Credit Suisse First Boston.

Federal Banking Supervisory Office of Germany (2001), comments to the Basle Committee on the New Capital Accord.

Finger, C. (1999), 'Conditional approaches for credit metrics portfolio distributions', *Riskmetrics Monitor*, April, 14–30.

Frye, J. (2000), 'Depressing recoveries', Federal Reserve Bank of Chicago, Emerging Issues Series, S&R-2000-8.

Goodhart, C. (2001), 'The inter-temporal nature of risk', mimeo.

Gordy, M. (2000), 'A comparative anatomy of credit risk models', *Journal of Banking and Finance*, January, 199–249.

Gordy, M. (2001), 'A risk-factor model foundation for ratings-based bank capital rules', Working paper, Finance and Economics Discussion Series No. 2001-55, Federal Reserve Board.

Gourinchas, P., R. Valdes and O. Landerretche (2001), 'Lending booms: Latin America and the world', NBER Working Paper 8249.

Hamilton, D., G. Gupton and A. Berthault (2001), 'Default and recovery rates of corporate bond issuers: 2000', Moody's Investors Service.

Hancock, D. and J. Wilcox (1997), 'Bank capital, non-bank finance, and real estate activity', *Journal of Housing Research*, **8**, 75–105.

Hancock, D. and J. Wilcox (1998), 'The "Credit Crunch" and the availability of credit to small Business', *Journal of Banking and Finance*, **22**, 983–1014.

International Monetary Fund (2001), 'IMF staff comments on the January 2001 proposals of the Basle Committee on Banking Supervision for a new capital adequacy framework for banks', comments to the Basle Committee.

Jackson, P., C. Furfine, H. Groeneveld, D. Hancock, D. Jones, W. Perraudin, L. Radecki and M. Yoneyama (1999), 'Capital requirements and bank behaviour: the impact of the Basle Capital Accord', Basle Committee on Banking Supervision Working Paper No. 1.

Jordan, J., J. Peek and E. Rosengren (2002), 'Credit risk modelling and the cyclicality of capital', Federal Reserve Bank of Boston, paper prepared by a conference on Changes in Risk through Time: Measurement and Policy Options, BIS, Basle, 6 March.

Lopez, J. (2002), 'The relationship between average asset correlation, firm probability of default and asset size', paper prepared for a conference Basle II: An Economic Assessment, Bank for International Settlements, May.

Nickell, P., W. Perraudin and S. Varotto (2000), 'Stability of rating transitions', *Journal of Banking and Finance*, **124**, 203–28.

Peek, J. and E. Rosengren (1997), 'Collateral damage: effects of the Japanese real estate collapse on credit availability and real activity in the United States', Federal Reserve Bank of Boston Working Paper, No. 99-5.

Saunders, A. and L. Allen (2002), *Credit Risk Measurement*, 2nd edn, New York: John Wiley and Sons.

Segoviano, M.A. and P. Lowe (2002), 'Internal ratings, the business cycle and capital requirements: some evidence from an emerging market economy', paper presented at a conference on The Impact of Economic Slowdowns on Financial Institutions and their Regulators, Federal Reserve Bank of Boston, 17–19 April.

Spanish Banking Association (2001), 'New Basle capital accord: comments by the Spanish Banking Association', comments to the Basle Committee.

COMMENT ON 'CREDIT RISK MEASUREMENT AND PROCYCLICALITY'

Henriëtte Prast

In my discussion I will focus on four issues:

- the behaviour of banks over the cycle;
- market discipline
- supervisory practices; and
- dynamic provisioning.

The Behaviour of Banks over the Cycle

My first question is about the behaviour of banks over the cycle. In the paper it is argued that some business cycle expansions sow the seeds of future contractions by generating imbalances in the financial system. These booms show rapid growth in credit and in asset prices. Obviously, in these cases the macroeconomy would benefit if banks were more cautious in their lending decisions at the top of the cycle and more generous at the bottom. Several explanations have been offered for the procyclical behaviour of financial institutions. Banks may have insufficient information about the business cycle. In that case, the behaviour of banks is individually rational given the available information. However, one might wonder why the banks themselves cannot infer from market conditions that the cycle embodies increased credit risk. Moreover, there are alternative explanations. The paper mentions an increased willingness of banks to take on risks, increased competition in credit markets, and easier availability of credit because of rising collateral values. Some simply argue that the forward discount rate of banks is too low. The theory of behavioural finance assumes that banks overestimate the creditworthiness of borrowers at the top of the cycle because of disaster myopia. In this case, bank asset quality deteriorates although the bank does not want to take on greater risk.[1]

My first question is, to what degree is procyclical behaviour of financial institutions in your opinion individually rational (although it obviously leads to collective irrationality), given the available information?

Market Discipline

My second question is about market discipline. In the paper, an important role is assigned to markets in preventing financial procyclicality. Thus, it is stated that under the new Capital Accord, markets can be expected to punish banks that increase lending in good times because their capital ratio has risen. This would lessen the potential procyclicality of the new regulatory ratios. However, it is often assumed that market prices themselves are procyclical and that the procyclical behaviour of financial institutions is a result of the procyclicality of markets.[2] Moreover, banks are accountable to shareholders and they are motivated to earn more dividends when the economy is booming.[3] In fact, shareholders may have a shorter horizon than bank management. Also, and I turn again to the behavioural finance theory, it has been suggested that market participants may over and underreact and display herding behaviour. Finally, banks may be tempted to underprice risk in order to preserve their position in an environment that is increasingly competitive.

My second question is, are you not too optimistic about the effects of market discipline when it comes to punishing procyclical behaviour by banks? Do you believe that shareholders have a longer horizon than banks? Do you not believe that the focus on shareholder value, in combination with increased competition, may have increased rather than decreased procyclicality by banks?

Supervisory Practices

The second pillar enables supervisors to take into account business cycle effects when assessing the capital adequacy of banks. The paper states that this may be hard to do because it may be difficult for supervisors to take a view on future macroeconomic conditions.

My third question is, should I interpret this as supervisors giving information to banks, and banks changing their behaviour because, given the new information, they have an incentive to do so, or should I interpret this as supervisors adapting capital requirements to the business cycle because it is in the interest of financial stability and the macroeconomy, but not necessarily of that of individual institutions?

Dynamic Provisioning

It has been argued that dynamic provisioning may encourage risk-adjusted pricing by banks, and reduce the procyclicality of bank lending. Dynamic provisioning would be forward looking and would imply that, as in the biblical story about the seven years of plenty followed by the seven years of famine in Egypt, buffers are created during good times in order to cushion shocks to capital in bad times.

The final question is, there is nothing in the paper about it, but do you see a role for dynamic provisioning as a remedy against procyclicality?

NOTES

1. J.J. Guttentag and R. Herring (1986), 'Disaster myopia in international banking', *Essays in International Finance*, **164**, Princeton University.
2. P. Turner (2000), 'Procyclicality of regulatory ratios?', CEPA Working Series III, Working Paper 13.
3. L. Clerc, F. Drumetz and O. Jaudouin (2001), 'To what extent are prudential and account-ing arrangements pro or countercyclical with respect to overall financial conditions?', BIS Papers No. 1, Basle: BIS, pp. 197–210.

REPLY

Philip Lowe

I would like to thank Henriëtte very much for her comments and for posing such interesting and thought-provoking questions. I hope you will forgive me, given the time constraint, if I take up just two of these questions.

The first is whether the paper is too optimistic on the issue of whether market discipline can serve to ameliorate the procyclical effects of higher minimum capital requirements in downturns and lower minimum requirements in booms. Here the short answer is that it is hard to tell, but I think there are grounds to be hopeful.

It is correct to say that markets are themselves highly procyclical. If calculated capital ratios increase because of favourable loan migration, banks may come under market pressure to enhance their return on equity by increasing their leverage. But at the same time, some market participants, including the credit rating agencies, are likely to be wary of such a response. Eventually, I think the agencies, and perhaps others, will require a bank that has benefited from favourable loan migration (and thus has a distribution of loans across ratings grades that is more skewed towards low risk grades than is usually the case) to report a higher than average regulatory capital ratio. This would be on the grounds that the average risk weight on the bank's assets (and thus its capital requirement) could increase to more normal levels if the economy deteriorated. While it is clear that the credit rating agencies also exhibit procyclical risk assessments, they often have a longer perspective than many other market participants, and are more likely than many to try to look through the business cycle.

While I think this form of market discipline will prove effective in the medium term, things are less certain in the short term. History is full of instances where changes in regulations have caused difficulties as people adjust to the new environment. Just as it took time for financial markets and institutions to adjust to the deregulation of the 1980s, it will take time for markets to understand why regulatory capital ratios change, and time for bank management to alter the way that they respond to movements in regulatory capital ratios. During this period of adjustment, supervisors will need to keep a particularly close eye on developments.

This process of adjustment can be made smoother by banks increasing the range of information that they provide to the market. In particular, information on the migration of loans across ratings grades and the effects of migration on capital ratios is important. Moreover, the early publication of meaningful stress tests, including the implications of these tests for the distribution of loans across rating grades should also help this process. While the reporting of stress tests to the supervisory authorities is also likely to be useful, the market needs to have access to the same, or similar, information if market discipline is to be effective.

The second question is whether there is a role for dynamic provisioning as a remedy to procyclicality. Here, the short answer is maybe, but by no means is it a magic solution.

Loan loss provisioning should be about valuing loans accurately (recall that the value of loans on a bank's balance sheet is the face value due less the provision). Accordingly, from this perspective, provisions should only increase in good times if the value of the loan portfolio falls below its face value. This may indeed be the case if default probabilities are rising due to an increased likelihood of an economic downturn. But, it need not be! If the underlying value is not declining, the automatic creation of provisions in good times can lead to the undervaluation of loans. While this might be useful from the point of procyclicality, it seems inconsistent with the idea that balance sheets should present a true picture of the value of bank's assets. What is needed is a system of provisioning that accurately reflects loan values. Such a system must by definition be forward looking.

A number of models of 'forward-looking' or 'dynamic' provisioning have been proposed. The best known is that recently introduced in Spain. This system will automatically create a rise in provisions in good times and allow those provisions to be run down in bad times, contributing to less cyclically sensitive bank profits. But some concerns have been raised about this approach, in particular whether it is appropriate to automatically create a provisions at origination on fairly priced loans and whether it will lead to loans being unvalued at certain points of the business cycle.

One idea worthy of further consideration is to apply the Spanish approach, not to provisions, but to capital. This would leave loan valuation to be governed by the accounting rules, but at the same time help ensure that the buffers against risk are not run down unduly in good times.

11. Economic versus regulatory capital for financial conglomerates

Jaap Bikker and Iman van Lelyveld[1]

INTRODUCTION

In a number of the larger financial institutions, firm-wide risk measurement and management currently experience significant growth. Recent methodological advances in measuring individual risk types, such as credit and operational risk, and sharply improved techniques for gathering and analysing information, are making truly firm-wide risk measurement systems feasible. An example of such a system is an economic capital model used to determine the total amount of capital needed to cover all risks, as perceived by the institution. However, a number of conceptual and practical difficulties still need to be resolved. This is especially the case where models seek to aggregate risks across risk areas, business units or even sectors, or alternatively across risk drivers.

Simultaneously with these developments in the financial industry, banking regulators are framing a new set of supervisory rules, especially with respect to minimum required capital. The most recent formulation of these rules by the Basle Committee has been tested in a third Quantitative Impact Study. In the near future, banks will be allowed to base their required capital in risk areas such as credit and operational risk on internal approaches and models, as currently is the case for market risk. The new rules will result in more risk sensitive regulatory capital. Insurance supervisors in a number of countries consider developing similar market-conforming and risk-sensitive capital requirements.[2] This advance of internal approaches and models contributes to the further development and application of economic capital models.

In addition to the minimum regulatory capital charges (referred to as Pillar I), the new Basle Accord distinguishes two further pillars, namely supervisory review and disclosure. Under the supervisory review pillar, banks are required to assess their economic capital and to have a strategic view on capital management. Only in the second instance would supervisors assess the process and result of banks' own evaluation. The question arises whether and, if so, how economic capital models may be employed in the supervisory review processes. Therefore, supervisors need to have a thorough understanding of the current and future state of economic capital models, not only with regard to their strengths and weaknesses in general, but especially with respect to their applicability in regulatory practice.

Since the early 1990s, banks and insurance companies in the Netherlands have been allowed to merge, which has resulted in a number of large financial conglomerates. Similar large financial groups have also emerged in other countries, albeit in more limited numbers. Owing to their size, the larger institutions are of major importance for financial stability, prompting the question of whether or not these conglomerates are more stable than their constituent parts. This could be the case when typical bank and insurance shocks are for the greater part uncorrelated or – even better – negatively correlated. If, on the other hand, contagion risk plays a major role, for example if both components are threatened with loss of reputation should problems arise in one of the constituent parts, financial stability would suffer from these cross-sector mergers. Closely related to this is the too-big-to-fail issue: is the moral hazard risk larger for large financial groups? Of course, these issues are tied in with the question of whether the simple sum of separate minimum capital requirements for banks and insurance firms is still adequate for a financial conglomerate.

The present chapter investigates the usefulness of economic capital models for the assessment of adequate capital requirements and the supervisory review process. First the rationale of supervision will be discussed: what makes banks and insurers so special that exceptional treatment is justified and are there differences in this respect between the two sectors? The current regulation for the components of the financial groups is analysed and we examine whether additional rules or different capital requirements for financial conglomerates are called for. The next section presents a theoretical basis for economic capital models and discusses the current state of the art regarding these models in practice. Where the aggregation of risk is certainly one of the more important issues in economic capital models, the aggregation of risk across sectors is a major problem. How are the various risk types correlated with each other and what are the effects of diversification? The subsequent section deals with these issues and provides empirical evidence from different angles. The first analysis investigates the sensitivity of bank and insurance balance sheets for stochastic shocks and assesses how the shock effects are correlated. The second analysis uses an option-pricing model to estimate the relative riskiness of banks, insurance companies and their (fictitious) combinations. The penultimate section contemplates the differences between economic and regulatory capital and the potential possibilities and shortcomings of economic capital models for supervisory purposes. The final section rounds off with a summary and conclusions.

MOTIVATION FOR CAPITAL REGULATION OF FINANCIAL INSTITUTIONS

Society wishes to regulate and supervise financial institutions for a number of reasons relating to consumer protection, the operation of financial institutions and markets, the incentives for participants, market imperfections and failures and, finally, the special nature of financial products.[3] Critics of regulation argue that market failures or imperfections are not serious or even that they do not exist at all.[4] Moreover, they say, regulation cannot prevent failures or imperfections, or is too costly, whereas some forms of regulation might even generate new sources of moral hazard.

We distinguish the following three objectives for the supervision of financial institutions: (1) consumer protection, (2) the promotion of systemic stability, and (3) maintaining the financial soundness of individual institutions.[5] Following Llewellyn (1999), the instruments at hand are *prudential regulation* and *conduct-of-business regulation*. The former aims to promote solvency and thus the general safety and soundness of institutions, while the latter concerns the customer–firm relationship. This chapter focuses on capital and hence concentrates on prudential regulation only.

The next three subsections consider the need for regulatory capital for banks, insurance firms[6] and financial conglomerates (FCs), respectively, in order to compare them.[7] In addition, the third subsection also seeks to establish whether the 'silo' approach or the 'integrated' approach is more appropriate for financial conglomerates. In the silo approach, total capital is a simple sum of sectoral capital requirements, whereas in the 'integrated' approach capital reduction for diversification effects or a capital add-on for contagion risk is incorporated.

Capital Regulation of Banks

Contrary to other firms, banks may use *deposits* for their funding needs. Deposits differ from other types of debt, in that a substantial part of deposits may be retrieved on sight. Demandable deposits generate the possibility of a bank run on an individual bank, which is suspected to be insolvent. The first come first served (FCFS) constraint, applicable for demand depositors, means that there is a strong incentive for depositors to be in the front of the queue (Chen, 1999). In regular near-bankruptcies it is more difficult to jump the queue and thus evade costs.

Another typical characteristic of banks (and other financial firms) is their *opacity*: it is hard to assess the total risk a bank is running. In particular, the value of longer-term investments that are not publicly traded is difficult to establish, let alone by relative outsiders such as depositors.[8] As the banking operations of different banks are fairly similar, financial stress emerging in one bank may indicate similar difficulties in others. In many cases it is difficult to distinguish bank-specific shocks from general shocks. Therefore, a run on one bank may generate runs on other banks, bringing about serious financial instability.[9] Contagion may also be reinforced because banks are interwoven through heavy interbank lending and cross participations. If bank runs are not triggered by true insolvency, they are detrimental to social welfare, because in a bankruptcy contracts will have to be renegotiated or traded at a discount. Hence, special measures are required to reduce welfare impairing bank runs and their threat of financial instability.

Banks also differ from other lines of business in that the contracts on both sides of the balance sheet have different maturities: funding is of a short-term nature, whereas lending is generally long-term. This creates both *liquidity risk*, which is often the immediate cause of a bank run, and *interest rate risk*, possibly damaging solvency. Therefore public authorities must act to control these risks and safeguard the public interest. Finally, banks have a pivotal role in the financial system, in the clearing and settlement of transactions and – above all – providing finance, in particular to small and medium-sized enterprises.

In industrial countries, two solutions for bank-run problems have been proposed and adopted. The first is the implementation of a *deposit insurance* scheme for the deposits of households.[10] Many deposits are insured up to a certain ceiling, which in the European Union (EU) is €20 000. In most countries, banks pay premiums to fill a fund, whereas in others, such as the Netherlands, banks need only to cover sustained losses after a failure. An additional motivation for deposit insurance is consumer protection.[11] The second solution for bank-run problems is the role of the central bank as the *lender of last resort*, which may provide funds to illiquid but solvent banks (in principle, only against collateral). The support can also go further, as the central bank or the supervisor may carry out a rescue operation.

Deposit insurance produces *risk-shifting* from the bank's deposit holders to all other banks or taxpayers. In this case the risk of deposit holders is not priced, which makes this type of funding cheap.[12] Risk insensitivity of funding creates an incentive for banks to expose themselves to more risky and thus more rewarding investment. Similarly, the lender-of-last-resort function implies that risk is shifted from all funding parties of the bank to the taxpayer, which may provoke more risky bank behaviour, because an unpriced insurance covers part of the possible damage. These *moral hazard* problems

Table 11.1 Arguments for supervision of financial conglomerates

Banks	Financial conglomerates[a]
Bank runs – deposit insurance (moral hazard)	Diversification (–)
Lender-of-last-resort (moral hazard)	Contagion risk (+)
Consumer protection	Supervisory arbitrage (+)
Financial stability	Too Big To Fail moral hazard risk (+)
Insurance firms	Cross-sector moral
Consumer protection	hazard (+)

Note: [a]The following arguments are in addition to those of their constituent parts.

brought about by instruments to reduce the fragility of banks imply a need to further refine banking regulation in order to prevent banks from overly risky behaviour at the expense of others. Table 11.1 summarizes the arguments for supervision of banks.

When it comes to safeguarding the financial soundness of banks and, more generally, achieving financial stability, minimum capital requirements are seen as the most effective tools of banking supervision, as they guarantee that banks have buffers to absorb unexpected losses. Ideally, the level of these requirements is linked to the probability of default on the part of the bank and reflects the degree of confidence society demands with respect to financial stability and the financial soundness of individual banks. Many banks choose a capital level that is substantially higher than the regulatory minimum for purely commercial reasons, for example in order to obtain a higher rating, as this makes capital market funding cheaper, or to avoid downgrading for reputational reasons.[13]

Capital Regulation of Insurance Firms

The main argument for bank supervision is banks' funding by deposit holders, with their special FCFS status, in combination with their long-term assets. Insurance firms, however, are not funded by deposit holders but by *policyholders*. These policyholders pay a lump sum or yearly premiums, for pensions, annuities, endowment insurance or property and casualty (P&C) policies. Particularly the life insurance policies generally have a long lifespan, up to as long as 60 years. Policyholders do not have the FCFS rights attributed to deposit holders. They have the right to surrender a policy, but refunding takes time, which allows the insurance firm to liquidate investments under normal conditions, which are much more favourable than those for banks in a bank-run situation. In the Netherlands refunding generally takes place under a certain discount, which covers at least administration and liquidation costs. Tax treatment is often less favourable if the policy is surrendered before legal minimum terms are met. Thus, commuting insurance policies comes with substantial costs and individual policyholders have no need to commute earlier than others. However, the situation may be different in other countries, where other legal conditions prevail for surrendering. Especially in the USA, the discounts may be lower and not always actuarially fair, which makes surrendering more likely and thus a greater risk for the firm.

In some respect, policyholders have a position similar to that of deposit holders: banks and life insurance firms are both *opaque* institutions, with a degree of riskiness that is hard to assess for the lay person. For this reason these institutions can afford to behave in a more risky fashion, because generally institutions do not fully incorporate their riskiness in their prices. Firms may attempt to gain market share with cheap policies against actuarially insufficient premiums and then proceed to gamble with the received monies. Hence, *consumer protection* is a strong argument for supervision. We have seen that consumer protection is an essential motive for deposit insurance too, where long-term fixed deposits without any demand characteristic are covered as well. For insurance firms it may even be the sole argument for regulation. For many life insurance policies, the case for consumer protection is even stronger than for deposits, as the contracts last much longer. Policy-holders are hardly able to assess the current riskiness of insurance firms, but even the most sophisticated experts cannot foresee a firm's behaviour in, say, five or 10 years, let alone over 40 or 60 years.

Morrison (2001) suggests that debtholders in insurance firms may reduce the need for supervision, as – different from deposit holders – they are able to judge the riskiness of the insurance firm and will demand a risk premium on their funding. In the Netherlands, however, the role of debtholders for insur-ance firms is very limited, as their share of the balance sheet is small, even smaller than in banks.

Where banks and insurance firms share their opacity and the ensuing need for consumer protection, they differ with respect to the other arguments for supervision. Insurance firms as stand-alone institutions do not constitute a major threat to financial stability, as far as their insurance products are con-cerned. Even where – due to the opacity of insurers – financial difficulties in one firm may contribute to doubts regarding other insurance firms, this will not lead to panic reactions similar to bank runs, as surrendering of policies takes time and involves costs for the policyholders. However, a certain contri-bution to the system risk may occur in as far as these institutions are heavily involved in credit derivatives. The possible negative effects on financial sta-bility caused by the interwovenness of insurers and banks will be discussed in the next section. Liquidity risk is not a major problem for insurance firms as their balance sheets generally have a reversed duration structure (life insurance firms) or payments of claims may be postponed somewhat (P&C insurers). Where banks have liabilities with a short contractual duration combined with longer-running assets, life insurers have long-term liabilities while their assets are of a much shorter duration; some of these assets can even be traded on a daily basis. Finally, insurance firms do not play a pivotal role in the financial system by lending and by maintaining the payment system, as banks do. Hence, the list of arguments for supervision of insurance firms is shorter: only consumer protection remains. It should be noted that this does not imply that capital requirements for insurers are lower than they are for banks. Even if the accepted probability of default for insurers were higher than the level acceptable for banks, one should take into account the long-term character of insurance policies, the ability of firms to recover from damaging shocks over time, and the possibility to raise new capital in time.

Capital Regulation of Financial Conglomerates

Morrison (2001) assumes that if the cost of capital in insurance is similar to that in banking, the *economic* capital requirements will be the same for both kinds of businesses. The cost of capital is related to the opacity of the respective line of business. If risk-averse investors are unable to evaluate the risk they are likely to run, they will tend to assume that the quality may be poor and adjust their required rate of return accordingly. In that respect, the question whether insurers are more opaque or less opaque than banks, is interesting. However, this consideration has little value in determining the optimal level of required *regulatory* capital, where probabilities of default – given the capital levels – are related to the different objectives of supervision.

The current regulatory regime for an FC is a silo approach, that is, the simple sum of capital requirements for banks and insurance firms.[14] The requirement that separate bank and insurance firms within the FC are working in distinct limited liability corporation structures constitutes a legal firewall. Separate minimum capital requirements hold for the bank and for the insurance firm, as if they were independent institutions. In determining the optimal level of economic capital, however, FCs themselves will be inclined to consider the total risk of the FC, including diversification effects, rather than the simple sum of bank and insurance requirements. For the moment, we will ignore the fundamental measurement problems in integrating bank and insurance risk (that is, a common unit of risk and a common time horizon. See the third section in this chapter).

In principle, FCs have an incentive to shift certain activities from, say, one of its banks to one of its insurance firms, where the insurance capital requirements are lower. Such regulatory arbitrage is particularly likely where the regulatory framework for banks and insurance firms differ in measuring risk and determining capital requirements. This may even be the case when the regulatory frameworks would be fully harmonized (after solving the fundamental measurement problems in integrating bank and insurance risk mentioned above), as different arguments for supervision may lead to different capital requirements. In any case, the current framework lowers the actual regulatory capital levels of FCs compared to the levels of their constituent parts. Therefore, an add-on (or other measures) for regulatory arbitrage in FCs would be called for.

Financial conglomerates may find themselves in a special position when their legal firewalls crack or are ignored by the public. This can be the case when financial difficulties in one of the subsidiaries in one sector have contagion or reputation effects on another subsidiary in a different sector, especially when they use the same brand name. In that case, the FC may be more vulnerable than its constituting subsidiaries. Similar contagion problems may also arise with non-regulated entities in a FC. If these entities can expect support when needed, a moral hazard problem arises, as they could be tempted to take on more risk than they would otherwise have done. Non-regulated entities would in a sense lean on the deposit insurance and/or the ignorance of policyholders (the so-called free-rider behaviour). Also banks and insurance subsidiaries themselves may expect help from the holding company in cases of financial stress and behave more risky in a FC than as a stand-alone institute. These possible contagion and, say, cross-sector moral hazard risks form an argument for minimum required capital of an FC that is higher than the simple sum of its financial components and that also includes capital requirements for non-regulated entities.[15]

Related to this contagion problem is the too-big-to-fail (TBTF) issue, yet another moral hazard problem. Big financial institutions with a large impact on financial stability may expect a rescue operation to be undertaken by the lender of last resort, when they encounter severe difficulties. Similar to the contagion argument, this TBTF-problem is another argument for additional capital requirements for FCs, as FCs tend to be large. The last column of Table 11.1 summarizes all additional arguments for supervision of FCs.

It might be thought rational for a bank to support an insurance firm of the same FC, or vice versa, in spite of the legal firewalls, in order to reduce contagion risk and to preserve shareholders' interests.[16] Any firewall is likely to have holes in it that make cross-sector support possible. The question arises how circumvention of legal firewalls in a FC would affect financial stability and consumer interests. Given the different arguments for regulation, we encounter rather complicated trade-offs in considering the effects of cross-sector support. Final conclusions regarding the desirability or undesirability of this kind of intra-group support cannot be drawn unless and until it is possible to weigh the arguments for regulation as presented in Table 11.1.

A certain degree of cross-sector support could also exist within the current limits of legal firewalls, in cases where capital in excess of minimum requirements for each of the two sectors is held at the holding level and is used to cover losses where necessary.[17] The possibility of cross-sector support raises the question central to economic capital models (ECMs), as to what diversification effect will occur for the FC as a whole. In the case of adverse (that is, compensating) shocks, cross-section support would be more acceptable from a supervisor's point of view, because the financial soundness of the FC is not at stake. Alternatively, when shocks tend to have a similar effect on the various subsidiaries, the contagion risk argument for additional minimum capital gains weight. A stipulation is that diversification effects should remain robust under stress where – contrary to normal conditions – correlation coefficients tend to approach one. In the fourth section of this chapter, this issue of diversification or correlation of risk across sectors is investigated further.

In determining economic capital of a FC, the diversification effect is an argument for holding less capital than would be required under the simple-sum rule of economic capital for subdivisions. However, from a regulatory point of view, the additional contagion risk, regulatory arbitrage, the increased TBTF-problem and other moral hazard issues constitute arguments for additional minimum capital requirements, if these partly or fully outweigh the diversification benefits. In extreme cases, the risk of a FC could even outstrip the simple sum of its components.

ECONOMIC CAPITAL IN THEORY AND PRACTICE

Economic capital is the amount of capital a financial firm itself deems necessary to operate normally, given its risk profile and its state of controls. This concept is not new but recent innovations in information technology and risk management have made it possible to measure economic capital in a firm-wide, comprehensive and model-based fashion. The motivation for determining economic capital and building capital models originates from the needs of the various stakeholders of a financial institution (Matten, 2000, p. 30): the treasurers, the regulators, the risk managers and the shareholders, are each affected differently by the risks of a financial institution. The treasurer is interested in the optimal use or allocation of economic capital across business lines, the regulator takes the interests of society or of depositors and policyholders into account, the risk manager wants to measure and control risk, whereas shareholders are primarily interested in the returns on their invested capital and the risk involved. In the end, all stakeholders face the same risk drivers, but their objectives – and hence their risk-return preferences – are different.

Institutions themselves increasingly feel the need for ECMs to allocate the scarce capital in order to maximize the risk-adjusted return on capital (RAROC) across different business lines. Measurement of firm-wide, interdependent risk on the various types of activities is a particular challenge for financial conglomerates, which include both banking and insurance activities. The RAROC approach allows management to make better informed strategic decisions and to recognize 'natural hedges', which are important in connection with possible new activities and in the event of a potential merger. Besides, this approach is also important for managerial compensation and pricing. Regulators might find the ECM a useful tool in the supervisory review process – required under Pillar II of the new Basle Capital Accord – where financial firms need to show that they have instruments in place to assess the appropriateness of their level of capital.

At first glance, the optimal amount of a financial institution's economic capital can be determined by applying portfolio selection theory. A firm decides to combine a number of activities, such as trading, lending or security investment that interact and have certain risk and return characteristics. After judicious aggregation, the portfolio will produce a certain risk profile. In practice, a number of technical issues have to be solved, such as the correct aggregation across various risk types and the adequate holding period. This approach has several shortcomings. First, the funding of activities is ignored by the model, although theoretically funding costs of financial firms would be sensitive to the risk profile, partially because of high leverage. A second inadequacy is that, in principle, the portfolio model addresses only one side of the balance sheet, whereas in an FC the risks are located at both sides: banking risk mainly on the asset side (as described above) and insurance risk chiefly on the liability side. Apparently, there is a need for a more comprehensive approach. The next subsection highlights insights into the more general framework of ECMs and their theoretical underpinnings, whereas the third sub-section describes the current state of the art of ECMs in practice and the difficulties associated with implementing ECMs.

A Theoretical Model for Economic Capital

Notwithstanding the needs felt in the financial industry, theoretical underpinnings for the formulation of firm-wide ECMs are rare. To quote Leland (1998): 'The theory addressing capital structure remains distressingly imprecise.' A relatively simple model that nevertheless provides a useful theoretical framework for our discussion has been developed by Froot and Stein (1998). Essential ingredients in their model are the understanding that external finance is costly and that at least a part of the risk taken by an institution is non-tradable and thus cannot be hedged. Given that there is some cost involved in holding capital, the issues of risk management, capital budgeting and capital structure policy become linked.

The model distinguishes three periods: an initial period (T_1) in which an institution decides how much capital to hold, a second period (T_2) in which new projects emerge and the institution can enter into these projects, and a final round (T_3) where the payout is determined. In the first round, the institution starts with a given initial portfolio and decides how much equity capital to hold. Raising capital at this point is costless but there is an increasing cost at the final period T_3, when a firm can go to the capital market. At T_2 a new product is introduced and the institution has to decide how much to invest in this activity. In addition, the institution has to decide how much too hedge (building on Froot, Scharfstein and Stein, 1993). Thus the amount of cash the institution has on hand at T_3 will depend on the realized returns of its old exposures, on its new product, and on its hedging positions, as well as on the amount of capital raised at T_1. The reason the institution cares about the distributional characteristics of cash balances is that at T_3 there are risk-free investment opportunities, which will require some level of investment. This investment can be funded by internal cash or by external funds, which are increasingly costly to raise. Hence, the marginal value of cash is positive but decreasing. Leaving out period T_2 reduces the model to a typical Myers and Majluf (1984) pecking-order model of equity. Adding period T_2 gives the institution two tools, besides keeping cash, to counter 'underinvestment distortions caused by costly external financing'. The institution can either adjust its risk-profile through a hedge or it can decide to be either more or less aggressive in investing in the new, risky activity at time T_2.

The fairly intuitive result emerges that if all risks are perfectly tradable, the value of the institution is maximized by hedging completely.[18] To make the model more realistic, Froot and Stein decompose the exposures in a tradable and a non-tradable part, such as private equity. It turns out that an institution will still hedge all tradable risks. Subsequently, the authors turn to the investment decision at T_2. If there is a single investment, the optimal amount to invest is shown to depend on how rewarding the investment is, on how strong the non-tradable risk is linked to market risk and on the risk aversion of the institution. If capital is infinite, the risk aversion is not important but with lower levels of capital, the probability that the institution has to access the external market (at some cost) increases. 'The greater the contribution of the new non-tradable risk to the variance of the institution's overall portfolio of non-tradable risk, the more pronounced the conservatism' (Froot and Stein, 1998, p. 65). Since the optimal amount to invest depends on how the investment opportunity is linked to the portfolio already held, there is no single unique hurdle rate (that is, the rate that individual investments have to pass to be accepted). Only for small investments an approximation can be found.

In the case of multiple investment opportunities, the amount to invest in a project depends not only on the old portfolio but also on the link with other investments evaluated. There are two sources of interdependence: (1) a *covariance spillover* effect, because projects will become more interesting if the covariance with other projects evaluated is low, and (2) an *institution-wide cost of capital* effect, because investing in a single, large opportunity might raise the risk aversion of the institution with negative repercussions for the other opportunities considered. These two effects would argue for central-ized decision making although there is a cost to this as well. Head office needs to gather data in order to determine the firm's risk aversion and the degree of non-tradable risks in the books. The central question turns out to be not whether some centralized decision-making is necessary but how often this should happen.

The authors then turn to the determination of the amount of capital the institution holds at T_1. Here the classic Modigliani-Miller result of debt-equity equivalence emerges, provided there is no cost attached to holding capital. Introducing capital holding cost results in cutting levels of capital and the introduction of the risk aversion of the institutions. Empirical evidence for the model proposed is difficult to find, because hurdle rates are difficult to observe and exogenous shocks to capital are hard to find.[19] The authors compare their model with the RAROC approach, which generally consists of applying some variant of the following three steps: (1) measure the expected return to capital given by $r_i = DCF_i / VaR_i$ ($\alpha\%$), where the rate of return on project i (r_i) is given by the discounted cash flows (DCF) divided by the value at risk (VaR) at some α percentile of the loss distribution. Thus the rate of return is framed in terms of expected return in relation to the capital at risk, (2) measuring the cost of capital (that is, the hurdle rate) $h_i = r_f + (r_m - r_f)\beta$, where r_f is the risk-free rate, r_m is the market rate of return and β is the relation with the market return. β is given by $\rho(i, M)\ \sigma_i/\sigma_M$,[20] and (3) maxi-mizing $r_i - h_i$.

Given the Froot and Stein model, three weak spots can be identified. First, RAROC can only deliver value maximization if it is applied on a post-hedged basis (that is, does not contain any tradable risk) which might be difficult to implement in practice. Secondly, the equation should include not only an asset or activity's variance but also its covariance with the existing portfolio. Finally, calculating the correct cost of capital or relevant beta is not easy (see also Chatterjee, Lubatkin and Schulze, 1999). A more practical criticism is voiced by Robinson (2001): decisions based on this framework may be arbitrary because the VaR($\alpha\%$)-amount is highly sensitive to the choice of α in combination with the actual loss distribution. The shape of the tail of the distribution differs significantly between different kind of returns and raising α will thus have significant effects on the relative expected returns. This in turn might change, depending on which projects eventually pass the hurdle rate.

In conclusion, the model presented by Froot and Stein (1998) is a concise model in which the capital budgeting and risk management within an institution is given a firmer theoretical footing, although some objections have been raised. Contrary to Modigliani-Miller there is a reason for managing the riskiness of an institution. An essential point in their story is that each investment decision will affect the (optimal) capital structure, which in turn influences the hurdle rate the particular investment has to pass.[21] This point gains in importance for FCs because their risk types are more diverse and their total risk is thus more unpredictable. Although it is impracticable to determine the impact of each individual investment on the hurdle rate, such feedback effects should be incorporated when investments are large, particularly if the covariance with the existing portfolio is large.

Economic Capital Models in Practice

In recent years a number of large financial institutions have shown an increasing interest in ECMs. The RAROC-type applications aiming at optimizing allocation of economic capital in order to improve returns constitute the main motive for developing these models. The need for a common measurement of returns increases with the diversity and complexity of financial organizations. In the Netherlands two financial conglomerates, namely, ING and Fortis, have developed such models, use them and even publish some results in their annual reports. Other financial conglomerates, which are known for developing such models, are Citigroup-Travellers, Credit Suisse and Dresdner Allianz. These large conglomerates have stronger incentives to develop and use such models as their activities are diverse and dispersed. Incidentally, the models mentioned above generally do not yet cover insurance activities.

Table 11.2 presents an overview of the various risk types applicable to a FC, as well as their definitions, measurement approaches, and underlying risk drivers. Market or asset-liability model (ALM), credit, operational and business risk occur in both banks and insurance firms, but the focus may differ (see Cumming and Hirtle (2001)). For instance, banks consider the risk of price changes regarding their trading activities based on a time horizon of one to 10 days. In addition, they examine the interest rate risk of their (long-term) assets and liabilities. Life insurance firms look at the risk of price changes of their assets and liabilities on a time horizon of many years or even decades, as their liabilities have extremely long maturities. This touches upon one of the fundamental problems in building ECMs, which is the choice of a com-

Table 11.2 Overview of risk types in economic capital models

Risk types	Subtypes	Descriptions	Typical measurement approaches	Risk drivers
Credit[a]		The risk of loss resulting from failure of obligors to honour their payments	Credit risk models, internal rating-based approach; expected loss, unexpected loss, probability of default, loss given default, exposure at default, maturity, correlation between credits[b]	Business cycle, sectoral developments, prices of shares, bonds, other financial products, commodities, commercial and residential real estate and other collateral
	Cross-border, transfer of country risk	Potential losses due to the possibility that funds in foreign currencies can not be transferred out of a country as a result of actions by the local authorities or of other events impeding the transfer	VaR, simulation model, credit risk models, internal rating based approach (country risk ranking model, foreign currency sovereign spread)	Foreign exchange rates, interest rates, local business cycle, political developments
Market or ALM	Market or trading, ALM, interest rate risk	The risk of adverse movements in market factors and their volatilities	VaR, scenario analysis, simulation models of the balance sheet	Share and commodities prices, foreign exchange rates, interest rates, equity and commercial and residential real estate prices; their volatilities

Type	Sub-type	Description	Methods	Factors
Life		The risk of loss due to unforeseen increases in life claims	Surplus, resilience, solvency and stress tests, second order foundation, ALM model	Lapses risk (surrender of policies), mortality and longevity expectancy, risk on expenses[c]
	Mortality	Deviations in timing and amount of the cash flows due to (non-)incidence of death		Mortality and longevity expectancy, risk on expenses
	Morbidity or disability	Deviations in timing and amount of the cash flows due to (non-)incident of disability and sickness		Morbidity and disability expectancy, risk on expenses[d]
P&C or non-life	Catastrophe P&C	The risk of loss due to catastrophes, such as hurricanes or earthquakes	Simulation, exceedence probability curves	Frequencies/severeties of insured risks (accidents, fires, etc.)
	Non-catastrophe P&C, including morbidity risk	The risk of loss due to unforeseen increase in non-catastrophe claims, such as car accidents, fires, etc.	Frequency severity modelling, loss triangle analysis, historical claim ratio	
Operational, including legal risk		The risk of loss resulting from inadequate or failed internal processes, people and systems or from external events	Non-parametric distribution, extreme value theory	Quality of control, volume of cash flows of other business measures

Table 11.2 (continued)

Risk types	Subtypes	Descriptions	Typical measurement approaches	Risk drivers
Business or strategic		The risk of loss due to adverse conditions in revenue/exposure, such as decreased demand, competitive pressure, etc.	Historical earnings volatility, analogues	Other risks, such as changes in volumes, margins and costs, strategic risk (choice of products and markets), risk of mergers, acquisitions and divestitures

Notes:

Reputation risk is an indirect loss, driven by one of the other risk types. In principle, all risk types include the following risk breakdown: (1) volatility, (2) model risk, that is, uncertainty about what is measured, and (3) event or tail risk. Liquidity risk is not considered in this survey, as it is questionable whether there is sense in covering it by capital.

a   This includes both on balance sheet credit risk as off balance sheet credit risk (counterparty risk in credit and other derivatives).

b   See Bikker (2000) and Bikker and Huijser (2001).

c   Future expenses are estimated over the entire term of the policy. Expenses may change due to inflation in prices or wages or improvement of efficiency.

d   It is difficult to distinguish risk drivers here. 'Frequencies or severities of catastrophes' would describe the extreme events, which occur in any risk category.

mon time horizon in order to assess risk integrated across business lines and sectors.[22] Credit risk is the major source of risk for universal banks. Much more than typical insurance risk categories such as mortality and (non-catastrophe) P&C risk, the so-called broad ALM risk (including market risk and embedded insurance options) is the dominant source of uncertainty for insurers, due to their long-lasting liabilities. The typical measurement approaches vary tremendously across the risk types. This indicates a second problem in building ECMs, namely the choice of a common unit of risk.

The level of sophistication of models for the various risk types varies significantly and is mainly determined by the availability of relevant data. In general, models for market risk are well developed. Data is available on a daily basis allowing back testing. The 1996 Amendment to the Basle Capital Accord allows banks to calculate their minimum capital requirement for trading risk activities using these models. Since then, these models have been developed and applied on a large scale. Insurance models for life and non-catastrophe P&C risk profit from a similar kind of data abundance. Credit risk models have come into vogue more recently. As the availability of default data is limited, these models are based on many assumptions, constraining their usefulness. The new Basle Capital Accord allows the internal rating based (IRB) approach for credit risk and models for operational risk for calculating minimum capital requirements, which is currently stimulating the development of these models and data collection efforts worldwide.

The various models or measurement approaches for the distinguished risk types constitute the building blocks of ECMs. Many problems regarding the unit of measurement, time horizon, and aggregation – each of them both *across types of risks* and *across types of business units or sectors* – need to be solved. The difficulties of the first problem, the search for a 'common currency' for risk, seem to be reduced because a common focus emerges on the potential for unexpected losses, either in earnings or economic value.[23] Practitioners have generally chosen a holding period of one year, because this best fits the control cycle (that is, budgets) and the time needed to raise new capital. One year is also an average value across the various measurement approaches, a mid-point between the short trading risk horizons and the long insurance risk horizons. Of course, such a standard period is unlikely to fit all activities perfectly.

The Froot and Stein model underlines that interaction between risks is of crucial importance. However, in most, if not all, financial institutions, risk measurement and management started as a bottom-up approach, resulting in a patchwork of differing approaches which makes aggregation across risk types and sectors rather complicated. In theory, all risks are interrelated, but in practice the correlation structure needs to be simplified. Oliver, Wyman and Company (OWC, 2001) observes that the coherence in the portfolio is often modelled on three levels: the portfolio, the business unit, and the holding level, termed level I, II, III, respectively. An alternative for levels II and III would be aggregation of, first, the risk for each risk type across the whole conglomerate and, secondly, across risk types. For most of the higher level correlations, financial institutions do not have the data required to obtain meaningful estimates. They rely on 'human judgement' or the consultant's perception of 'industry practice'. Some institutions set correlation values at rather conservative levels, whereas others use rough approximations such as correlations between – baskets of – appropriate share prices. As correlations determine the diversification effects, they are crucially important for determining the ultimate level of economic capital. An issue is whether correlations should reflect normal conditions, like those reflected in the building blocks of the ECM, or stress conditions under which capital is really needed to absorb losses. In practice, large diversification effects are found at the portfolio level (80 to 90 per cent), smaller ones at the business line level (40 per cent), whereas minor effects (5 to 10 per cent) are assumed at the cross-sector level (OWC, 2001). In the next section we proceed to investigate correlations and diversification effects on the holding level by providing various empirical estimates.

CORRELATIONS, AGGREGATION AND DIVERSIFICATION

In the theoretical model developed by Froot and Stein (1998), we need to establish the degree of correlations between all individual investments. As mentioned above, the more pragmatic approach of OWC (2001) distinguishes three levels of diversification: the portfolio, the business unit, and the holding level. The question we would like to answer is, what are sensible and reasonable empirical values to be used in the economic capital models? In particular we will focus on the holding level. The literature in this area is understandably very scarce. On the one hand, the consulting firms that implement economic capital have no incentive to publish and jeopardize their livelihood; on the other hand, the institutions treat their data as confidential.

Data for the OWC level I or within portfolio correlations is plentiful. For the higher levels one may think of a number of different sources. Conversely, finding an adequate source for correlation on the business unit level (level II) is difficult. One possibility is to analyse how, for a certain market, the market index, as an indicator of market risk, is related to credit spreads on corporate bonds, as an indicator for credit risk.[24] Correlations between insurers and banks on the holding level (level III) could, among other things, be based on the returns on equity or bonds.[25] More specifically, one may ask to what degree the results from pure banking and insurance firms are correlated? In this vein the American bank holding companies have been examined using various methods (see 'Bank holding company literature' subsection below).

In addition to values for 'normal times' we are also interested in the levels of correlation during recessions or crisis periods. There is an extensive literature studying the linkage between various markets in various countries.[26] Generally these studies focus on how turmoil in one market 'spills over' into other markets during crisis periods. Recent studies investigate whether the correlation, often derived from ARCH-type Auto Regressive Conditional Heteroscedasticity models, becomes stronger during a crisis.[27] Although this issue does merit attention, we will abstract from it in the light of the scarcity of consensus about reasonable values for empirical parameters and investigate two different approaches. The first, presented in the next section, investigates the sensitivity of banks' and insurance firms' balance sheets for stochastic shocks and assesses how the effects of these shocks are correlated. The second analysis uses an option-pricing model to estimate the relative riskiness of banks, insurance companies and their (fictitious) combinations.

A Simple ALM Model to Simulate Diversification between Banks and Life Insurers

The balance sheets of banks and life insurers are each others' counterparts in the sense that bank assets have a longer maturity than bank liabilities, whereas for insurers it is the other way around. This creates asymmetry in the sensitivity to interest rate shocks of these institutions, in particular for changes in the slope of the yield curve. This asymmetry is often mentioned as an argument for the existence of negative correlation between interest rate risk of banks and insurance firms, or in terms of OWC (2001), of diversification on level III. On the other hand, both sectors invest in shares, participations and subsidiaries, which contributes to a positive correlation. This section develops a strongly stylized ALM for banks' and insurance firms' balance sheets. In this model, we consider life insurers only, as P&C insurers have just limited balance sheet sizes, so that interest rate and asset price risk only play a minor role.[28] Moreover, the main risk types P&C insurers run are P&C risk, operational and business risk (see Table 11.2), which are assumed to be uncorrelated to the risk run by banks and life insurers.[29] For the same reason, we ignore non-regulated entities. Note that these activities with uncorrelated risk would contribute to further diversification at the holding level.

Our model simulates the balance sheet values in a stochastic environment, where values of interest rates and asset prices are subject to shocks. Economic capital models (ECMs) or the ALMs of individual banks, insurance firms and FCs are able to provide a much more detailed description of the dependence of the balance sheet items on such external shocks, as they have more information available. However, only a few FCs are able to model simultaneously interest rate and asset price shocks for both their banks and insurance firms. In particular, we do not have sufficient data on off-balance sheet positions of banks. However, our simple stylized model can provide a general picture of the diversification effects with respect to shocks in interest rates and asset prices.

Our model exercises are based on the aggregated balance sheets of domestic bank activities of the five largest commercial bank conglomerates in the Netherlands (covering 79 per cent of all Dutch domestic banking activities) and of domestic insurance activities of Dutch insurance firms.[30] To illustrate our model, the Appendix at the end of this chapter provides stylized versions of the aggregated balance sheets used in the calculations. As an alternative, the calculations have also been executed with consolidated data of all Dutch banks. The analyses on an aggregated level provide *average* effects of interest rate and asset price shocks on the profit or wealth of banks and insurance firms and their mutual interdependence. Our ALM model distinguishes a large number of interest rates. A set of interest rate equations, presented in the Appendix, link these rates to two core rates: the short-term rate (reflecting monetary policy) and the long-term rate (reflecting capital market conditions). The value of each balance sheet item is linked to one – or more – of the interest rates or to an asset price. Where useful and possible, balance sheet items have been split using internal data. Many of these interest-link equations are based on distributed lags (DLs) of interest rates, of which the length reflects the maximum maturity of the respective balance sheet item (see also the Appendix). These equations take lags in interest payments into account as well. For banks, the average lag of the DL is set to reflect the average duration found in the interest rate risk surveys of De Nederlandsche Bank. Similar information and details on the (distribution of the) remaining length of life insurance contracts are obtained from insurance firms.

A first complication in incorporating bank and insurers' balance sheets into one model, is the difference in accounting rules. Dutch banks use the Dutch accounting authority's rules for their annual public statement and quite similar supervisory rules for their reports to their supervisor. The value of the trading portfolio, which in Dutch banks is small compared to the banking book portfolio, is recorded at market prices. Bonds and promissory notes are recorded at their nominal value. In principle, other financial assets are booked at acquisition values, adjusted downwards if necessary, whereas participations show up at the lowest of acquisition values and market prices. Subsidiaries are recorded at net wealth or revenue value, and real estate investment is booked at market prices, but after deduction of depreciations.[31] In the near future, the EU will implement a new International Accounting Standards

Board (IASB) accounting regime for firms quoted on the stock exchange, which relies more on market values.[32]

Valuation rules in the insurance sector vary from firm to firm. In general, insurers record shares, other non-fixed income securities and real estate investment at market prices. This also holds for investments, which is at the risk of policyholders or insured thrift clubs. The valuation of life insurance liabilities (technical life insurance reserve) is based on a fixed 'calculation interest rate' of 3 per cent. Investment in fixed-income securities stemming from insurance policies, which are based on a guaranteed expiration benefit or sold at a 'level of interest rate' discount (in Dutch, *rentestandskorting*), are recorded at redemption value.[33] For insurance balance sheets items we use actual values, as far as possible.

For our simulations, we have to bridge the different accounting regimes. For asset price scenarios, we assume that the shock effects are based on (changes in) market value. This does not reflect current accounting practice, but is in line with economic theory. For interest rate scenarios, we distinguish two regimes for presentational reasons. First an accrual accounting regime, where the value of the fixed-income securities and the technical life insurance reserves remain unchanged, so that the shock effects reflect only changes in net interest income. Secondly, a fair value type of accounting regime, where all interest rate sensitive balance sheet items, including saving accounts and technical provisions on life insurance policies are marked-to-market (as will be explained below). These distinguished regimes reflect two extremes, which encompass the actual regime.

We checked the model by an *ex post* forecasting test. For banks we compared predicted paid and received interest with actual values. For insurance firms, we forecasted and compared investment revenues and funding costs to actual outcomes on a balance sheet item basis, because realizations are known in greater detail for insurers (PVK, 2001a, Table 24). The forecast errors were fairly small.

Interest rate shocks under an accrual accounting regime

In this section we assume an accrual accounting regime, where the only changes are on net interest income.[34] We evaluate the following four interest rate scenarios: (1) a two percentage point short-term interest rate rise where the long-term rate is defined in the model,[35] (2) a two percentage point short-term interest rate rise with a fixed, unchanged long-term rate, (3) a two percentage point long-term interest rate rise,[36] and (4) a two percentage point increase in the yield curve's slope, caused by a one percentage point increase of the long-term rate and a one percentage point fall in the short-term rate. These shock sizes are realistic: over the last two decades, the average absolute annual change in the short and long rates were more than 1 and 0.75 per cent, respectively, and over two year periods 1.75 and 1.25 per cent, respectively. All shocks are one-off events (that is, not repeated) but permanent, unexpected and occurring at the start of the year.

For banks and insurers, Table 11.3 shows the net interest income in the base line scenario and presents the *changes* in net interest income, all in billions of guilders, in the four interest rate scenarios considered.[37] As part of the investment of insurance firms is purely at the policyholders own risk, we do not incorporate the corresponding changes in net interest income in these shock effects. Table 11.3 presents the yearly effects, as they would show up in the book-keeping, and which illustrate the dynamic nature of the model. In reality, new shocks may occur and banks and insurers may change their balance sheets, blurring the original impulses. All presented effects assume that the behaviour of banks and their customers remains constant.[38] Of course, banks, insurers and customers might react to changed interest rate conditions, in general reducing the shock effects, but probably only slightly for reasons of continuity and lacking alternatives. In any case, banks and insurers have to accept the inescapable losses or gains, as shown here but made most clear from fair-value accounting. Furthermore, it should be emphasized that our analysis does not include off-balance sheet positions. Hence, our model ignores full or partial coverage of interest rate mismatches of banks or insurers by, say, interest rate swaps, and also disregards speculative positions of banks or insurers on future interest rate developments.

In the first three years, a 2 per cent rise in the short-term-interest rate would eat into the net interest income of banks, as funding costs would rise (see the first row of Table 11.3). As the long-term interest rate rises too, according to the underlying term–structure relationship, banks will receive additional interest revenues from lending and investment, gradually rising over time due to the longer maturity and hence later interest rate adjustment of these assets. After four years this would compensate for the higher funding costs. In a simulation where the long rate would remain unchanged, further flattening the yield curve, the full funding cost rise shows up (see the second row). The effect rises over time as part of the deposits have a fixed interest rate for up to five years. A rise in the long-term rate has only favourable effects, gradually increasing over time, as more new loans and investment yields are based on the new interest rate level (see the third row). According to our model, the short-term interest rate is not affected by the long-term rate and so remains unchanged in this scenario.

For insurers, all scenarios with rising interest rates are favourable, as investment dominates funding by far, in spite of the fact that the higher rates feed through with substantial delays. For banks and insurers, the effects of a long-term interest rate rise are similar and hence are correlated, whereas for the short-term interest rate rise, they diverge, indicating negative correlation.

Table 11.3   *The effects of two percentage point interest rate shocks on net interest income of domestic activities of banks and insurers (in billions of guilders)*

Year:	1	2	3	4	5	Total
Banks						
Net interest income in baseline	30.6	28.3	28.0	29.0	30.0	
Changes in net interest-income						
Short-term interest rate rise (free long rate)	−3.2	−4.6	−3.4	−1.3	1.1	−11.5
Short-term interest rate rise (fixed long rate)	−3.2	−5.3	−6.5	−6.8	−6.9	−28.8
Long-term interest rate rise	1.4	5.5	7.9	10.5	13.4	38.7
Steeper slope yield curve	2.3	5.4	7.2	8.7	10.1	33.7
Insurers						
Net interest income in baseline	20.9	20.9	21.1	21.5	21.8	
Changes in net interest-income						
Short-term interest rate rise (free long rate)	1.5	1.8	2.7	3.8	4.7	14.6
Short-term interest rate rise (fixed long rate)	1.5	1.5	1.5	1.5	1.5	7.6
Long-term interest rate rise	0.6	2.2	3.3	4.1	4.9	15.1
Steeper slope yield curve	−0.4	0.3	0.9	1.3	1.7	3.8

In the latter case, a hypothetical FC would encounter a strong diversification effect. The last simulation exercise, a steeper slope of the yield curve, has favourable interest revenue effects for both types of institutions, gradually increasing over time (see the fourth row in Table 11.3). However, the effect for banks is far stronger, owing to the lower short rate.[39] The first-year effect for insurers is negative, as the short-rate drop makes itself felt directly, whereas the long-rate hike affects interest income with more delay.

Table 11.4 presents the simulation results of Table 11.3 scaled by profit before taxation. The effects in percentages of profits indicate how sizeable the observed changes in net income are for banks and insurers, normally hidden from view, as day-to-day interest rate shocks follow an erratic pattern. In order to obtain further insight into the diversification effects of FCs, the lower part of Table 11.4 calculates the effects of imaginary mergers of (all) banks and insurers, assuming that banks and insurers within an FC continue to operate independently from each other as before, but pool their profits on the holding level.[40] It is clear from the first four FC rows that the impact of short-term shocks on the profit of the FC is far smaller, compared to the profits of their components, reflecting the negative correlation between banks and insurers (due to different funding behaviour). The long-term shock effects for the FC are slightly smaller than for their constituent banks, but somewhat greater than for their insurers. For the yield curve shocks, a similar conclusion may be drawn, be it that the differences are larger.

The diversification effects can best be illustrated by expressing the changes in profits of FCs as shares of those of banks (last four rows of Table 11.4).[41] Changes in profits, however, are lower for FCs than for their constituent banks in all cases, due to the two well-known facets of diversification. On the one hand, profit shocks are smaller where correlations are negative, as for short rate shocks (the 'hedging' effect) and, on the other hand, profit shocks for FCs *tend* to be lower, as they are the weighted average of the two underlying profit shocks (the 'levelling out' or 'spread' effect of averages).[42]

The considerable diversification effects suggest that a hypothetical merger is rewarding. However, two remarks should be made here. First, the diversification effects of Table 11.4 do not imply any kind of synergy; investors could also achieve these gains by holding both bank and insurance shares in their portfolio. Second, the diversification effects suggest some gain in terms of financial stability, as insurers can absorb bank shocks and vice versa although legal firewalls between banks and insurers should limit financial cross-sector support.[43] In practice, however, such firewalls may prove less robust under crisis conditions.

Table 11.4 The effects of two percentage point interest rate shocks on profits of banks, insurers and (imaginary) financial conglomerates

Year:	1	2	3	4	5
Changes in profit (%)					
Banks					
Short-term interest rate rise (free long rate)	-18	-26	-19	-8	6
Short-term interest rate rise (fixed long rate)	-19	-30	-37	-39	-39
Long-term interest rate rise	8	31	45	60	77
Steeper slope yield curve	13	31	41	50	58
Insurers					
Short-term interest rate rise (free long rate)	20	23	36	49	61
Short-term interest rate rise (fixed long rate)	20	19	20	20	20
Long-term interest rate rise	8	28	43	53	64
Steeper slope yield curve	-6	4	12	17	22
Imaginary financial conglomerates (FC)					
Short-term interest rate rise (free long rate)	-7	-11	-3	10	23
Short-term interest rate rise (fixed long rate)	-7	-15	-20	-21	-21
Long-term interest rate rise	8	30	44	58	73
Steeper slope yield curve	7	23	32	40	47
Changes in profit of FC compared to banks (index)					
Short-term interest rate rise (free long rate)	0.37	0.43	0.13	a	a
Short-term interest rate rise (fixed long rate)	0.37	0.50	0.53	0.54	0.54
Long-term interest rate rise	0.99	0.97	0.98	0.97	0.95
Steeper slope yield curve	0.57	0.74	0.78	0.80	0.81

Note: [a]This index is less useful where the denominator – change in bank profits – is close to zero.

Interest rate shocks under a fair-value accounting regime

Under fair-value accounting, assets are valued at market prices. This approach takes changes in all future interest flows, such as described in the former section, into account immediately. Approximating a fair value regime, we use a broad-brush approach for our balance sheets. In case of an interest rate hike the value of a fixed rate instrument diminishes with the net present value of all future interest rate differences.[44] This subsection presents the effects of a two percentage point rise in all interest rates, where the current level of the long-term rate is 5 per cent. Other fixed-income securities, including credits, have been treated more or less like bonds. This is not apparent for credit loans, where in general no market prices are observed and uncertainty may exist about creditworthiness. Moreover, many credits have embedded options such as early settlement or renegotiation of the interest rate.[45] Of course, such options only come into the money when the interest rate *declines* and are worthless in our scenario of an interest rate *rise*. For most long-term fixed income assets, we assume a term structure of 12 years and a duration of around three years (or, in the case of mortgages, close to five years), in line with interest rate risk reports of banks in the Netherlands. This generates discounts of 5 to 7 per cent (see the Appendix). The revaluation of liabilities has been treated likewise, as is obvious for fixed-income time deposits and debentures. Of course, the discounting of debt is favourable for the wealth of the bank or the insurer. Serious difficulties arise in revaluation of the various savings accounts and demand deposits or current accounts. The interest rates on these accounts are not very sensitive to movements in model rates. Therefore, the 'value' of these accounts rises, as this cheap debt becomes relatively cheaper. Naturally, the account holders have the permanent option to move their funds to other more rewarding investment. However, as most of the account holders do not use this option under the current rates, we assume that many of them will not do so under the higher rates.[46]

The valuation of the balance sheet of insurers has been dealt with in a similar way, taking into account that a part of these assets is held at the policyholders' own risk. A problem is how to revalue the technical provision for life insurance policies. Formally, the technical provision for life insurance is based on a certain 'calculation' rate that remains unchanged when market rates move. The required funds to cover the liabilities of the policy portfolio (or the debt) decrease. However, when interest rates rise, it is easier to satisfy the corresponding liabilities or to make a profit on this portfolio.[47] Based on a gradually declining term structure of 40 years for the technical life insurance reserve (in line with what can be observed in large insurance companies), the interest rate rise from 5 to 7 per cent would imply a reduction of required reserves (or investment) of more than 13 per cent (see the Appendix).[48] However, part of the policies has profit sharing. This is typical for individual policies with payment of premiums and for part of the collective policies. Most of the other policies have a fixed 'level of interest rate' discount in advance, whereas the rest has no profit sharing at all. Based on figures of the shares of individual policies and of policies with annual premiums, we assume that half of the total profit is shared, that is, that half of the policies would collect all gains on investment or that all policyholders would share half the gains and profit on investment. Further on, we will relax this assumption. As in the earlier simulations, we calculate the effects of the interest rate changes, assuming unchanged behaviour of banks and insurers. In any case, gains and losses due to unexpected market price changes are unavoidable (except in the case of hedging).

Table 11.5 presents the simulated revaluation results of a two percentage point interest rate rise. Due to, amongst other things, the optionality embedded in credit loans and savings accounts, these effects would differ from a similar interest rate fall, since the effects are asymmetric. Obviously, the revaluation effects of the interest rate shock are large, dwarfing the effects on net interest income in Table 11.3. We will compare these effects below. The major impact of the interest rate rise on banks is the drop in market value of their assets. Although the fair value of their debt also falls significantly (which reflects a certain degree of hedging of interest rate risk), a large net loss remains, significant in terms of both profits and capital. This mirrors the fact that banks transform short money into long money. For insurers, the opposite is true: although the value of their investment portfolio declines, the reduction in the burden to meet their policy obligations dominates by far. This reflects that insurers transform short- or medium-term investment into long- or extremely long-term investment. These results indicate the significant diversification gains of a pro forma merger between banks and insurers with respect to a revaluation resulting from an enduring interest rate shock. This is best expressed in the last column of Table 11.5, where the shock effects on the pro forma FC are compared to the effects on banks. The joint revaluation effect for FCs is only 60 per cent of the revaluation effect for banks. Expressed in percentages of profit or capital, the diversification effect is even higher.

The diversification effect of revaluation is very strong due to the observed negative correlation for revaluations. Of course, the precise figures depend on the relative sizes of the 'merged' sectors and on the underlying assumptions. This is illustrated by the following sensitivity analysis. Until now, we have assumed 50 per cent profit sharing by policyholders. Were we to assume that all policyholders would share only one-third of the gains and profit on investment, the figures in parentheses in Table 11.5 would apply.[49] The diversification effect would be even stronger, illustrating the sensitivity of the results to this assumption.

Table 11.5   The revaluation effects of a two percentage point interest rate rise on the fair value balance sheets of banks, insurers and (pro forma) financial conglomerates

	Banks	Insurers	Financial conglomerates	FC compared to banks (index)
Profit in 2000[a]	17.5	7.7	25.2	
Capital and reserves, end 2000[a]	93	62	155	
Revaluation effect, billions of guilders	−32.7	13.7 (18.4)	−19.0 (−14.3)	0.58 (0.44)
Revaluation effect, in % of profit	−186.4	177.9 (238.4)	75.4 (−56.9)	0.40 (0.31)
Revaluation effect, in % of capital	−35.1	22.1 (29.6)	−12.3 (−9.3)	0.35 (0.26)

Notes:
Figures between parenthesis refer to 33 per cent instead of 50 per cent profit sharing by policyholders.
[a]   Billions of guilders.

The net interest income or accrual accounting effects of Table 11.3 and the revaluation or fair-value effects of Table 11.5 complement each other in the sense that they do not overlap. The additional net interest income would show up under each accounting regime, reflecting the higher income from new investment or from current investment but with adjusted interest rates, as well as the higher cost of new funding or current funding but with adjusted interests. So under the fair-value regime this effect should be added to the revaluation effect. Note that the revaluation effect appears immediately but is followed subsequently by gradual opposite moves in the value, so that the total effect fades away over time. This is similar to the behaviour of bond prices: they fall after an interest rate rise, but recover over time, up to the notional amount. Therefore, in the long run, only the (cumulative) net interest income effect remains.

Table 11.6 gives an overview of the various simulations. The first six columns are based on Tables 11.3, 11.4 and 11.5 and show the effect of a combined short- and long-term interest rate rise of two percentage points on net interest income (that is, the sum of simulations two and three). In the first year, a clear diversification effect occurs, as the effects are negatively correlated; in fact, the effects almost cancel each other out. In the subsequent years the diversification effect diminishes until in the final year the positively correlated long-term effect dominates, resulting in equal effects on banks and insurers in guilders. As observed above, the revaluations in bank and insurance balance sheet items show a strong diversification. The final column presents the marked-to-market effects of a 25 per cent fall in shares prices and the value of participations and subsidiaries. The respective losses for banks and insurers are positively correlated; the same would hold for gains from share price rises.

Of course, there is a limitless list of other shocks that could affect banks and insurers. Some probably have positively correlated effects on banks and insurers, such as higher wages, lower demand due to business cycle downturns, or lower real estate prices, and would thus contribute little to diversification. Other shocks are likely to have effects on banks and insurers that are uncorrelated and would therefore contribute more to diversification – such as losses from operational risk, unfavourable developments in lapses, mortality, longevity, morbidity and disability expectancies and tax rules with respect to life insurances or interest rates.[50] Another example would be that an increase in credit losses due to business cycle deterioration is likely to hurt banks much more than insurers.

The simulation model is based on many assumptions and the data used is not representative for all FCs, so the results should be evaluated with some caution. Nevertheless, the results provide ample evidence that part of the risks within an FC – in particularly, the short-term interest rate movements –

Table 11.6 Overview of interest rate and share price change effects

	Interest rate rise of 2 percentage points							Share price drop of 25%
Year:	1	2	3	4	5	Total	Revaluation[a]	
In billions of guilders								
Banks	−1.8	0.2	1.4	3.7	6.5	9.9	−32.5	−26.5
Insurers	2.1	3.7	4.8	5.6	6.4	22.7	13.7	−22.8
FC	0.3	3.9	6.2	9.3	12.9	32.6	−19.0	−49.3
In % of profit								
Banks	−11	1	8	21	38		−186.4	−151
Insurers	28	47	63	73	84		177.9	−295
FC	1	15	25	37	51		−75.4	−195

Note: [a]Figures refer to 50 per cent profit sharing by policyholder.

is negatively correlated and that the diversification effect of the combination of bank and insurance activities may be considerable, depending on the origin of changes and the employed accounting regime. This outcome is reassuring in the sense that this diversification gain compensates for increased risk of financial stability and contagion as discussed in the section on motivation for capital regulation of financial institutions.

Diversification Estimates from Market Data

Bank holding company literature

A useful literature, if we want to analyse the degree to which the risks in financial sector activities are interrelated, is the primarily American discussion as to what activities are permitted for bank holding companies.[51] The relative impact of mixing banking activities with various other kinds of activities has been discussed in depth and this discussion is nested in the more general one whether diversification is always a good thing for any company, to which the answer is often thought to be negative (cf. Berger and Ofek, 1995; Lamont and Polk, 2002).

Research can be categorized into studies that look at activities already permitted (Wall, 1987) and at 'forbidden' activities (Boyd, Graham and Hewitt, 1993).[52] Another distinction that can be drawn is between studies using market information and studies using book values (for example, Estrella, 2001, versus the work of Boyd and Graham, 1988). There is some debate as to whether accounting or market data provide the best measure of risk and return.[53] It is well known that accounting data show a smoothed picture of profits, partly because assets and liabilities are shown at historical cost rather than at market value. Stock prices, in contrast, quickly reflect all relevant information as it becomes known. However, equity price series show substantial volatility indicating that other factors than just developments relevant to the value of the firm itself are reflected. Some of the studies on hypothetical mergers have been criticized because the variability of profits has been used instead of the more appropriate probability of bankruptcy (Santos, 1998). Other studies use measures aggregated over industries, introducing an aggregation bias. Finally, it has been pointed out that a merger is more than just combining balance sheets. Following a merger, policies are very likely to be changed to take advantage of the new situation. In that case, pro forma hypothetical mergers would be less informative.

The conclusions reached are mixed. Life insurance seems to be unambiguously a good choice for banks looking for a reduction of risk. Diversification into real estate seems to generally increase risk but the strength of this result might be driven by particular sample selections. The effect of diversification into securities activities seems to be unclear, depending on method, period or definition. The only study using European data is Gully, Perraudin and Saporta (2001), and is different in the sense that the institution's risk is modelled in a bottom-up fashion, starting with the assets on the balance sheet of the banks and insurers.

Diversification: an empirical peek

The first question that comes to mind, if we want to look at whether or not there are possible diversification benefits, is: does a given stock move with those of its own sector or move more in line with the movements in the other sector? To analyse this we computed the correlations between all possible combinations of equity series, excluding combinations of two equal series, in each country, as shown in Table 11.7. We limit ourselves to within country analysis because we feel that differences in regulatory, tax, and institutional conditions between countries are too large to ignore.

Table 11.7   Median correlation of stock prices between the sectors, by country, 1990–2000

	France	Germany	Netherlands	UK	USA	Japan
Bank-bank	**0.53**	0.85	**0.86**	0.79	0.77	0.87
	(132)	(90)	(30)	(90)	(132)	(86)
Bank-ins.	0.54	0.71	0.92	**0.77**	**0.72**	**0.81**
	(210)	(180)	(36)	(160)	(264)	(240)
Ins.-ins.	0.73	**0.60**	0.94	0.83	0.85	0.85
	(64)	(72)	(6)	(56)	(110)	(132)

Note: The number in parentheses is the number of within country combinations available. The bold figures are the lowest correlations by country (column).

   The bold figures in Table 11.7 are the lowest correlations by country. Table 11.7 shows that in a number of countries (UK, USA and Japan) the correlations between sectors are as expected: those between banks and insurers are the lowest of all possible combinations. Diversification benefits would thus be the highest in mergers across sectors. Judging by Table 11.7, it is likely that French banks might attain the most diversification benefit within the banking (or any financial) sector. For the USA the results correspond to previous results (Estrella, 2001, p. 2373).

   Most of the larger banks and insurers in the sample are already well diversified and the deck is thus stacked against finding substantial diversification benefits. Smaller institutions generally operate largely in a single sector and should thus give us a better picture of sector risk. To see whether smaller

Table 11.8   *Median correlation of stock prices of small firms between the sectors, by country, 1990–2000*

	France	Germany	Netherlands	UK	USA	Japan
Bank-bank	0.43	0.79	0.94	**0.50**	0.75	**0.80**
	(20)	(20)	(2)	(20)	(20)	(20)
Bank-ins.	0.56	**0.61**	**0.92**	0.61	0.75	0.86
	(28)	(40)	(4)	(40)	(50)	(50)
Ins.-ins.	**0.07**	0.67	—	0.68	**0.70**	0.94
	(6)	(12)		(12)	(20)	(20)

Note: The number in parentheses is the number of within country combinations available. The bold figures are the lowest correlations by country (column).

institutions are indeed more likely to see benefits in merging, we split the sample in two using the median market capitalization (within country and sector) as an indicator variable. Table 11.8 shows the combinations involving just small firms.

Here, compared with Table 11.7, a different, rather erratic, picture emerges. However, the number of available observations in some countries, especially the Netherlands, is so low as to make the results somewhat fragile. The interesting – counterintuitive – results emerge that in most countries smaller institutions would benefit most from mergers with their own kind, contrary to the results shown in the previous table where cross-sector mergers looked most promising. Note that the correlations discussed are the correlations over the full sample period. These are more or less the 'going concern' correlations. Table 11.8 thus does not address issue that these correlations might increase significantly in times of stress as discussed above.

An option-pricing method
Following an approach similar to Estrella (2001) and Santomero and Chung (1992), we apply an option-pricing model to estimate the volatility of assets and a measure of the likelihood of failure of a firm.[54] Using the standard Black-Scholes (BS) model, we compare the likelihood of various pro forma combinations of firms. The model assumes that the market value of a firm's assets follows a stochastic process

$$dV_A + \mu V_A dt + \sigma_A V_A dz \qquad (11.1)$$

where V_A and dV_A are the firm's asset value and its change, μ is the firm's growth rate, σ_A the firm's asset volatility and dz is a Wiener process. A simplifying assumption in the BS model is that there is just a single class of both debt and equity. The market value of equity (V_E) and the market value of assets are related by

$$V_E = V_A\Phi(d_1) - e^{-rT}L\Phi(d_2) \qquad (11.2)$$

where Φ is the cumulative normal distribution, r denotes the risk free interest rate, T is the expiration date of the option, L stands for the firm's liabilities and

$$d_1 = \frac{\ln(V_A/L) + (r + \sigma_A^2/2)T}{\sigma_A\sqrt{T}} \qquad (11.2\ \text{cont.})$$

$$d_2 = d_1 - \sigma_A\sqrt{T}$$

In addition it can be shown that

$$\sigma_E = \frac{V_A}{V_E}\Phi(d_1)\sigma_A \qquad (11.3)$$

where σ_E is the volatility of equity. The market value of assets and the volatility of assets are not directly observable but are implied by the market price and its volatility. V_A and σ_A are found through solving (11.2) and (11.3) simultaneously by iterative imputations. Given equation (11.2) we can derive a function for the probability of failure. However, for the firms in our sample the probability of failure at short horizons are typically very small and thus analysing the argument in the distribution function of the failure equation, also known as the distance to default or z^*, is more fruitful

$$z^* = \frac{\ln(V_A/L) + (\mu - \sigma_A^2/2)T}{\sigma_A\sqrt{T}} \qquad (11.4)$$

z^* is the number of standard deviations that the firm is away from default. A standard assumption is that the leverage ratio, V_A/L, is constant over time. Firms, however, adjust their gearing as they approach default (Bliss, 2001, Crosbie and Bohn, 2002) and, unfortunately, this biases our measure in an opposite way.

To compute the measures of risk just discussed we need values for L, V_E, σ_E, μ, r, and T. Book values for liabilities (L) for the year 2000 are taken from Bankscope and ISIS databases, for banks and insurance companies, respectively. The value of equity, V_E, and equity prices are taken from Datastream and Bloomberg, running from 1990 to 2000. The volatility of equity prices, σ_E, is computed as the standard deviation of log price differences for each month, which is then annualized by multiplying by the square root of 12 (months). For μ, the expected rate of asset growth, we use the average yearly growth rate of the share price of each institution over the last five years.[55] The risk free rate, r, is the long-term government bond yield average of December 2000, taken from the IMF International Financial Statistics. T, the expiration date, is set to 12 months.[56] We include the largest 20 institutions by country, aiming at an equal split between insurers and banks, except for the Netherlands for which we took all the institutions available.

The results of the option-pricing model provide a fuller picture of risk. Next to the average return, μ, and its variability it estimates the variability of assets, as implied by market perceptions, and z^*, the markets' expectation of default. As discussed previously, z^* is an inverse measure of risk; higher values of z^* indicate lower risk. In Table 11.9 we show the risk and return characteristics of the firms in our sample.

Table 11.9   Risk and return characteristics by country and industry

Industry		France	Germany	Netherlands	UK	USA	Japan
Banks	z^*	**10.6730**	1.4719	**6.6638**	1.3644	0.2792	−1.2504
	σ_A	0.0100	0.0100	0.0600	0.1535	0.3010	0.1110
	σ_E	0.2331	0.2960	0.2852	0.3738	0.5102	0.3234
	μ	0.1077	0.0645	0.1611	0.1845	0.1800	−0.1374
	N	7	7	3	8	10	9
Insurance	z^*	5.6357	**2.9613**	0.6479	**3.4848**	3.5909	**−0.6002**
	σ_A	0.0355	0.0390	0.2690	0.0490	0.1325	0.2440
	σ_E	0.2057	0.2572	0.3739	0.3622	0.4142	0.3478
	μ	0.0877	0.0718	0.2481	0.0726	0.1700	−0.0740
	N	6	7	3	7	8	10

Note: μ is the median value of the average return by firm over the sample. σ_E is the annualized standard deviation of stock prices. σ_A is the estimated standard deviation of asset values implied by market values. N is the number of observations.

Table 11.9 clearly shows the decade-long decline in Japanese equity prices. Furthermore, banking is on average the more profitable activity in half of the countries. The fuller measure of risk, z^*, shows that banking is generally the more risky sector.

The next step in our analysis is the construction of pro forma mergers between the banks and insurers in our dataset. Again we limit ourselves to mergers within each country. To construct an observation of a merged bank we weigh the appropriate values by market capitalization (Table 11.10).

Looking at the z^* values, two groups can be discerned with regard to the pro forma mergers. On the one hand, we have the continental European

Table 11.10　　*The effects of pro forma mergers, weighted by market capitalization*

		France	Germany	Netherlands	UK	USA	Japan
Bank-bank	z^*	**31.9622**	**28.1148**	**15.6132**	−0.1368	1.7603	5.0692
	σ_A	0.0150	0.0110	0.0980	0.6820	0.3260	0.1100
	σ_E	0.2328	0.2789	0.2952	0.3882	0.5037	0.3528
	N	75	57	19	70	107	37
Bank-ins.	z^*	25.8278	27.3863	4.7246	2.4294	2.8081	4.8059
	σ_A	0.0215	0.0215	0.1910	0.4585	0.3140	0.1265
	σ_E	0.2235	0.2684	0.3279	0.3813	0.4617	0.3528
	N	104	126	28	124	218	130
Ins.-ins.	z^*	13.9754	8.7715	1.8017	**4.7920**	**6.4965**	**11.4867**
	σ_A	0.0335	0.0820	0.2925	0.3240	0.2990	0.1435
	σ_E	0.2057	0.2572	0.3739	0.3622	0.4147	0.3634
	N	30	51	6	42	86	86

Note: σ_E is the annualized standard deviation of stock prices. σ_A is the estimated standard deviation of asset values implied by market values volatility. All variables are median values. N is the number of observations.

countries France, Germany and the Netherlands, where the combination of just insurers leads to the lowest z^* values, implying the largest probability of default. On the other hand, we find the Anglo-Saxon countries and Japan, where the combination of just banks leads to the lowest z^*.

Again, we split the sample into smaller and larger firms and construct fictitious combinations. The results in Table 11.11 seem to suggest that hypothetical mergers of just small banks are relatively more risky than their insurance counterparts.

What do these results imply for regulatory or economic capital? The first observation is that there is no clear international pattern in the various results. Depending on the particular country and sectors involved in the pro forma merger, merges could reduce or increase risk. A second observation is that some of the more robust USA findings are difficult to replicate using the current sample. The banks and insurance companies in our sample are the large and hence more diversified firms. The more fragmented USA firms are more focused and are thus more likely to be less than perfectly correlated, leading to diversification gains for at least one of the prospective merger candidates. Since the FCs in our analyses are already highly diversified, gains are likely to be less impressive. Nevertheless, some mergers would yield diversification gains although, again, the pattern of these gains would differ from country to country.

Table 11.11 The effects of pro forma mergers of small firms, weighted by market capitalization

		France	Germany	UK	USA	Japan
Bank-bank	z^*	33.2452	15.8618	3.5676	3.1307	1.8889
	σ_A	0.0230	0.0100	0.3815	0.2160	0.0530
	σ_E	0.1075	0.1162	0.4600	0.5166	0.3528
	N	15	18	18	18	15
Bank-ins.	z^*	**64.1046**	67.5561	6.0584	6.5103	4.7268
	σ_A	0.0245	0.0130	0.3385	0.2345	0.1220
	σ_E	0.1873	0.1193	0.4469	0.5100	0.3322
	N	24	35	38	50	44
Ins.-ins.	z^*	55.1670	**235.3528**	**13.3447**	**8.3980**	**24.8102**
	σ_A	0.0205	0.0160	0.2820	0.1725	0.1285
	σ_E	0.1880	0.2489	0.4204	0.4887	0.2699
	N	6	8	12	18	20

Note: σ_E is the annualized standard deviation of stock prices. σ_A is the estimated standard deviation of asset values implied by market values and volatility. All variables are median values. N is the number of observations. The Netherlands is not included due to lack of observations.

SUPERVISORS' VIEW ON ECONOMIC CAPITAL

As mentioned above, economic capital is the buffer that a financial institution itself considers as necessary to absorb unexpected losses, given its risk profile, controls and degree of risk aversion. One of the tools for measuring the risks of a financial institution and determining the level of economic capital is an economic capital model. It is beyond the scope of this chapter to give a detailed outline of the requirements these models should meet. In this section we will, however, briefly discuss the merit and possible shortcomings of economic capital (models) for supervisors.

Since economic capital models can play an important role as an instrument for firm-wide risk management, their development should be encouraged strongly. However, at the present stage of developments, the existing models have several shortcomings. The measurement of some of the risk types, as distinguished in Table 11.2, is well developed, but the measurement of many other risk types is still in its infancy. In most cases this is due to insufficiencies in the data. For some areas this problem will solve itself over time, as data continue to be collected and stored and measurement techniques are developed further. For other areas, however, the problem of data inadequacy will probably persist, as many relevant phenomena, such as major catastro-phes, large-scale frauds and defaults of high-rated corporates, occur only rarely. With respect to certain risk types, lack of data will hinder the correct measurement of correlations. In addition to these practical difficulties, there are several fundamental problems, in particular regarding cross-sector risk measurement, such as the issue of choosing a unit for risk measurement and an appropriate time horizon. Yet, despite these inadequacies, the ECM is the most promising tool for FCs to measure and manage their firm-wide risk. Besides, ECMs can be used for commercial purposes, in particular, to meas-ure the (risk-adjusted return) performance of the various units in the FC and to allocate economic capital in order to increase shareholder value.

The supervisor might employ ECMs in a number of ways. First, an FCs ECM can be used to increase the knowledge and understanding of the risk profile of a supervised financial institution. Particularly under the second pillar of Basle II, where banks are required to have instruments in place to assess the adequacy of their (economic) capital, given their particular risk profile. Secondly, the ECM can be utilized to evaluate whether the current (simple sum) minimum capital requirements for FCs are adequate and, espe-cially, to assess what the level III type diversification is in cross-section institutions. One might even consider whether – in the distant future – an ECM could be used by financial institutions to calculate their minimum required capital, as they already do for market risk.

Both supervisory uses make strong demands on an ECM. As a central requirement, the financial institution should be able to convince the supervi-sor that the ECM is able to measure all material risk accurately and reliably. As has been argued above, this may currently be the case for some risk types, but it is not universally true, and hence not for the model as a whole. Nevertheless, ECMs might be acceptable as long as they are the best avail-able tool, as is probably the case for Pillar II risk assessment. It is worth mentioning that the general problem of model validation might be rather similar for FCs and for supervisors. An FC's central risk management unit may find itself facing the situation where a large number of legal entities provide building blocks for the ECM (describing their risk levels), while at the same time these entities may have incentives to underestimate their risks. Similarly the supervisor could encounter institutions that might have stimuli to underrate their own riskiness.

For the second supervisory goal – the assessment of the current mini-mum required capital – ECMs have a further shortcoming as they ignore risks, such as contagion risk, that are important for the supervisor. Here a difference between economic capital (optimized in the eyes of the firm's management) and regulatory capital (minimum requirement as seen by the supervisors) emerges. In theory, supervisors would be able to compute the magnitude and likelihood of all ignored risks and social costs. Knowing the expected value, the supervisor would then be able to charge an institution accordingly, either through the formation of a fund or requiring the allocation of some risk-bearing capital. The current state of risk measurement, however, has not yet attained a level that would make the practical implementation of this theoretical exercise feasible.

A second issue in this respect is the risk aversion of a supervisor relative to that of – the management of – an institution. In all likelihood, both parties will have divergent perceptions of risks. It is also common for supervisors to stress prudence and, if there is model uncertainty, an additional capital surcharge is often added. Hence we may expect that an economic capital model constructed from a number of sub-models (of, for example, market risk, credit risk, and so on) may have several representations of 'prudence' concealed in its inner working. Care should be taken that such accumulation does not result in a too high a minimum requirement.

A third issue is that supervisors will be inclined to focus on the parameter values used to represent conditions in periods of stress. In other words, a supervisor will place more weight on the role of an ECM as a risk measurement system under all circumstances than on the other functions of an ECM (pricing and management fees, for example).

SUMMARY AND CONCLUSIONS

Economic capital models can improve firm-wide risk management substantially, particularly in mixed conglomerates, and their development and use should therefore be strongly encouraged. However, at the present stage of development, such models have a number of serious shortcomings, most of them owing to lack of data. Although ECMs can be useful for some regulatory purposes, such as the 'supervisory review', we conclude that their immaturity and insufficient validation possibilities prohibits their use in a wider regulatory context. This holds true especially for the assessment of the adequate minimum required capital for cross-sector FCs. The main determinant of a FC's optimal regulatory capital is the correlation or diversification of risk across sectors. Neither ECMs nor other measurement instruments provide convincing results regarding the degree of diversification. This chapter addresses this issue by presenting two empirical analyses, which are quite different and therefore complement each other. The first analysis is based on an asset and liability model and identifies diversification effects for FCs under various shocks. The diversification effects appear to be very strong for some scenarios, particularly when the full fair-value effects are taken into account, but rather weak for other shocks. The second investigation employs correlations across share prices and option models and finds that diversification occurs not only when banks and insurers merge, but also when banks are combined with other banks or insurers with insurers. The correlations between share prices make clear that, except for the Netherlands, diversification effects for FCs are substantially larger than found by OWC (5 to 10 per cent). The option model suggests that FCs have lower default probabilities than separate bank or insurance firms. A caveat applies as the model estimated is relatively stylised. On the whole, however, empirical evidence reveals that diversification effects are substantial and possibly somewhat larger than suggested by OWC. This is important information for regulatory purposes, but insufficient for any conclusions regarding minimum capital requirements as far as deviating from the current simple sum. After all, these studies ignore the non-negligible additional risk run by FCs, namely contagion risk, regulatory arbitrage and cross-sector and TBTF moral hazard risks.

APPENDIX: A SIMPLE ALM SIMULATION MODEL

The ALM simulation model is based on expanded versions of the balance sheets in Table 11.12.

Table 11.12   Aggregated balance sheets of Dutch banks and insurance firms (domestic, 2000)

Banks		Life insurance firms	
Assets	Billions	Assets	Billions
Cash	19	Deposits	9
Short-dated government paper	7	Mortgage loans	62
Banks	334	Other loans	55
Loans and advances to government	11	Bonds	93
Loans and advances to private sector	999	Shares	78
Interest-bearing securities	209	Investment in affiliated undertakings	12
Shares	53	Investment in land and buildings	28
Participations	53	Other financial investment	12
Property and equipment	22	Investment for policyholders' own risk[a]	156
Other assets	12	Debtors	19
Prepayment and accrual income	32	Other assets	6
Total	1751	Prepayment and accrual income	10
		Total	540
Liabilities		Liabilities	
Banks	485		
Savings accounts	309	Total debt	46
Other funds entrusted	470	Other liabilities	16
Debt securities	179	Accrual and deferred income	9
Other liabilities	81	Capital and reserves	62
Accrual and deferred income	40	Technical provisions	
Subordinated liabilities	37	Life insurance policies	262
Other provisions, capital and reserves	150	'Own risk' life insurance policies[a]	145
Total	1751	Total	540

Note: [a]The risk of investment is borne by the life insurance policyholders.

In addition, the model contains the following interest rate and discount equations. The interest rate equations are based on, among others, Bikker et al. (1994), van Els and Vlaar (1996) and DNB (2000), where necessary adjusted for the introduction of the euro. Some of the interest rates are base rates, which may be liable to surcharges, depending on, for example, credit risk.

Interest rate equations:[57] · *Describing:*

$rd_t = 0.8\, rd_{t-1} + 0.15\,(0.3\, rs_t - 0.1\, rs_{t-1})$ — Demand deposits

$rsa_t = rsa_{t-1} + 0.25\,(0.33\,(rs_t - rs_{t-1})$ — Savings accounts < 10.000 Dfl
$\qquad + 0.67\,(rl_t - rl_{t-1})$

$rsa1_t = rsa1_{t-1} + 0.5\,(0.33\,(rs_t - rs_{t-1})$ — Savings accounts > 10.000 Dfl
$\qquad + 0.67\,(rl_t - rl_{t-1})$

$rt_t = 0.5\,(rs_t + rl_t)$ — Time deposits

$rb_t = 0.8\, rl_t + 0.2\, rs_t$ — Bank debt

$rl_t = 0.5\, rl_{t-1} + 0.5\, rs_t + 0.5$ — Long-term interest rate

$rm_t = rl_t + 1$ — Mortgages

$rl_t^* = 0.02\, rl_t + 0.21\, rl_{t-1} + 0.17\, rl_{t-2}$ — Distributed lag rl
$\qquad + 0.15\, rl_{t-3} + 0.13\, rl_{t-4} + 0.11\, rl_{t-5}$
$\qquad + 0.09\, rl_{t-6} + 0.07\, rl_{t-7} + 0.05\, rl_{t-8}$

$rt_t^* = 0.2\, rt_t + 0.4\, rt_{t-1} + 0.3\, rt_{t-2} + 0.1\, rt_{t-3}$ — Distributed lag rt

$rsa_t^* = 0.5\,(rsa_t + rsa_{t-1})$ — Distributed lag rsa

$rsa1_t^* = 0.5\,(rsal_t + rsal_{t-1})$ — Distributed lag rsa1

$ro_t^* = 0.1\, rl_t + 0.3\, rl_{t-1} + 0.2\, rl_{t-2}$ — Distributed lag of government
$\qquad + 0.15\, rl_{t-3} + 0.15\, rl_{t-4} + 0.1\, rl_{t-5}$ — bonds

$rh_t^* = ro_t^* + 1$ — Distributed lag rh

$rb_t^* = 0.8\, rl_t^* + 0.2\, rs_t$ — Distributed lag rb

Discount equations:

$D(T) = \Sigma_{t=1,\dots,T}\,(w(i)\, r\,\{(1 - 1/(1 + d)t)/d$ — Weighted sum of discounts for
$\qquad + 100/(1 + d)t\}$ — various T's and weighting
schemes w(i). The weighting
scheme is parameterized on
the interest rate risk reports
submitted to DNB

$D(40) = \Sigma_{t=1,\dots,40}\,((41 - t)/82)\, r\,\{(1 - 1/$ — Weighted sum of discounts for
$\qquad (1 + d)t)/d + 100/(1 + d)t\}$ — technical provisions for life
policyholders

NOTES

1. De Nederlandsche Bank, Directorate Supervision, Section Banking and Supervisory Strategies, PO Box 98, 1000 AB Amsterdam. E-mail addresses: j.a.bikker@dnb.nl and
i.p.p.van.lelyveld@dnb.nl. The views expressed in this chapter are those of the authors
and not necessarily those of De Nederlandsche Bank. The authors are grateful to R.T.A.
de Haas, K.H.W. Knot, G.C.M. Siegelaer and H.L.T. Wanders for valuable comment, R.
Lammers for essential information and D. van den Kommer for excellent research assistance.
2. The International Accounting Standards Board (IASB) is developing an international
accounting standard. See IAA (2002) for comments.

3.   Llewellyn (1999) distinguishes between regulation (setting specific rules), monitoring (observing compliance) and supervision (general observations of bank behaviour).
4.   The fiercest opponents to government regulation can be found in the Free Banking School. See for instance Dowd (1994), Rolnick and Weber (1984) and White (1984). More recent criticism can be found in Benston and Kaufman (1996) and Benston (2000).
5.   See Allen and Herring (2001), Table I, for a discussion of additional motives, including measures employed.
6.   Pension funds are not yet subsidiaries of FCs, but this may change in the future. Their position with respect to supervision is similar to that of insurers.
7.   Reflecting continental European practice, we consider FCs which combine universal banking and insurance activities and not FCs which combine banking and securities activities, as is more common in Anglo-Saxon countries.
8.   For that reason, the new Basel capital accord introduces a set of disclosure requirements to encourage greater transparency and reduce uncertainty.
9.   Seminal contributions in this area are Bryant (1980) and Diamond and Dybvig (1983).
10. For an overview, see Garcia (2000). Deposits held by households in the Netherlands amount to €190 billion, that is 54 per cent of all deposits held by the private and government sector. Note that this insurance scheme only covers deposits held by bank offices in the Netherlands.
11. For instance, in the Netherlands, all deposits are covered, not only the deposits which are directly demandable and hence contribute to the bank-run risk, but also non-demandable liabilities such as fixed long-term time deposits. Moreover, securities in trust are also covered to some extent.
12. Unless the deposit insurance is based on risk sensitive premiums, as is the objective in a growing number of countries (Garcia, 2000).
13   Some argue that financial firms do not directly target a certain probability of default (PD) level but try to avoid a downgrade during a severe downturn. Hence, one can not draw the conclusion that an AA rating reflects the management's target of, at the worst, only one default in 1000 years.
14. Supervision of FCs is based on the so-called silo plus approach, as additional rules – not directly regarding capital requirements – apply for FCs.
15. An integrated capital requirement regime for FCs would also raise practical problems, as supervision of insurance firms is based on host country control, whereas supervision of banks is based on home country control. As capital requirements of insurance firms are not based on an international agreement (such as the Basel Accord for banks), domestic and foreign insurance divisions face different regulatory treatment.
16. See Rule (2001) for a description of the various channels that are employed.
17. Note that there are limits to shifting of surplus capital. For instance, a bank in the Netherlands needs a vvgb (declaration of no objection) by the supervisor to distribute a supernormal dividend to the holding company.
18. This is an oversimplified result because it is assumed that risk hedging is costless. More importantly, the whole balance sheet is hedgeable. The very existence of intermediaries, however, is explained in the second section by informational asymmetries, meaning that they specialize in products that are opaque and thus not easily traded, let alone hedged.
19. With regard to (2): in a credit crunch, reduced bank capital leads to substantial declines in lending volumes, implying that capital matters for lending. However, if a reduction in bank capital is only symptomatic of a bad lending environment, then falling lending volume could reflect a scarcity of good lending opportunities instead of changing hurdle rates.
20. M is the market index, i the value of project i and σ_M and σ_i their respective standard deviations.
21. Note that the hurdle rate is only one criterion. Activities should also be judged on their value for other business lines and future prospects.
22. The time horizon is the period which is chosen to investigate the potential unexpected loss of a portfolio.
23. As noted by Cumming and Hirtle (2001, p. 11), who also note that 'other potential

definitions of risk could involve pure volatility measures, such as standard deviations of earnings or economic value, or sensitivity measures that capture the deviations of earnings or economic value with respect to particular risk factors, such as the "value of a basis point"'.

24.   OWC finds, after an analysis of 'normal times' that the correlation between market and credit risk is 0.8. For more general studies of non-crisis cross-asset interdependency, see, for example, Longin and Solnik (1995), Fleming, Kirby and Ostdiek (1998), and Bodart and Reding (1999).

25.   Using market rates does not guarantee a clear answer because of for instance the distortions caused by tax incentives. Moreover, does the market perceive that a conglomerate can cash in on the (risk) benefits of conglomeration? If risk is not centrally managed, there are still benefits from scope and scale but not a reduction in risk. An alternative source of information, not pursued here, could be to use accounting data and for instance measure to what degree the results of the banking and insurance part in a financial conglomerate are related.

26.   See De Bandt and Hartmann (2001) for an excellent survey of the financial market crises and contagion literature.

27.   A related literature examines whether currency crises are contagious as in for instance Eichengreen, Rose and Wyplosz (1996). Finally, Borio and McCauly (1996) study bond market spill-overs in volatile periods.

28.   In the Netherlands, the aggregated balance sheet total of P&C insurers in 2000 is only 80 billion guilders against 541 billion guilders for life insurers, where net premium income has a similar size (36.5 versus 52.5 billion guilders) (PVK, 2001a; 2001b).

29.   That is uncorrelated with interest rate and market price risk, central in these analysis, as well as credit risk, life risk and the operational and business risk banks and insurers run.

30.   Bank supervision is based on home control, whereas insurance supervision is based on host control. Therefore banks publish consolidated figures, including domestic and foreign activities, whereas (Dutch) insurance firms only publish domestic figures.

31.   Subsidiaries are investments with control, but not necessary *full* control.

32.   EU Member States require this new regime for all banks.

33.   The difference between the actual interest rate at the moment of the sale and the 'calculation rate' 3 per cent, which determines the insured nominal amount (endowment insurance or annuity) can be used for a discount off the single premium insurance policy or for a rise of the guaranteed expiration benefit.

34.   These changes in net interest income are identical to those in a fair-value accounting regime. The latter regime also considers revaluation effects.

35.   We assume that the long-term rate of the euro depends in part on its short-term rate.

36.   Which does not effect the short-term rate.

37.   The base line scenario consists of imaginary model predictions for 2001–05 for unchanged balance sheet items in an environment without (new) shocks. This base line scenario shows changes in the interest rates due to the dynamic structure of the various interest equations.

38.   Banks can adjust the allocation of their asset and the composition of their funding, whereas customers can reduce their lending and hold more or less monies on deposits. However, the simulations use balance sheet items, which are constant over time.

39.   By approximation, the changed yield curve slope simulation is equal to the third shock minus the second one, both divided by two.

40.   In fact, the aggregated balance sheets of banks and insurers are added together.

41.   This index is less meaningful where the denominator – change in bank profits – is close to zero, as for the fourth and fifth year in the first row. For similar failures, an alternative index – changes in profits of FCs as shares of those of *insurers* – would be less useful.

42.   This can be illustrated as follows, assuming that x and y are stochasts with zero expectation; var $(\alpha x + (1 - \alpha) y) = \alpha^2$ var $(x) + (1 - \alpha)^2$ var $(y) + 2 \alpha (1 - \alpha) \rho \sqrt{(\text{var}(x) \text{var}(y))}$. For, say, $\alpha = 0,5$, and var $(x) = $ var (y), this implies var $((x + y)/2) = 0,5 (1 + \rho)$ var $(x) <$ var (x), where the inequality holds, as long as $\rho < 1$. For $\rho = 0$, the variance of the average is half the variance of x or y. In our case, $\alpha = p/(p + q)$ stands for the share of bank profits in the FC profits, $(1 - \alpha) = q/(p + q)$ for the share of insurance profits, $x = X/p$ is the profit

shock of banks and y = Y/q stands for the profit shock of insurers (p and q are profits of banks and insurers, respectively, and X and Y are net interest income shocks of banks and insurers, respectively). Thus a linear combination of shocks has a lower variance than its components (the more so the lower ρ is), and hence, given the zero expectations of x and y, that, in general, it is *probable* that this combination is closer to zero than its components, and thus the index below 1.

43. An alternative view is that financial conglomerates harm financial stability, as banks can be dragged down by severe problems of insurers.
44. Comparing the lower interest rate of an existing bond with the higher interest rate of a newly emitted bond.
45. Other counterparties do not have these options, for instance, because (i) they cannot find another bank willing to lend, (ii) their creditworthiness has declined since the loan was granted, or (iii) a penalty clause applies (as in the case of mortgages).
46. Which is in line with the assumed duration of these accounts in the interest rate risk reports of banks.
47. 'Interest rate discounts' and 'return guarantees' for policyholders are not taken into account as they are fixed. We ignore optionality in the policy portfolio, in particular, the possibility to surrender. In general, surrender is not profitable, as the insurers discount the surrender value and its tax treatment may be unfavourable.
48. This reduction does not apply to technical provision for life insurance reserve for those policies, where policyholders bear the risk of the related investment themselves.
49. Alternatively we could assume that half of the policyholders would collect two-thirds of the related gains on investment.
50. There may be negative correlation and stronger diversification when unfavourable tax rule changes for life insurance products cause a shift from investment in these products towards savings.
51. This debate was especially relevant in the run-up to the abolition of the Glass-Steagall Act (see Kwan and Laderman, 1999). The literature is discussed in Laderman (2000). Contributions are for instance Boyd and Graham (1988), Boyd, Graham and Hewitt (1993), Estrella (2001), Gully, Perraudin and Saporta (2001), Kwan and Laderman (1999), Kwast (1989), Lown et al. (2000) and Santomero and Chung (1992).
52. See Boyd, Graham and Hewitt (1993) for an overview of many of the relevant papers.
53. Where the standard measure of risk used is volatility. See Harrison and Kreps (1979) for alternative measures of risk.
54. See Crosbie and Bohn (2002, p. 14 and onward) or Hull (2000, ch. 11) for derivation and discussion of this kind of model. An alternative route would be to recast the problem using a different type of option, such as f.i. a barrier-option, along the lines of Avellaneda and Zhu (2002). Ritchken, et al. (1993) find a barrier-option framework to be useful for explaining the behaviour of bank equity prices.
55. Admittedly this is not the most forward looking proxy. We have computed other variants (namely, the risk free rate, supplemented with an equity premium). The results are not very sensitive to this assumption. See also formula (4).
56. We ran the estimations for T = 18 and 24 months with qualitatively similar results.
57. An n-year lag is denoted by the subscripted t–n. The short rate and the long rate are rs and rl, respectively.

REFERENCES

Allen, F. and R. Herring (2001), 'Banking regulation versus securities market regulation' Working Paper, Wharton University, 01/29.
Avellaneda, M. and J. Zhu (2002), 'Distance to default', *RISK*, **15**, 125–9.
BCBS (2001), 'The new Basle Capital Accord, second consultative document?', Basle, Bank for International Settlements.

Benston, G.J. (2000), 'Is government regulation of banks necessary?', *Journal of Financial Services Research*, **18**, 185–202.

Benston, G.J. and G.G. Kaufman (1996), 'The appropriate role of bank regulation', *Economic Journal*, **106**, 688–97.

Berger, P.G. and E. Ofek (1995), 'Diversification's effect on firm value', *Journal of Financial Economics*, **37**, 39–65.

Bikker, J.A. (2000), 'Kredietrisicomodellen: een nieuw instrument voor risicobeheer' (in Dutch: Credit risk models: a new instrument for risk management), *Risico & Rendement*, **28**, 1–25.

Bikker, J.A. and A.P. Huijser (2001), 'De opmars van de interne ratings (I en II)' (in Dutch: 'Basle II: the advance of interne ratings (I & II)'), *Bank- en Effectenbedrijf*, **50**, 10–13 March, 11–14 April.

Bikker, J.A., W.C. Boeschoten, G.J. de Bondt, J.W.D. Bos, I.T. van den Doel and P.J.A. van Els (1994), 'Euromon: een macro-economisch model voor de Europese Unie' (in Dutch: 'Euromon: a macro-economic model for the European Union'), De Nederlandsche Bank Research Series WO&E No. 416.

Bliss, R. (2001), 'The pitfalls in inferring risk from financial market data', Federal Reserve Bank of Chicago, Working Paper.

Bodart, V. and P. Reding (1999), 'Exchange rate regime, volatility and international correlations on bond and stock markets', *Journal of International Money and Finance*, **18**, 133–51.

Borio, C.E.V. and R.N. McCauly (1996), 'The economics of recent bond yield volatility', BIS Economic Paper, 45.

Boyd, J.H. and S.L. Graham (1988), 'The profitability and risk effects of allowing bank holding companies to merge with other financial firms: a simulation study', *Federal Reserve Bank of Minneapolis Quarterly Review*, **12**, 3–20.

Boyd, J.H., S.L. Graham and R.S. Hewitt (1993), 'Bank holding company mergers with nonbank financial firms: effects on the risk of failure', *Journal of Banking & Finance*, **17**, 43–63.

Bryant, J. (1980), 'A model of reserves, bank runs, and deposit insurance', *Journal of Banking & Finance*, **4**, 335–44.

Chatterjee, S., M.H. Lubatkin and W.S. Schulze (1999), 'Towards a strategic theory of risk premium: moving beyond CAPM', *Academy of Management Review*, **4**, 556–67.

Chen, Y. (1999), 'Banking panics: the role of the first-come, first-served rule and information externalities', *Journal of Political Economy*, **107**, 946–68.

Crosbie, P.J. and J.R. Bohn (2002), 'Modelling default risk', KMV Corporation White Paper.

Cumming, C.M. and B.J. Hirtle (2001), 'The challenges of risk management in diversified financial companies', *Federal Reserve Bank of New York Economic Policy Review*, **7**, 1–17.

De Bandt, O. and P. Hartmann (2001), 'Systemic risk: a survey', CEPR Discussion Paper Series, 2634.

Diamond, D.W. and P.H. Dybvig (1983), 'Bank runs, deposit insurance, and liquidity', *Journal of Political Economy*, **91**, 401–19.

DNB (2000), *Euromon: The Netherlandsche Bank's Multi-Country Model for Policy Analysis in Europe*, Amsterdam: De Nederlandsche Bank/NIBE-SVV, Monetaire Monografieën 19.

Dowd, K. (1994), 'Competitive banking, bankers' clubs, and bank regulation', *Journal of Money, Credit & Banking*, **26**, 289–308.

Eichengreen, B., A.K. Rose and C. Wyplosz (1996), *Contagious Currency Crises*, Berkeley: University of California, Graduate Institute of International Studies.

Estrella, A. (2001), 'Mixing and matching: prospective financial sector mergers and market valuation', *Journal of Banking & Finance*, **25**, 2367–92.

Fleming, J., C. Kirby and B. Ostdiek (1998), 'Information and volatility linkages in the stock, bond, and money markets', *Journal of Financial Economics*, **49**, 111–37.

Froot, K.A. and J.C. Stein (1998), 'Risk management, capital budgeting, and capital structure policy for financial institutions: an integrated approach', *Journal of Financial Economics*, **47**, 55–82.

Froot, K.A., D.S. Scharfstein and J.C. Stein (1993), 'Risk management: coordinating corporate investment and financing policies', *Journal of Finance*, **48**, 1629–58.

Garcia, G.G.H. (2000), 'Deposit insurance: a survey of actual and best practices', International Monetary Fund Occasional Paper, 197.

Gully, B., W. Perraudin and V. Saporta (2001), *Capital Requirements for Combined Banking and Insurance Activities*, London: Bank of England.

Harrison, J.M. and D.M. Kreps (1979), 'Call options and the risk of underlying securities', *Journal of Financial Economics*, **13**, 425–34.

Hull, J.C. (2000), *Options, Futures, & Other Derivatives*, Upper Saddle River, NJ: Prentice Hall.

IAA (2002), 'Report of solvency working party: prepared for IAA insurance regulation committee', International Actuarial Association, February.

Kwan, S.H. and E.S. Laderman (1999), 'On the portfolio effects of financial convergence: a review of the literature', *Federal Reserve Bank of San Francisco Economic Review*, **2**, 18–31.

Kwast, M.L. (1989), 'The impact of underwriting and dealing on bank returns and risks', *Journal of Banking & Finance*, **13**, 101–25.

Laderman, E.S. (2000), 'The potential diversification and failure reduction benefits of bank expansion into nonbanking activities', Federal Reserve Bank of San Francisco Working Paper, 2000–01.

Lamont, O.A. and C. Polk (2002), 'Does diversification destroy value? Evidence from the industry shocks', *Journal of Financial Economics*, **63**, 51–77.

Leland, H.E. (1998), 'Agency costs, risk management, and capital structure', *Journal of Finance*, **53**, 1213–43.

Llewellyn, D.T. (1999), 'The economic rationale for financial regulation', FSA Occasional Paper Series, 1.

Longin, F. and B. Solnik (1995), 'Is the correlation in international equity returns constant: 1960–1990?', *Journal of International Money and Finance*, **14**, 3–26.

Lown, C.S., C.L. Osler, P.E. Strahan and A. Sufi (2000), 'The changing landscape of the financial services industry: what lies ahead?', *Federal Reserve Bank of New York Economic Policy Review*, **6**, 39–55.

Matten, C. (2000), *Managing Bank Capital*, Chichester: John Wiley and Sons.

Morrison, A.D. (2001), 'The economics of capital regulation in financial conglomerates', Working Paper.

Myers, S.C. and N.S. Majluf (1984), 'Corporate financing and investment decisions when firms have information that investors do not have', *Journal of Financial Economics*, **13**, 187–221.

OWC (2001), *Study on the Risk Profile and Capital Adequacy of Financial Conglomerates*, London: Oliver, Wyman and Company.

PVK (2001a), *Financiële gegevens levensverzekeraars 2000* (in Dutch: Financial Data of Life Insurance Firms), Apeldoorn: Pensioen- & Verzekeringskamer.

PVK (2001b), *Financiële gegevens schadeverzekeraars 2000* (in Dutch: Financial data of property and casualty insurance firms), Apeldoorn: Pensioen- & Verzekeringskamer.
Ritchken, P., J.B. Thomson, R.P. DeGennaro and A. Li (1993), 'On flexibility, capital structure and investment decisions for the insured bank', *Journal of Banking & Finance*, **17**, 1133–46.
Robinson, G. (2001), 'The destructive power of best practice', *RISK*, September, 123–5.
Rolnick, A.J. and W.E. Weber (1984), 'The causes of free bank failures', *Journal of Monetary Economics*, **14**, 267–91.
Rule, D. (2001), 'Risk transfer between banks, insurance companies and capital markets: an overview', *Financial Stability Review*, Bank of England, December, 137–59.
Santomero, A.M. and E.J. Chung (1992), *Evidence in Support of Broader Bank Powers*, New York: New York University, Salomon Centre.
Santos, J.A.C. (1998), 'Commercial banks in the securities business: a review', *Journal of Financial Services Research*, **14**, 35–60.
Van Els, P.J.A. and P.J.G. Vlaar (1996), *Morkmon III: een geactualiseerde versie van het macro-economische beleidsmodel van de Nederlandsche Bank* (in Dutch: Morkmon III: An Updated Version of the Macro-economic Policy Model of De Nederlandsche Bank), De Nederlandsche Bank Research Series WO&E No. 471, Amsterdam: De Nederlandsche Bank.
Wall, L.D. (1987), 'Has bank holding companies' diversification affected their risk of failure?', *Journal of Economics and Business*, **39**, 313–26.
White, L.H. (1984), *Free Banking in Britain: Theory, Experience, and Debate, 1800–1845*, Cambridge: Cambridge University Press.

COMMENT ON 'ECONOMIC VERSUS REGULATORY CAPITAL FOR FINANCIAL CONGLOMERATES'

Gaston Siegelaer

The paper 'Economic versus regulatory capital for financial conglomerates' by Jaap Bikker and Iman van Lelyveld discusses some issues that have yet to be resolved by regulators and supervisors. Therefore, I consider the paper very valuable in the way it stimulates further thinking and discussion. The main theme of the paper is the question as to what level of regulatory capital should apply to a financial conglomerate as a whole compared to the sum of the capital requirements that apply to the banks and insurance companies that are part of the financial conglomerate.

Since a decade, regulators and supervisors in the Netherlands have paid attention to supervision on financial conglomerates, but the regulatory discussion has gained momentum in the past few years. While the co-ordination of supervision for the constituent parts of a financial conglomerate has been regulated, it is precisely this question about (additional) capital requirements at holding company level that is being debated.

What makes financial conglomerates so special in terms of capital requirements on holding company level? Or to put in a different way: why is a financial conglomerate different from the sum of its parts? The answer is twofold.

First, it can be argued that there is room for risk diversification across the constituent licensed parts of the financial conglomerate. Following this line of reasoning, the amount of capital at holding company level should not necessarily be at least equal to the sum of the capital requirements of the constituent licensed parts, but could be lower, depending on the effective level of risk diversification. Little wonder that this argument is advocated by the financial industry.

The second aspect that makes a financial conglomerate different from the sum of its parts, is contagion risk across the constituent parts. I will elaborate on both aspects.

Risk Diversification

What are the main determinants of risk diversification within a financial conglomerate? The scope of the paper is limited to the impact of interest rate changes and share price changes, so let us focus on these risk drivers. First, consider the impact of interest rate changes on a bank's or an insurer's balance sheet. The duration mismatch between the asset side and the liability side of the balance sheet determines the level of interest rate

sensitivity. In this respect, banks and insurers typically show opposite exposures. Banks suffer from interest rate increases, as their assets have
longer maturities than their liabilities. Life insurers profit from interest rate
increases, as their liabilities have longer maturities than their assets. The
paper gives a quantification of the interest rate sensitivity using different
scenarios. The impact of interest rate changes on a fictitious financial conglomerate, consisting of a bank and a life insurer, is modelled. This combined
impact is determined by two factors: (1) the duration mismatch of the bank
relative to the duration mismatch of the insurer; and (2) the weights of the
bank's equity relative to the insurer's equity on the combined balance sheet.
   A numerical example, excerpted from Table 11.5 from the paper, will give
some insight. We calculate the modified duration for a bank's equity on the
balance sheet and for an insurer's equity on the balance sheet as approxi-
mated by the formula $- (\Delta E/E)/\Delta r$, where $(\Delta E/E)$ is the percentage change in
equity due to the interest rate change Δr. The capital and reserves as mentioned in Table 11.5 are regarded as equity.

Modified duration for the bank: $- (\Delta E/E)/\Delta r = - (-32.7)/93/2\% = 17.5$
Modified duration for the life insurer: $- (\Delta E/E)/\Delta r = -27.4/62/2\% = -22.1$

Notice that the interest rate mismatch of the life insurer is larger than the
bank's mismatch.
The combined impact is the weighted sum of both individual modified
durations. The bank's equity weight is $93/155 = 0.6$, while the insurer's
equity weight is $62/155 = 0.4$.

So the combined impact is $0.6 \times 17.5 + 0.4 \times -22.1 = 1.7$

This can be checked by calculating the modified duration of the fictitious
financial conglomerate:

$- (\Delta E/E)/\Delta r = - (-5.3)/155/2\% = 1.7$.

   So, because the bank is larger than the insurer in terms of capital and
reserves, the combined impact is a small but positive modified duration,
which implies a slightly negative interest rate sensitivity. If either the bank or
the insurer's balance sheet dominated the consolidated balance sheet, there
would hardly be any levelling out of interest rate sensitivities.
   Thus, when considering only the impact of interest rate changes, one is
inclined to draw the following conclusion from the paper: the more the
balance sheets of the bank and insurer are sized in the same order of magnitude, the higher the level of risk diversification will be.

The impact of the other risk driver, share price changes, can easily be seen in Table 11.6. While interest rate changes lead to changes in the equity of the bank and the life insurer in opposite directions, share price changes lead to changes in the equity of the bank and insurer in the same direction. So the more the bank and the life insurer have invested in shares, the lower the level of risk diversification within the financial conglomerate will be.

A third effect comes into play, however, which has to do with the stochastic behaviour of interest rates and share prices and therefore cannot be inferred from the deterministic scenarios used in the paper. Interest rates and share prices are negatively correlated, which means that share prices tend to drop when interest rates increase. As can be seen from Table 11.6, for a bank, the combined scenario of rising interest rates and declining share prices leads to an accumulation of losses on the fair value balance sheet. The life insurer however suffers less from it, because the two effects partly cancel each other out. This leads to the conclusion that banks are typically more volatile than life insurers. However, the empirical findings in Table 11.9 suggest that banks are less volatile than insurers in the Netherlands. The authors leave us here with an unresolved puzzle.

The second conclusion one could draw from this combined effect is that financial conglomerates where the banking part is more dominant are more volatile than financial conglomerates where the life insurance part is more dominant. Also, one could argue that a pro forma merger of a bank and a life insurer would lead to more risk diversification than a pro forma merger of two banks or two life insurers. The empirical findings as presented by the authors, however, do not give a clear and unambiguous picture of the effect of pro forma mergers of banks and insurers.

We end up with the conclusion that there is no clear empirical evidence underpinning the theoretically assumed risk diversification, regrettably so for the advocates of lower capital requirements for financial conglomerates. So far, so good. But for supervisors, who are trained in finding risks where others only see opportunities, it is not the end of the story about financial conglomerates.

Reputational Contagion Risk

The authors put forward two reasons for setting additional capital require-ments at holding company level: contagion risk and moral hazard risk. Moral hazard risk is linked to the too-big-to-fail syndrome of large financial con-glomerates. I doubt however whether moral hazard risk can be offset by additional capital requirements. Moral hazard has to do with management behaviour that exploits the possibility of a bailout at the expense of taxpay-ers. It can be countervailed by mechanisms that prevent financial institutions from excessive risk-taking behaviour, such as risk-sensitive capital requirements and disclosure of the risk profile to market participants, which are precisely the first and third pillar of the Basle 2 approach.

Contagion risk is not a new concept. It is often used in explaining banking crises and systemic risk. However, when attributed to a financial conglomerate, we have to be more precise about what we mean by the specific financial conglomerates' contagion risk. In other words, what contagion risk would not have been present if the financial conglomerate were merely a separate bank and a separate insurer. In my opinion, it is the possible contagion of reputational damage when using the same brand name in banking and insurance. Reputational contagion occurs when one part of the financial conglomerate gets into trouble while the other is in a financially sound condition, but subsequently gets swept away due to the fact that the public loses confidence in the brand name of the financial conglomerate. Therefore I would prefer to call this the financial conglomerate's reputational contagion risk, thus distinguishing it from systemic contagion risk that is assumed as a consequence of the interrelationship between banks in the financial system.

We then arrive at the question, is there a trade-off between capital requirements and the impact of reputational contagion risk? Can you measure it? I think it is possible to model 'reputational contagion scenarios'. As they can be quantified, capital buffers can offset them. Let me give two examples of such reputational contagion scenarios. Both examples apply to a financial conglomerate consisting of a bank and an insurer using the same brand name.

First example of reputational contagion scenario
Suppose the banking part of a financial conglomerate gets into financial trouble because of large losses in the credit portfolio. The public then starts losing confidence in the insurer and new sales of insurance products decline heavily, subsequently leaving the insurer in a run-off situation.

Second example of reputational contagion scenario
Suppose you have a financial conglomerate of which the life insurance part has invested heavily in shares. A large share price drop leads to the near insolvency of the insurer. Although the banking part is financially sound, customers start panicking and want their money back from the bank. A classical bank run then takes place and the bank runs into liquidity problems. This scenario illustrates how problems outside the bank can end up with a classical bank run. So the vulnerability of a bank becomes leveraged in a financial conglomerate that is using the same brand name for its insurance and banking parts.

In both cases there is additional risk of a financial conglomerate compared to a stand-alone bank and stand-alone insurer.

Conclusion

When addressing the question as to what level of regulatory capital should apply to financial conglomerates, one should elaborate on the balance between risk diversification and reputational contagion risk. By using (stochastic) scenarios, one could try to get a feeling for the quantitative impact of reputational contagion risk. Then it is not a matter of pure speculation as to what the impact will be, but a matter of calculation, or at least estimation. And calculated risk instead of speculation; that should appeal to supervisors.

REPLY

Jaap Bikker and Iman van Lelyveld

We are pleased that Gaston Siegelaer has taken ample time and effort to provide meaningful comment on our analysis. After summarizing our work, he makes a number of valuable remarks about diversification and reputational contagion risk. Here is our reaction to the following four of his observations.

Because, in terms of duration, the typical balance sheet structures of banks and insurers are each other's counterparts, interest rate shocks have opposite effects on each type of financial institution. Siegelaer raises the point that a significant diversification effect will generally emerge only if the two sectors are more or less equal in size, and that if one sector dominates the other, there will be hardly any levelling out of interest rate sensitivities. We do not agree with this comment, particularly the latter part. In our empirical analysis we use the aggregated balance sheet of the domestic activities of the largest five Dutch banks and that of all Dutch insurance companies. Total assets of banks are three times those of insurers, a proportion that is also found within ING and Fortis. Nevertheless, we observe significant diversification, whether in guilders (42 per cent) or in percentages of capital (65 per cent; see Table 11.5). Of course, diversification would be higher if we reduced the number of banks in our fictitious merger (increasing the share of insurers) until the optimal mix of cross-sector components showed 100 per cent diversification. On the other hand, any cross-sector diversification is in itself valuable, even where the hedge is only partial, because it always reduces risk.

Siegelaer further notes that interest rate and share price risks tend to be negatively correlated and hence that banks are expected to be more volatile than insurers where interest rate and share price risk partly cancel each other out. In his view, this contradicts our results in Table 11.9, which suggest that banks are less volatile. We think there is no such contradiction, for two reasons. First, there are differences in the two types of analysis with respect to the sample (all firms versus large firms with traded equity, balance sheet effects versus share price effects, level of leverage). And second, the combined interest rate and share price shock scenario is only one (although an important one) of the many sources of volatility affecting the wealth and income of financial institutions. There are many circumstances conceivable which might increase the volatility of insurance shares.

A second possible puzzle perceived by Siegelaer is that even where diversification effects are obvious, the results in Table 11.7, for some countries including the Netherlands, suggest that mergers among banks may be more profitable than cross-sector mergers. It is indeed unexpected that, at least for some countries, hypothetical cross-sector mergers are not the most promising ones. We are not able to fully explain this, but it does not mean that 'there is no clear empirical evidence underpinning diversification', as Siegelaer states. Each of the two analyses in our chapter confirms the existence of cross-sector diversification. The only puzzle is that in some countries intra-sector diversification might be even somewhat greater.

Siegelaer elaborates on our analysis of other risk types typical for FCs by better defining and explaining 'reputational contagion' risk. He advocates running reputational contagion scenarios as a means to achieve quantification of the impact of contagion or reputational shocks and gives two examples of possible scenarios. We agree that any quantification of the risk types typical for FCs would be very welcome and indeed needed to improve future regulation on FCs.

Scenario analysis might indeed be an interesting avenue to explore, but, unfortunately, we are far from convinced that they will generate serious evidence. The central question is how to parameterize any model for this purpose, given the lack of relevant data. This would make any outcome purely dependent on the underlying assumptions. Nevertheless, any step forward in this area would be extremely helpful and should be encouraged.

Index

Titles of publications are shown in *italics*.

ABN bank 21
accountability of regulator 86–8
accrual accounting regime, interest rate
   shocks 189–92
Acharya, V. 83
advanced IRB approach, LGD 149
ALM simulation model 187–99, 207,
   209–10
Altman, E. 150
Amro bank 21
Amsterdam Bank Associatie 13
asset and liability model (ALM)
   187–99, 207, 209–10
authorization requirements for bank
   management 28
Autoriteit Financiële Markten (Netherlands Authority for the Financial
   Markets) 31

BaFin (Bundesanstalt für
   Finanzdienstleistungsaufsicht)
   56–8
bancassurance, *see* financial conglomerates
Bangia, A. 145
Bank Act, 1903, Netherlands 12
bank assurance, *see* financial conglomerates
bank holding companies (BHCs),
   activities 199–200
Bank for International Settlements (BIS)
   64–5
bank runs 172
banking crises 46–7
   Netherlands 13
banking industry, internationalization
   27, 41–2
banking stability, Netherlands 45–6
banking supervision, *see* supervision

Banking Supervision Committee of the
   European System of Central Banks
   61–2
banks
   behaviour over business cycle 164
   commercial, and central bank 14–15
   credit rating systems 144
   failure 70–71, 83–4
   and interest rate changes 194–9,
      217–18, 222
   and share price changes 219, 222
   supervision charges 112
Basle Capital Accord 27
Basle 2 Capital Accord 64–6, 70,
   90–100, 105–7, 108
Bernanke, B. 98
BIS (Bank for International Settlements)
   64–5
Bliss, R. 81
Blum, J. 98
Bolt, W. 133, 135
borrower credit ratings 141–4
Bundesanstalt für
   Finanzdienstleistungaufsicht
   (BaFin) 56–8
Bundesbank, role in supervision 56–7
business cycles and credit risk 136–60,
   164–5
business supervision 18–19; *see also*
   prudential supervision

Calomiris, C. 98
Capital Accord, *see* Basle Capital
   Accord
capital buffers 158
capital regulation 145–6, 171–7
capital requirements
   Basle 2 Accord 169
   changes through time 151–6

and economic capital models 206–7
and incentives 79–80
Caprio, G. 81, 82
Carling, K. 154
Catarineu-Rabell, E. 154
central banks
and commercial banks 14–15
as lender-of-last-resort 172–3
Netherlands, *see* Nederlandsche
Bank, De
and prudential supervision 60–61
charges, bank supervision 112
Chung, E.J. 201
commercial banks
and Basle 2 Accord 64–6
and central bank, Netherlands 14–15
competition, Basle 2 Accord 97–8
competition policy and deposit insurance 133
competitive neutrality, Basle 2 Accord 96–7
conglomerates, *see* financial conglomerates
consumer protection
deposit insurance 113–14
motive for supervision 174
contagion risk, financial conglomerates 176, 219–20
contract regulation 89–90
corporate governance 85–6
costs, bank supervision 112
Council of Financial Supervisors (Raad Financiële Toezichthouders) 30
credit ceilings 18, 20–21
credit ratings systems 138–40, 141–4; *see also* IRB risk assessment approach
credit risk
management 157
measurement 136–60, 164–5, 167–8
Basle 2 Accord 91–2
Credit System Supervision Act, *see* Supervision of the Credit System, Act on the
Crockett, A. 5–6
cross-sector support, financial conglomerates 177

Davies, B. 94, 96, 98
debtholders 174

default losses (LGD) 149
Demirguc-Kunt, A. 116–22, 123
deposit guarantee schemes, EU 115
deposit insurance 24–5, 110–29, 172–3
fair pricing 132
and supervision 110–12
Deposit Insurance and Crisis Management 115
Deposit Insurance Working Group 115
Detragiache, E. 116–22, 123
Diebold, F. 145
disciplines on the regulator 86–8
diversification, banks and insurers 187–201
estimates from market data 199–205
DNB, *see* Nederlandsche Bank, De
Drake, L. 98
Drees, B. 78
dynamic provisioning and procyclicality 165, 168

economic capital 177–86
Basle 2 Accord 94
economic capital models (ECM) 178–86, 207–8
use by supervisors 205–7
emergency regulations 25
entry barriers, Basle 2 Accord 96
ESCB (European System of Central Banks), Banking Supervision Committee 61–2
Estrella, A. 90, 201
European Central Bank and DNB 29
European Union (EU)
deposit guarantee schemes 115
financial services market 27
prudential supervision 51–2, 60–63
explicit deposit protection systems 123–4

fair pricing, deposit insurance scheme 132
fair-value accounting regime, interest rate shocks 194–9
Federal Authority for Financial Services Supervision, Germany 56–8
Federal Deposit Insurance Corporation Improvement Act (FDICIA) 111, 134
financial conglomerates
capital regulation 175–7

Netherlands 26–7, 30–31, 42, 48,
170
risk diversification 217–19
risk types 181–6
financial industry internationalization
41–2
financial regulation, *see* regulation,
financial
Financial Services Authority (FSA) 87
financial services market, EU 27
financial system stability
and deposit insurance 113–14
Netherlands 45–6
Financial Stability Forum (FSF) 115–21
financial supervision, *see* supervision
Finger, C. 147
Fischer, S. 115
Flannery, M. 81, 85
foundation IRB approach 105–6, 108
LGD 149
Freixas, X. 132, 134
Froot, K.A. 178–81
FSA (Financial Services Authority) 87
FSF (Financial Stability Forum) 115–21

Garcia, G.G.H. 70, 116–21, 122
Germany, single regulator 55–8
Goodhart, C. 98, 99
Griffiths-Jones, S. 98
Gully, B. 200

Hall, M. 115
Hellman, T. 132, 134
Hellwig, M. 97–8
Honohan, P. 81

IADI (International Association of
Deposit Insurers) 115
IMF and deposit insurance 114–15
incentive-compatible deposit insurance
systems 116
incentive structures 74, 78–80
insurance and banking, *see* financial
conglomerates
insurers
and interest rate changes 194–9,
217–18, 222
and share price changes 219, 222
integrated financial supervision,
Germany 55–8

interest rate changes
accrual accounting regime 189–92
fair-value accounting regime 194–9
impact on banks and insurers 217–18
internal allocation of capital, Basle 2
Accord 95
internal ratings based risk assessment
approach 91–2, 105–6, 149
International Association of Deposit
Insurers (IADI) 115
internationalization and banking
supervision 27, 41–2, 51–3
intervention by regulatory agencies 83–5
IRB risk assessment approach 91–2,
105–6, 149

Jackson, P. 154, 156
Jordan, J. 152

Kane, E. 84
KMV ratings system 142–4
Knight, A. 97
Kyei, A. 122

Lamfalussy procedure agreement 62
Lang, W. 81
Lannoo, K. 98–9
Lee, W. 78
Leland, H.E. 178
lender-of-last-resort, central bank 172–3
LGD (loss given default) 149–50
liberalization, and banking supervision
26–31
licence requirements, credit institutions
23–4
life insurers, ALM model 187–99
Lindgren, C.J. 70
Llewellyn, D.T. 98, 171
loss given default (LGD) 149–50
Lowe, P. 154
Lown, C. 98

macroeconomic effects
Basle 2 Accord 98
risk-based capital 156–9
MAE (Monetary and Exchange Affairs
Department) 115
market-based ratings systems 142–4
market data, diversification estimates
199–205

market discipline
on banks 80–82
Basle 2 Accord 92, 100
and procyclicality 164–5, 167
market integration, *see* financial
conglomerates
Marx and Company's Bank 13
Mendelssohn & Co. Bank 14
mergers
banking and insurance, *see* financial
conglomerates
banks, Netherlands 21
Mexico, bank internal rating 154–6
Milne, A. 99
minimum required capital, *see* capital
requirements
Monetary and Exchange Affairs
Department (MAE) 115
monetary supervision, Netherlands 14,
16–18, 23–4
monitoring financial firms 77–8
Monro-Davies, R. 96, 98
Moody's credit rating 144
moral hazard risk 4, 176, 219–20
Morrison, A.D. 174, 175
Murdock, K. 132, 134

Nakaso, H. 80
national central banks, *see* central
banks
Nederlandsche Bank, De (DNB)
independence 29
supervisory role 11–32, 45–7, 48–50
Netherlands
Authority for the Financial Markets
(Autoriteit Financiële Markten)
31
banking performance 46–7
banking supervision 10–32, 41–3,
44–50, 59–60
central bank, *see* Nederlandsche
Bank, De
financial conglomerates 26–7, 30–31,
42, 48, 170
ALM model 188–99

Oliver, Wyman and Company (OWC)
185–6
optimal regulatory environment 69–101,
105–7

option-pricing model, risk measurement
201–4
OWC (Oliver, Wyman and Company)
185–6

PCA (prompt corrective action) 84, 111
PD, *see* probabilities of default
Peek, J. 152
Pension and Insurance Supervisory
Authority, Netherlands (PVK) 50
Perraudin, W. 200
policyholder rights 173
portfolio
Basle 2 Accord 97
correlation 185–7
selection theory 178
pricing
bank supervision 112
deposit insurance scheme 132
probabilities of default (PD) 142–4
correlation across borrowers 146–9
correlation with LGD 150
procyclicality
Basle 2 Accord 98
and credit risk management 164–5,
167–8
and credit risk measurement 136–60
project finance, Basle 2 Accord 66
Prompt Corrective Action (PCA) 84, 111
prudential supervision 44–7, 50
and Eurosystem 61–3
Nederlandsche Bank 14
Netherlands Act on Supervision
18–19
regulation 51–2
role of central banks 60–61
PVK (Pension and Insurance Supervisory Authority, Netherlands) 50

Raad Financiële Toezichthouders
(Council of Financial Supervisors)
30
RAROC (risk-adjusted return on capital)
178, 180
regulation, financial 69–101
objectives 5, 171–7
regulator
accountability 86–8
impact on incentive structures 74
single, Germany 55–8

regulatory arbitrage, Basle 2 Accord
    95–6
regulatory capital 145–6, 171–7
    Basle 2 Accord 94
Regulatory Impact Analysis (RIA) 87–8
regulatory regimes 72–88
    Basle 2 Accord 90–100
reputational contagion risk 219–20, 223
Resti, A. 150
revaluation effects 195–7
reward systems 78–80
RIA (Regulatory Impact Analysis) 87–8
risk-adjusted return on capital (RAROC)
    178, 180
risks
    analysis systems, Basle 2 Accord 91,
        94–5
    diversification 217–19
    financial conglomerates 181–6
    measurement
        using economic capital models
            (ECM) 206
        option-pricing method 201–4
    pricing, Basle 2 Accord 95
    see also credit risk
Robaver (Rotterdamsche Bank
    Vereeniging) 13
Robertson, D. 81
Robinson, G. 180
Robinson, J. 11
Rochet, J.C. 132, 134
Rosengren, E. 152
Rotterdamsche Bank Vereeniging
    (Robaver) 13

Saal, M. 70
Santomero, A.M. 201
Saporta, V. 200
Saunders, A. 77
Schinasi, G. 78
Schuermann, T. 145
Segoviano, M.A. 154
SEIR intervention 84
share price changes, impact of 219, 222
Simpson, D. 74
single regulator, Germany 55–8
Sironi, A. 150
South Holland Credit Union 11–12
Spratt, S. 98
Stein, J.C. 178–81

Stiglitz, J. 132, 134
structural supervision, Netherlands 24
Summer, M. 70, 71, 83
supervision
    business cycle effect 165
    costs for banks 112
    and deposit insurance 110–12
    Germany 55–8
    and internationalization 27, 41–2, 51–3
    Netherlands 10–32, 41–3, 44–50,
        59–60
    regulatory agency role 77–8
    risk-based capital system 159
    see also prudential supervision;
        systemic supervision
Supervision of the Credit System, Act
        on the, Netherlands
    1952 16–19, 50
    1956 Amendment 19–22
    1978 22–6, 46
    1992 28–9
supervisors
    discretionary powers, Basle 2 Accord
        65–6
    and economic capital models (ECM)
        205–7
Supervisory Review Process, Basle 2
        Accord 90–91, 169–70
supervisory system, Netherlands 59–60
Sweden, bank internal ratings 154
systemic financial instability 4–5
systemic supervision 5, 52–3

Teixeira de Mattos bank 21–2
Tieman, A. 133, 135
Tilburg Mortgage Bank (Tilburgsche
        Hypotheek Bank) 25
too-big-to-fail (TBTF) syndrome,
        financial conglomerates 170, 176
*Towards a Framework for Financial
        Stability* 115
trade-offs within regulatory regime 74–5
transition matrices, borrower credit
        ratings 144–5
Tsomocos, D. 154

value-at-risk (VaR) models 141
    and PD–LGD correlation 150

Wallman, S. 75

Wet Toezicht Kredietwezen, *see*
    Supervision of the Credit System,
    Act on the
Wilson, B. 77, 98

World Bank and deposit insurance 114

Zuid-Hollandsche Crediet-Vereeniging
    11–12